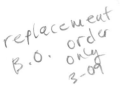
A Citizen's Guide to Frequently Asked Tax Questions and the Answers the IRS Wants You to Know

Gladson I. Nwanna, Ph.D., Editor

Frontline Publishers
Baltimore, Maryland

Library of Congress Cataloging-in-Publication Data

A citizen's guide to frequently asked tax questions and the answers the
    IRS wants you to know / Gladson I. Nwanna, editor.
      p. cm.
    Includes index.
    ISBN-13: 978-1-890605-38-4 (pbk.)
    ISBN-10: 1-890605-38-7 (pbk.)
    1. Income tax--Law and legislation--United States--Popular works.
    2. Income tax--Law and legislation--United States--Miscellanea.
    I. Nwanna, Gladson I.
    KF6369.6.C488 2006
    343.7305'2--dc22

                                        2005030117

10-digit ISBN: 1-890605-38-7
13-digit ISBN: 978-1-890605-38-4

Cover Design by David E. Ricardo

Printed in the United States of America

Visit Frontline Publishers Website at **http://www.frontlinepublishers.com**

Acknowledgement

This book benefited from the encouragement and advice of a lot of people, all of whom I am indebted. I would especially, like to thank, Mrs. Phyllis Desbordes for her editorial support and other valuable suggestions.

My gratitude and indebtedness also goes to the Internal Revenue Service whose work I have reproduced in several parts of this book, and in particular, several IRS employees who assisted me with answers to my questions.

Preface

U.S. taxpayers both pros and newcomers share one common characteristic in the seemingly unending myriad of questions relating to taxes, and their responsibilities and obligations; that is, questions that often range from the simple and obvious to the complex, from income tax related and non income tax related, from Federal income tax-related to non federal income-tax related.

Incidentally these taxpayers have good reason to ask their questions. Not only is the issue of taxes important to both the individual taxpayers, businesses, and taxing authorities, the subject of taxes is by its very nature complex and taxing. Not even the best tax accountant or tax preparer can guarantee their clients the correct answers or responses all of the time. Let alone the average taxpayer with no background in accounting, taxes or tax laws.

Finding correct or reliable answers to their tax-related questions will an important relief to taxpayers as much as it is of interest to the government.

What many taxpayers fail to understand are the numerous available sources to seek answers to their tax –related questions and the efforts of the government to ensure that their questions are answered accurately. The Federal Government, through the Internal Revenue Service (IRS), provides various avenues to meet taxpayer's needs. They can do so in person at IRS offices, by phone, by accessing the IRS TELETAX TOPICS, by fax, by writing to the IRS, through the internet at the IRS website or by reading various IRS publications.

A good number of taxpayers, however, are either not aware of these avenues or find them overwhelming and confusing. Many others do not have the time or the patience to seek out the various sources for answers to many of their questions.

This book comes as a service and guide to these taxpayers. In this book, I pull together most of the taxpayers' frequently asked federal income tax-related questions, and importantly, the answers the IRS would want them to know. In this sense, the information contained in this book can be considered accurate and reliable since they reflect the IRS answers and in IRS' own words.

This book focuses primarily on questions related to the federal income tax and makes no attempt to answer questions related to any other taxes such as state, county, City or non-income tax issues. Both individual taxpayers as well as small businesses should benefit from this book.

I hope you will find this book and the information contained in it useful and time saving. In any book such as this, typos and errors are inevitable despite my best efforts to ensure that there are none. Should you find any, I would certainly welcome your bringing them to my attention so that they may be corrected in future editions. Please forward/mail your letters to: Editorial, Frontline Publishers, P.O. box 32674 Baltimore, MD 21282-2674.

TABLE OF CONTENTS

APPENDIXES:

Chapter 1

IRS Procedures

~~~~~

Keyword(s): Payment Voucher (1040-ES); Keyword(s): Address Changes; Keyword(s): IRS Will Figure Your Tax; Keyword(s): 1040X Amended/Corrected Tax Return; Keyword(s): 1040-ES; Keyword(s): 1040-ES; Keyword(s): Bill/Debt/Liability; Keyword(s): Tax Bill/Debt/Liability; Keyword(s): Estimated Tax Payments; Keyword (s): Owe Tax Bill/Debt/Liability;

1.1 General Procedural Questions

Q. I'm concerned because my check payment to the IRS has not been cashed yet. What should I do?

A. You can call (800) 829-1040 and ask an IRS representative if the payment has been credited to your account. If it has not and the check has not cleared your financial institution, you may choose to place a stop-payment on the original check and send another payment.

Q. Will IRS figure the amount of tax and credits for taxpayers?

A. If you choose, the IRS will figure your tax on Form 1040EZ, Form 1040A, or Form 1040. Refer to Tax Topic 552, Tax and Credits Figured by IRS, for more information.

References:
• Form 1040, U.S. Individual Income Tax Return
• Form 1040A, U.S. Individual Income Tax Return
• Form 1040EZ, U.S. Individual Income Tax Return for Single and Joint Filers with No Dependents
• Tax Topic 552, Tax and credits figured by the IRS
• Publication 967, the IRS Will Figure Your Tax

Q. What are the new changes for 2006?

A. Refer to Tax Topic 302, *Highlights of 2006 Tax Changes*, for a brief overview of the tax law changes that are effective in 2006. Some items will be discussed in more detail in separate topics. Remember, this information is effective for your current 2006 return. For more detailed information, refer to Publication 553, *Highlights of 2006 Tax Changes.*

References:
* Publication 553, Highlights of 2006 Tax Changes
* Tax Topic 302, Highlights of Tax Changes

Keyword(s): Address Changes

1.2 Address Changes

Q. *Should I notify the IRS of my change of address?*

A. If you moved, you need to notify the IRS of your new address. The IRS can change its records so that any tax refunds due you or any other IRS communications will reach you in a timely manner. Refer to Tax Topic 157, *Change of Address - How to Notify IRS*, for additional information.

References:
• Tax Topic 157, Change of Address - How to Notify IRS
• Form 8822, Change of Address

Keyword(s): 1040X Amended/Corrected Tax Return

1.3 Amended Returns & Form 1040X

Q. *What should I do if I made a mistake on my federal return that I have already filed?*

A. It depends on the type of mistake that was made. Many mathematical errors are caught in the processing of the tax return itself. If you did not attach a required schedule the service will contact you and ask for the missing information.

If you did not report all your income or did not claim a credit, you are entitled to file an amended or corrected return using Form 1040X, Amended U.S. Individual Income Tax Return. Include copies of any schedules that have been changed or any Forms W-2 you did not include. The Form 1040X should be submitted after you receive your refund or by the due date of the return, whichever, is earlier. Generally, to claim a refund, the Form 1040X must be received within three years after the date you filed your original return or within two years after the date you paid the tax, whichever is later.

References:
• Form 1040X, Amended U.S. Individual Income Tax Return
• Tax Topic 308, Amended returns

Q. *I received a refund that is more than I should have received because I've discovered I made a mistake on my return. I have not yet cashed this check. What should I do now?*

A. Many mistakes are corrected in processing and a letter of explanation is mailed at the time the refund is issued. If the mistake was not corrected in processing, you need to file an amended or corrected return using Form 1040X, *Amended U.S. Individual Income Tax Return*, as soon as possible. Include copies of any schedules that have been changed or any Forms W-2 you did not include. If you return the refund check with a letter of explanation, a refund in the correct amount will be issued when the amended return processes.

References:
• Form 1040X, Amended U.S. Individual Income Tax Return
• Tax Topic 308, Amended returns

Q. *How can I check the status of my amended return?*

A. You will need to contact the IRS assistance line at (800) 829-1040 to receive information on the processing of your amended return. Amended/corrected returns are processed as quickly as possible. However, it could take 8 to 12 weeks to process an amended return.

References:
• Form 1040X, Amended U.S. Individual Income Tax Return
• Tax Topic 308, Amended Returns

Q. *If I call the automated tax line to check the status of a refund on an amended return, do I enter the total amount of my original refund, or only the amended amount?*

A. You cannot check the status of a refund for an amended return on the automated tax line. Amended/corrected returns are processed as quickly as possible. However, it may take 8 to 12 weeks or longer to process the return. If 8 weeks have elapsed and you have not received your refund, call (800) 829-1040.

References:
• Form 1040X, Amended U.S. Individual Income Tax Return
• Tax Topic 308, Amended returns

Q. *What should I do if I made a mistake on my federal return that I have already filed?*

A. It depends on the type of mistake that was made. Many mathematical errors are caught in the processing of the tax return itself. If you did not attach a required schedule the service will contact you and ask for the missing information.

If you did not report all your income or did not claim a credit, you are entitled to file an amended or corrected return using Form 1040X, Amended *U.S. Individual Income Tax Return*. Include copies of any schedules that have been changed or any Forms W-2 you did not include. The Form 1040X should be submitted after you receive your refund or by the due date of the return, whichever, is earlier. Generally, to claim a refund, the Form 1040X must be received within three years after the date you filed your original return or within two years after the date you paid the tax, whichever is later.

References:
• Form 1040X, Amended U.S. Individual Income Tax Return
• Tax Topic 308, Amended returns

Q. *How do I amend, or make changes on a tax return I had already filed?*

A. File Form 1040X to change a return you already filed. Generally, Form 1040X must be filed within 3 years after the date the original return was filed, or within 2 years after the date the tax was paid, whichever is later. But you may have more time to file Form 1040X if you are physically or mentally unable to manage your financial affairs. Refer to Pub. 556 for details.

Keyword(s): **Letter** **Ruling;** **Keyword(s):** **Revenue**
Procedure/Ruling/Regulations

1.4 Code, Revenue Procedures, Regulations, Letter Rulings

Q. How would I obtain a private letter ruling?

A. Visit Tax Regs in English where you can download Internal Revenue Bulletin 2005-01 which includes Revenue Procedure 2005-1 A request for a letter ruling should be submitted under Revenue Procedure 2004-1 including the applicable user fee to:

Ruling Request Submission
Internal Revenue Service
Attn: CC: PA:LPD:DRU
P.O. Box 7604
Ben Franklin Station
Washington, DC 20044

The procedure for requesting a private letter ruling is updated annually. It is always the first revenue procedure in the first Internal Revenue Bulletin of the year.

Keyword(s): Installment Agreement/Payment Plan; Keyword(s): Due date/Dateline; Keyword(s): Penalty For Underpayment; Keyword(s): Monthly Payment Plan/Installment Agreement; Keyword(s): Payment Plan/Installment Agreement

1.5 IRS Procedures: Collection Procedural Questions

Q. I am unable to pay my delinquent taxes. Will the IRS accept an Offer in Compromise?

A. You may qualify for an Offer in Compromise if you are unable to pay your taxes in full or if you are facing severe or unusual economic hardship. Refer to Tax Topic 204, *Offers in Compromise*, for additional information.

References:
• Tax Topic 204, Offers in Compromise
• Form 656 , Offers in Compromise
• Additional topics Offer in Compromise

Q. *Is there any special assistance available on unresolved tax matters which are creating a hardship?*

A. If you are suffering, or about to suffer a significant hardship because of the way Internal Revenue laws are being carried out, you may ask for special help from the IRS' Taxpayer Advocate Program. The Taxpayer Advocate represents your interests and concerns within the IRS by protecting your rights and resolving problems that have not been fixed through normal channels. You can reach that office by dialing (877) 777-4778.

Q. *Can I ask to make installment payments on the amount I owe?*

A. Yes. If you cannot pay the full amount due as shown on your return, you can ask to make monthly installment payments. However, you will be charged a one time user fee of $43.00, as well as interest on any tax not paid by its due date, and you can be charged a late payment penalty unless you can show reasonable cause for not paying the tax by April 15, even if your request to pay in installments is granted. Before requesting an installment agreement, you should consider less costly alternatives such as a bank loan.

To request an installment agreement, send Form 9465, *Installment Agreement Request*, with your return or call (800) 829-1040. You should receive a response within 30 days. For more details on installment payments, refer to Tax Topic 202, *What to do if You Can't Pay Your Tax*, or Publication 594, *Understanding the Collection Process*
.

References:
• Publication 594, Understanding the Collection Process
• Form 9465, Installment Agreement Request
• Tax Topic 202, What to do if You Can't Pay Your Tax

Q. *What kind of penalties and interest will I be charged for paying and filing my taxes late?*

A. Interest, compounded daily, is charged on any unpaid tax from the due date of the return until the date of payment. The interest rate is the federal short-term rate plus 3 percent. That rate is determined every three months.

For current interest rates, go to *News Releases and Fact Sheets* on the IRS website (www.irs.gov) and find the most recent Internal Revenue release entitled Quarterly Interest Rates. In addition, if you filed on time but didn't pay on time, you'll generally have to pay a late payment penalty of one-half of one percent of the tax owed for each month, or part of a month, that the tax remains unpaid after the due date, not exceeding 25 percent. However, you will not have to pay the penalty if you can show reasonable cause for the failure. The one-half of one percent rate increases to one percent if the tax remains unpaid after several bills have been sent to you and the IRS issues a notice of intent to levy.

Beginning January 1, 2000, if you filed a timely return and are paying your tax pursuant to an installment agreement, the penalty is one-quarter of one percent for each month, or part of a month, that the installment agreement is in effect.

If you did not file on time and owe tax, you may owe an additional penalty for failure to file unless you can show reasonable cause. The combined penalty is 5 percent (4.5% late filing, 0.5% late payment) for each month, or part of a month, that your return was late, up to 25%. The late filing penalty applies to the net amount due, which is the tax shown on your return and any additional tax found to be due, as reduced by any credits for withholding and estimated tax and any timely payments made with the return. After five months, if you still have not paid, the 0.5% failure-to-pay penalty continues to run, up to 25%, until the tax is paid. Thus, the total penalty for failure to file and pay can be 47.5% (22.5% late filing, 25% late payment) of the tax owed. Also, if your return was over 60 days late, the minimum failure-to-file penalty is the smaller of $100 or 100% of the tax required to be shown on the return.

Also, refer to Tax Topic 653, IRS Notices and Bills and Penalty and Interest Charges.

References:
• Tax Topic 653, IRS notices and bills and penalty and interest charges
Q. What Do I do If Haven't Received a Form W-2?

A. You should receive a Form W-2, "Wage and Tax Statement," from each employer you worked for to use in preparing your federal tax return. According to the IRS, employers must furnish this record of 2005 earnings and withheld taxes no later than Jan. 31, 2006 (if mailed, allow a few days for delivery). If you do not receive your Form W-2, contact your employer to find out if and when the W-2 was mailed. If it was mailed, it may have been returned to your employer because of an incorrect or incomplete address, so be sure to verify your address.

After contacting your employer, allow a reasonable amount of time for your employer to re-mail or to issue the W-2. If you still do not receive your W-2 by Feb. 15, contact the IRS for assistance toll free at 1-800-829-1040.

When you call, have the following information handy:
- The employer's name and complete address, including zip code, the employer's identification number (if known) and telephone number;
- Your name, address, including zip code, Social Security number, and telephone number; and
- An estimate of the wages you earned, the federal income tax withheld, and the dates you began and ended employment.

If you misplaced your W-2, contact your employer and be prepared with the information listed above. Your employer can replace the lost form with a "reissued statement." Be aware that your employer is allowed to charge you a fee for providing you with a new W-2. You still must file your tax return on time even if you do not receive your Form W-2. If you cannot get a W-2 by your tax-filing deadline, you may use Form 4852, *"Substitute for Form W-2, Wage and Tax Statement,"* but it will delay any refund due while the information is verified. If you receive a corrected W-2 after your return is filed and the information it contains does not match the income or withheld tax you reported on your return, you must file an amended return on Form 1040X, *"Amended U.S. Individual Income Tax Return"*. You can download Forms 4852 and 1040X and their instructions or order them by calling toll free to 1-800-TAX-FORM (1-800-829-3676).

References:
- Form 4852, Substitute for Form W-2, Wage and Tax Statement
- Form 1040X, Amended U.S. Individual Income Tax Return
- Instructions for Form 1040X

Keyword(s): Tax Forms; Keyword(s): Financial Aid; Keyword(s): Forms/Publications; Keyword(s): Copy of Return; Keyword(s): W-2; Keyword(s): Past/Previous Years' Returns

1.6 Copies & Transcripts

Q. How do I request a copy of my tax return for last year?

A. If you need an exact copy of a previously filed and processed return and all attachments (including Forms W-2), you must complete Form 4506 , *Request for Copy of Tax Return* and mail it to the IRS address in the instructions along with a $39 fee for each tax year requested. Copies are generally available for returns filed in the current and past 6 years.

In cases where an exact copy of the return is not needed, tax return and transcripts may be ordered. The tax return transcript shows most line items contained on the return as it was originally filed, including any accompanying forms and schedules. In most cases, a tax return transcript will meet the requirements for lending institutions for mortgage verification purposes.

The transcript can be ordered by completing a Form 4506-T or calling (800) 829-1040 and following the prompts in the recorded message. There is no charge for the transcript and you should receive it in 10 business days from the time the IRS receives your request. Tax return transcripts are generally available for the current and past three years. If you need a statement of your tax account which shows changes that you or the IRS made after the original return was filed, you must request a "Tax Account Transcript". This transcript shows basic data including marital status, type of return filed, adjusted gross income, taxable income, payments and adjustments made on your account. Tax return and account transcripts are generally available for the current and past 3 years.

Form 4506-T can also be used to get proof from the IRS that you did not file a tax return for a particular tax year. Forms can be downloaded at Forms & Pubs or ordered by calling (800) 829-1040.

References:
- Form 4506 Request for Copy of Tax Return
- Form 4506-T Request for Transcript of Tax Return

Q. *Can I get copies of my prior year Forms W-2 from the IRS?*

A. The quickest way to obtain a copy of a prior year Form W-2 is through your employer. If that is not possible, you can order and pay for copies of your entire return (attachments include Form W-2) from IRS, or order W-2 information at no charge from IRS. IRS can provide W-2 information for up to 10 years. Information for the current year is generally not available until the year after it is filed with the IRS. For example, W-2 information for 2005, filed in 2006, will be available from IRS until 2007.

To receive a copy of your return or transcript, complete and mail Form 4506, *Request for Copy of Tax Return* or Form 4506-*T Request for Transcript of Tax Return*. You should allow 60 calendar days for a response.

References:
- Form 4506, Request for Copy of Tax Return
- Form 4506-T Request for Transcript of Tax Return

Q. *How do I get a Copy of My Tax Return?*

A. If you need a copy of your tax return, use Form 4506. There is a $39 fee for each return requested. If you want a free transcript of your tax return or account, use Form 4506-T or call the IRS.

Q. *How do I get a copy of my tax Return Information?*

Taxpayers have two easy and convenient options for getting copies of their federal tax return information — tax return transcripts and tax account transcripts — by phone or by mail.

A. A tax return transcript shows most line items from the tax return (Form 1040, 1040A or 1040EZ) as it was originally filed, including any accompanying forms and schedules. It does not reflect any changes you, your representative or the IRS made after the return was filed. In many cases, a return transcript will meet the requirements of lending institutions such as those offering mortgages and student loans.

A tax account transcript shows any later adjustments either you or the IRS made after the tax return was filed. This transcript shows basic data, including marital status, type of return filed, adjusted gross income and taxable income.

Request either transcript by calling 1-800-829-1040, or order by mail using IRS Form 4506-T, Request for Transcript of Tax Return. The IRS does not charge a fee for transcripts, which are available for the current and three prior calendar years. Allow two weeks for delivery.

If you need a photocopy of a previously processed tax return and attachments, complete Form 4506, *Request for Copy of Tax Form,* and mail it to the IRS address listed on the form for your area. There is a fee of $39 for each tax period requested. Copies are generally available for the current and past 6 years.

Forms 4506-T and 4506 are free and can be downloaded to your computer or you can order them by calling the IRS at 1-800-TAX-FORM (1-800-829-3676).

References:
*   Form 4506-T, Request for Transcript of Tax Return
*   Form 4506, Request for Copy of Tax Form

Keyword(s): U.S. Citizen Abroad; Keyword(s): Foreign Country; Keyword(s): Extensions

1.7 Extensions

Q. I am filing my U.S. tax return from the U.K. and am eligible for the automatic 2-month extension. Do my forms need to be in Philadelphia by June 15th, or do they just need to be postmarked by June 15th?

A. Your return must be postmarked by June 15.

References:
• Publication 17, Your Federal Income Tax

Keyword(s): Forms, Publications; Keyword(s): Forms & Publications

1.8 Forms & Publications

Q. How do I obtain forms (including prior year) and publications not available on your site?

A. By phone: Call (800) 829-3676 (available M-F 7:00 am - 10:00 pm).

Keyword(s): Injured Spouse; Keyword(s): Child Support

1.9 Injured & Innocent Spouse

Q. My ex-spouse is delinquent in paying child support. The attorney general has filed some sort of paperwork with the IRS to withhold my ex-spouse's tax refund. How would I receive the withheld refund?

A. The answer is different for each state. You need to contact the state link to the U.S. Department of Health and Human Services Administration for Children & Families Office of Child Support Enforcement where you live to get this information.

References:
• Form 8379, Injured Spouse Claim and Allocation
• Publication 504, Divorced or Separated Individuals
• U.S. Department of Health and Human Services Administration for Children & Families Office of Child Support Enforcement

Q. Is there any way to find out if I need to file an injured spouse claim before I file a return?

A. Your spouse can ask the agency that might be claiming the refund for a past-due debt. Another source of information is the Financial Management Service Help Desk at (800) 304-3107.

References:
• Form 8379, Injured Spouse Claim and Allocation

Q. Can I file my return electronically even though I am filing a Form 8379, Injured Spouse Claim and Allocation?

A. Yes, you can file electronically.

References:
• Form 8379, Injured Spouse Claim and Allocation

Q. How can I collect child support from my ex-spouse?

A. You must contact your local child support agency.

References:

• Form 8379, Injured Spouse Claim and Allocation
• Publication 504, Divorced or Separated Individuals
• U.S. Department of Health and Human Services Administration for Children & Families Office of Child Support Enforcement.

Q. Are there any relief available to Innocent Spouses?

A. You may qualify for relief from liability for tax on a joint return if (a) there is an understatement of tax because your spouse omitted income or claimed false deductions or credits, (b) you are divorced, separated, or no longer living with your spouse, or (c) given all the facts and circumstances, it would not be fair to hold you liable for the tax. Refer to Form 8857 or Pub. 971 for more details.

Keyword(s): Maiden/Married Name; Keyword(s): Married Filing Jointly; Keyword(s): Name Changes/Corrections; Keyword(s): Newly wed; Keyword(s): Recently got divorced

1.10 Name Changes & Social Security Number Matching Issues

Q. If I go to the Social Security Administration office to change my name, how long does it take the IRS to update its records?

A. IRS records are generally updated 10 days after the records at the Social Security Administration are changed.

References:
• Social Security Administration

Q. Do I need to change my maiden name to my married name on my social security card for us to file jointly?

A. You can still file Married Filing Jointly without changing your name with the Social Security Administration. However, you do need to show your maiden name on the tax return instead of your married name.

Q. I got married and I have not changed the name on my social security card to my married name. My Form W-2 is in my married name but my tax forms came in my maiden name. Should I file with my maiden name or married name?

A. It is important that the name the Social Security Administration has in its system for your social security number agrees with the name on your tax return. You have a choice. You can file with your maiden name and contact the Social Security Administration after you file your return. Or, if you have enough time before the due date of your return, you can contact the Social Security Administration and have your records changed. Please wait 10 days to file your tax return.
To change the name shown on your social security card, you need to complete SSA Form SS-5, *Application for a Social Security Card.* Form SS-5 is available at you can also obtain Form SS-5 by calling SSA at 1-800-772-1213 or visiting your local SSA office. *Note:* Form SS-5 is filed with SSA. The Social Security Administration will issue you a new security card reflecting your married name and automatically send an update to us.

References:
•Social Security Administration
 Form SS-5

Q. How can I correct the spelling of my name with IRS?

The name on the refund check is spelled the way it appears on your tax return. If the address label you receive is spelled wrong, do not use the label. Instead, print the information on the tax return. You can also call (800) 829-1040 and the IRS can change the spelling of your name over the phone.

A. *What could happened if both the Name and SSN on my Tax Forms do not Agree With my Social Security Card?*

If not, certain deductions and credits may be reduced or disallowed, your refund may be delayed, and you may not receive credit for your social security earnings. If your Form W-2, Form 1099, or other tax document shows an incorrect SSN or name, notify your employer or the form-issuing agent as soon as possible to make sure your earnings are credited to your social security record. If the name or SSN on your social security card is incorrect, call the Social Security Administration at 1-800-772-1213.

Q. *I am a newly wed and my friend recently got divorced. Is there anything we may have to do to avoid tax problems?*

Marriage or Divorce — Check Your Social Security Number

A. Newlyweds and the recently divorced should make sure that names on their tax returns match those registered with the Social Security Administration (SSA). A mismatch between a name on the tax return and a Social Security number (SSN) could unexpectedly increase a tax bill or reduce the size of any refund.

For newlyweds, the tax scenario can begin when the bride says "I do" and takes her husband's surname, but doesn't tell the SSA about the name change. If the couple files a joint tax return with her new name, the IRS computers will not be able to match the new name with the SSN.

Similarly, after a divorce, a woman who had taken her husband's name and had made that change known to the SSA should contact the SSA if she reassumes a previous name.

It's easy to inform the SSA of a name change by filing Form SS-5 at a local SSA office. It usually takes two weeks to have the change verified. The form is available on the agency's Web site, www.ssa.gov, by calling toll free 1-800-772-1213 and at local offices. The SSA Web site provides the addresses of local offices.

Generally, taxpayers must provide SSNs for each dependent claimed on the tax return. For adopted children without SSNs, the parents can apply for an adoption taxpayer identification number, or ATIN, by filing Form W-7A with the IRS. The ATIN is used in place of the SSN on the tax return. You can download the form or order it by calling the IRS toll free 1-800-TAX-FORM (1-800-829-3676).

References:
* Form W-7A, Application for Taxpayer Identification Number for Pending U.S. Adoptions

Keyword(s): Social Security Number; Keyword(s): Rejected Return; Keyword(s): Letter/Notice; Keyword(s): Exemption/Support Issues

1.11 Notices & Letters

Q. I received a letter from the IRS indicating that due to my misprint of my daughter's social security number, the exemption was rejected. Can I make the correction and still receive the exemption?

A. You are entitled to the exemption if your child qualifies as your dependent. To correct the return, you must provide the correct social security number information for your daughter. You can return it with a copy of the IRS letter in the envelope provided or contact the phone number listed in the upper right-hand corner of the letter for assistance.

Q. I received a Notice/Letter from the IRS I thought it was a refund, but it wasn't. What should I do?
A. It's a moment any taxpayer dreads. An envelope arrives from the IRS — and it's not a refund check. But don't panic. Many IRS letters can be dealt with simply and painlessly.

Each year, the IRS sends millions of letters and notices to taxpayers to request payment of taxes, notify them of a change to their account or request additional information. The notice you receive normally covers a very specific issue about your account or tax return.

Each letter and notice provides specific instructions explaining what you should do if action is necessary to satisfy the inquiry. Most notices also give a phone number to call if you need further information. Most correspondence can be handled without calling or visiting an IRS office, if you follow the instructions in the letter or notice. However, if you have questions, call the telephone number in the upper right-hand corner of the notice, or call the IRS at 1-800-829-1040. Have a copy of your tax return and the correspondence available when you call so your account can be readily accessed.

Before contacting the IRS, review the correspondence and compare it with the information on your return. If you agree with the correction to your account, no reply is necessary unless a payment is due. If you do not agree with the correction the IRS made, it is important that you respond as requested. Write an explanation why you disagree, and include any documents and information you wish the IRS to consider. Mail your information along with the bottom tear-off portion of the notice to the address shown in the upper left-hand corner of the IRS correspondence. Allow at least 30 days for a response.

Sometimes, the IRS sends a second letter or notice requesting additional information or providing additional information to you. Be sure to keep copies of any correspondence with your records.

For more information about IRS notices and bills, see Publication 594, *Understanding the Collection Process*. Information about penalties and interest charges is available in Publication 17, *Your Federal Income Tax*. Both publications are available on IRS.gov or by calling 1-800-TAX-FORM (1-800-829-3676).

References:
- Publication 594, Understanding the Collection Process
- Publication 17, Your Federal Income Tax
- Tax Topic 651

Keyword(s): Refunds; Keyword(s): Refund Inquiries

1.12 Refund Inquiries

Q. *Can my refund be used to pay other debts?*

A. Under the law, state and Federal agencies refer to the IRS the names of taxpayers who are behind in their support payments, taxes, and loans. Your tax refund may not be refunded to you if you are delinquent in child or child and spousal support payments, have a past due Federal debt (such as a student loan), or owe state income taxes. Therefore, your refund will be used to pay other debts you owe. For additional information, refer to Tax Topic 203, *Failure to Pay Child Support and Other Federal Obligations.*

References:
- Tax Topic 203, Failure to Pay Child Support and Other Federal Obligations

Q. *Can a person receive a tax refund if they are currently in a payment plan for prior year's federal taxes?*

A. As a condition of your agreement, any refund due you in a future year will be applied against the amount you owe. Therefore, you may not get all of your refund if you owe certain past-due amounts, such as federal tax, state tax, a student loan, or child support. The IRS will automatically apply the refund to the taxes owed. If the refund does not take care of the tax debt; you must continue the installment agreement.

Q. *How long does it take after you've filed to receive a refund?* ✓

A. Processing time for refund returns depends on the method used for filing. If you e-file opting for direct deposit and have not received your refund within 3 weeks after filing your return (eight weeks if you filed a paper return opting for a paper check), you can check your refund status online at the IRS website (www.IRS.gov) by clicking on "Where's My Refund " then go to *Get My Refund Status* " (after inputting the required data). Or, you can call the Refund Hotline at (800) 829-1954. Be sure to have available a copy of your current tax return because you will need to know your social security number shown on your return, the filing status and the exact whole dollar amount of your refund. If you have requested direct deposit, the refund should take one week less time to be issued as opposed to getting a paper check.

Q. *I have filed my tax return and expect a refund. How can I check on the status of my refund?*

A.   Refund information does not become available until it has been 6 weeks since you filed your tax return (3 weeks if you filed electronically or through TeleFile). After waiting the appropriate number of weeks, the fastest, easiest way to find out about your current year refund is to log onto www.irs.gov. Click on *Where's My Refund* then go to Get My Refund Status or you can call Refund Hotline at (800) 829-1954. Be sure to have a copy of your current tax return available because you will need to know your social security number shown on your return, the filing status and the exact whole dollar amount of your refund. Generally, if you already filed your federal tax return and are due a refund, you have several options for checking on the status of your refund. One way is to use *"Where's My Refund?"* an interactive tool on IRS.gov. Simple online instructions guide taxpayers through a process that checks the status of their refund after they provide identifying information shown on their tax return. Once the information is processed, results could be one of several responses, including:
• 		Acknowledgement that a return was received and is in processing,

17

- The mailing date or direct deposit date of the taxpayer's refund, or
- Notification that the refund has been returned to the IRS because it could not be delivered.

The results also include References to customized information that is based on the taxpayer's specific situation. The References guide taxpayers through the steps they need to take to resolve any issues that may be affecting their refund. The *Where's My Refund?* service meets stringent IRS security and privacy certifications. Taxpayers enter identifying information that includes their Social Security number, filing status and the exact amount of the refund shown on the return. This specific information verifies that the person is authorized to access that account and avoids an unsuccessful response. *Where's My Refund?* is accessible to visually impaired taxpayers with the Job Access with Speech (JAWS) screen reader used with a Braille display and is compatible with different JAWS modes. If it has been at least four weeks since you filed your return, you can call the toll-free IRS TeleTax System at 1-800-829-4477. When you call, you will need to provide the first Social Security number shown on the return, your filing status and the amount of the refund. If the IRS has processed your return, the system will tell you the date your refund will be sent. The TeleTax refund information is updated each weekend. If you do not get a date for your refund, please wait until the next week before calling back. Another option is the IRS Refund Hotline. Please call the toll-free hotline number at 1-800-829-1954. It is staffed from 7 a.m. to 10 p.m. weekdays, and from 10 a.m. to 3 p.m. on Saturdays through April 9. All times are local, except for Alaska and Hawaii, which are on Pacific Time. The IRS updates refund information every seven days. Refer to Tax Topic 152, *Refunds - How Long They Should Take,* for additional information.

References:
- Where's My Refund?
- Tax Topic 152, Refunds - How Long They Should Take

Q. I lost my refund check. How do I get a new one?

A. Call the IRS at (800) 829-1954. If your refund check has not been cashed, the IRS can normally provide a replacement within six to eight weeks. If your refund check has been cashed, the Financial Management Service (FMS) will provide a copy of the check and a Form 3911 Taxpayer Statement Regarding Refund, to initiate a claim. The signature on the cancelled check will be reviewed before determining whether another refund can be issued.

Q. Is it possible to find out if a federal tax refund check has been cashed?

A. If you need to know whether a federal tax refund check that was issued to you has been cashed, you can call (800) 829-1954 and request Form 3911, *Taxpayer Statement Regarding Refund.*

If you are inquiring about a check that was issued to someone other than yourself, the IRS is not allowed under the Privacy Act of 1974 to disclose any information.

References:
• Form 3911, Taxpayer Statement Regarding Refund

Keyword(s): Fraud

1.13 Reporting Fraud

Q. *How can I make sure no one files under my name using my social security number?*

A. The IRS has security measures in place to verify the accuracy of tax returns and validity of social security numbers submitted. If however, you have knowledge of tax fraud being committed, you can make an anonymous report toll free to (800) 829-0433. You can contact the Social Security Administration to verify if there is another taxpayer using your social security number. The telephone number for the Social Security Administration is (800) 772-1213. For information on how to prevent identity theft contact the Federal Trade Commission (FTC) Identity Theft Hot-line (877) 438-4338.

Keyword(s): Joint Return ✓

1.14 Signing the Return

Q. *My husband passed away last year, and I will be filing a joint return. Are any special return notations required to indicate my husband is deceased?*

A. If you are a surviving spouse filing a joint return and no personal representative has been appointed, you should sign the return and write in the signature area, "filing as surviving spouse." The final return should have the word "Deceased, " the decedent's name, and the date of death written across the top of the return. For additional information, refer to Tax Topic 356, *Decedents.*

References:

• Tax Topic 356, Decedents

Keyword(s): W-2; Keyword(s): W-2 – Additional, Incorrect, Lost, Non-receipt, Omitted; Keyword(s): I haven't received a Form W-2

1.15 W–2 - Additional, Incorrect, Lost, Non-receipt, Omitted

Q. May an employer provide me my Form W-2 electronically?

A. Yes, an employer may furnish your Form W-2 electronically provided certain criteria are met. You must affirmatively consent to receive the Form W-2 in an electronic format and prior to, or at the time of, your consent, your employer must provide you a disclosure statement containing specific disclosures. Additionally, the electronic version of the Form W-2 must contain all required information and comply with applicable revenue procedures relating to substitute statements to recipients. If the statement is furnished on a Website, then your employer must notify you, via mail, electronic mail, or in person, that the statement is posted on a Website and provide instructions on accessing and printing the statement.

References:
• Treas. Reg. 31.6051-1(j)

Q. I didn't get my W-2 by January 31, so I asked my employer for it, but I still don't have it. What should I do?

A. If you don't receive your Form W-2 by February 15, contact the IRS for assistance at (800) 829-1040. Also, you may want to refer to Tax Topic 154, Form W-2 - *What To Do if Not Received,* to Refer to the specific information the IRS will need in order to prepare Form 4852, *Substitute For a Missing Form W-2.*

References:
• Form 4852, Substitute For a Missing Form W-2
• Tax Topic 154, Form W-2 - What To Do if Not Received

Q. I have already filed my return and now I have received another Form W-2. What can I do?

A. If you find that you have done any of the following, you should file an amended return 1) you did not report some income; 2) you claimed deductions or

20

credits you should not have claimed; 3) you failed to claim some deductions or credits you are entitled to; or 4) you used an incorrect filing status. The form you use to correct the Form 1040, Form 1040A, Form 1040EZ, or TeleFile you already filed is Form 1040X, Amended U.S. Individual Income Tax Return. Refer to Tax Topic 308, Amended Returns, for additional information.

For additional information on when, where, and how to file, refer to Tax Topic 301, When, Where, and How to File.

References:
• Form 1040, U.S. Individual Income Tax Return
• Form 1040A, U.S. Individual Income Tax Return
• Form 1040EZ, U.S. Individual Income Tax Return for Single and Joint Filers with No Dependents
• Form 1040X, Amended U.S. Individual Income Tax Return
• Tax Topic 301, When, where, and how to file
• Tax Topic 308, Amended Returns

Q. I received an incorrect W-2 form. I can't get my former employer to issue a corrected W-2? What should I do?

A. If your attempts to have an incorrect Form W-2 corrected by your employer are unsuccessful and it is after February 15th, contact the IRS at (800) 829-1040. An IRS representative can initiate a Form W-2 complaint. Form 4598, Form W-2 or 1099 Not Received or Incorrect, will be sent to the employer and a copy will be sent to you along with Form 4852, Substitute for a Missing Form W-2, *Wage and Tax Statement,* or Form 1099-R, *Distributions from Pensions, Annuities, Retirement or Profit-Sharing Plans, IRAs, Insurance Contracts,* etc. The copy that the employer receives will advise him or her of the employer's responsibilities to provide a correct Form W-2 and of the penalties for failure to do so. When you call the IRS or visit an IRS Taxpayer Assistance Center (TAC), please have the following information available: Your employer's name and complete address, including zip code, employer identification number (if known - Refer to prior year's Form W-2 if you worked for the same employer), and telephone number, Your name, address, including zip code, social security number, and telephone number; and An estimate of the wages you earned, the federal income tax withheld, and the period you worked for that employer. The estimate should be based on year-to-date information from your final pay stub or leave-and-earnings statement, if possible.

If you file your return and attach Form 4852 to support the withholding amount claimed instead of a Form W-2, your refund can be delayed while the information you gave us is verified.

If you receive a Form W-2 after you file your return and it does not agree with the income or withheld tax you reported on your return, file an amended return on Form 1040X, Amended U.S. Individual Income Tax Return.

References:
• Form 4852, Substitute for a Missing Form W-2
• Tax Topic 154, Form W-2 - what to do if not received
• Tax Topic 308, Amended returns
• Form 1040X, Amended U.S. Individual Income Tax Return

Keyword(s): W-4; Keyword(s): Withholding Allowances (Form W-4); Keyword(s): Withholding Taxes; Keyword(s): Social Security Tax; Keyword(s): Employment Taxes; Keyword(s): FICA Taxes; Keyword(s): Medicare Tax

1.16 W–4 - Allowances, Excess FICA, Withholding

Q. *What can be done if an employer will not withhold income taxes, social security, and Medicare from my pay?*

A. Generally, in situations such as this, the employer is not considering you to be an employee. Rather, you are being treated as an independent contractor (self-employed person). If you cannot resolve this matter with your employer, and if you feel that an employer-employee relationship exists, you should submit a Form SS-8, *Determination of Employee Work Status for Purposes of Federal Employment Taxes and Income Tax Withholding.* The factors used to determine if an employer-employee relationship exists are covered in Chapter 2 of Publication 15-A, *Employer's Supplemental Tax Guide.*

If your status as an employee is not at issue, it may be that you are in a category of employment whose earnings are not defined as wages under U.S. federal tax and social security law. Find out from your employer the reason that social security and Medicare taxes and income taxes are not being withheld from your pay. If you have further questions, contact the IRS at 800-829-1040 or visit an IRS walk-in office for assistance.

References:
• Form SS-8 , Determination of Employee Work Status for Purposes of Federal Employment Taxes and Income Tax Withholding
• Publication 15-A, Employer's Supplemental Tax Guide
• Publication 1779, Independent Contractor or Employee

Q. *What could I do if the amount I owe is large?*

A. If the amount you owe is large, you may want to file <u>a new</u> Form W-4 with your employer to change the amount of income tax withheld from your pay. For details on how to complete Form W-4, Refer to Pub. 919. In general, you do not have to make estimated tax payments if you expect that your next years Form 1040 will show a tax refund or a tax balance due of less than $1,000 (<u>for 2005</u>). If your total estimated tax (including any household employment taxes or alternative minimum tax) will be more that $1,000 (<u>for 2005</u>), Refer to Form 1040-ES. It has a worksheet you can use to Refer to if you have to make estimated tax payments. For more details, Refer to Pub. 505.

Q. *What could I do if the amount I overpaid is large?*

A. If the amount you overpaid is large (i.e. you got a big refund), you may want to file <u>a new</u> Form W-4 with your employer to change the amount of income tax withheld from your pay. For details on how to complete Form W-4, Refer to Pub. 919.

Chapter 2

Filing Requirements/Status/Dependents/Exemptions
~~~~~

Keyword(s): Single Filing Status

2.1 Filing Requirements

Q. How much does a student have to make before he or she has to file an income tax return?

A. If you are an unmarried dependent, you must file a tax return for 2005 if you have earned income of more than $5,000, unearned income of more than $800, or if your gross income is more than $800 and exceeds your earned income by more than $250. If part of your earned income is from tips, Refer to Tax Topic 402, *Tips.*

Even if you do not have to file, you should file a federal income tax return to get money back if any of the following apply:
• You had income tax withheld from your pay.
• You qualify for the earned income credit.
• You qualify for the additional child tax credit. Refer to Publication 501, Exemptions, Standard Deduction and Filing Information, for an explanation of the five exemption tests and filing requirement rules.
For additional information Refer to Tax Information for Students

References:
• Publication 501, Exemptions, Standard Deduction and Filing Information
• Tax Information for Students

Q. Do I Have to File a Tax Return?

A. Use Chart A, B, or C found in any current Form 1040-INSTRUCTIONS booklet to Refer to if you must file a return. U.S. citizens who lived in o income from a U.S. possession should Pub. 570. Residents of Puerto Rico can use TeleTax topic 901 to refer to if they must file.

Note: Even if you do not otherwise have to file a return, you should file one to get a refund of federal income tax withheld. You should also file if you are eligible for the earned income credit, the additional child tax credit, or the health coverage tax credit.

Exception for children under age 14. If you are planning to file a tax return for your child who was under age 14 at the end of the tax year you are filing and certain other conditions apply, you can elect to include your child's income on your return. But you must use Form 8814 to do so. If you make this election, your child does not have to file a return. For details, use TeleTax topic 553 or Refer to Form 8814.

Nonresident aliens and dual-status aliens. These rules also apply to nonresident aliens and dual-status aliens who were married to U.S. citizens or residents at the end of the tax year who have elected to be taxed as a resident aliens. Other nonresident aliens and dual-status aliens have different requirements. They may have to file 1040NR or Form 1040NR-EZ. Specific rules apply to determine if you are a resident or nonresident alien. Refer to Pub. 519 for details, including the rules for student scholars who are aliens.

Q. *When Should You File?*

A. Not later than April 15, 2006 for the 2005 tax year. If you file after this date, you may have to pay interest and penalties.

Q. *What If You Cannot File on Time?*

A. You can get an automatic 4-month extension if, no later than April 15, 2006, you either file for an extension by phone or you file Form 4868. For details, including how to file by phone, Refer to Form 4868. *An automatic 4-month extension to file does not extend the time to pay your tax. Refer to Form 4868.*

It you are a U.S. citizen or resident may qualify for an automatic extension of time to file without filing Form 4868 or filing for an extension by phone. You qualify if, on the due date of your return and meet one of the following conditions:

• You live outside the United States and Puerto Rico and your main place of business or post of duty is outside the United States and Puerto Rico.

• You are in military or naval service on duty outside the United States and Puerto Rico.

This extension gives you an extra 2 months to file and pay the tax, but interest will be charged from the original due date of the return on any unpaid tax. You must attach a statement to your return showing that you meet the requirements.

Q. *Where Do I File my Tax Return?*

A. Refer to Appendixes I-L for filing instructions and addresses. Including details on using a private delivery service to mail your return or payment.

Keyword(s): Support/Exemption Issues; Keyword(s): Separate Returns; Keyword(s): Living Together Tax Issues; Keyword(s): Child Care Credit; Keyword(s): Dependent Care Credit; Keyword(s): Dependents/Exemptions; Keyword(s): Divorced or Separated Spouses/Parents; Keyword(s): Earned Income Tax Credit; Keyword(s): Filing Status

2.2 Filing Status

Q. *If two single people (never married) have a child and live together, providing equal support for that child, can they both claim head of household status?*
A. Only the person who paid more than half the cost of keeping up a home for the year would qualify for the head of household filing status. If both people paid exactly the same amount, neither would qualify for the head of household filing status. Refer to Publication 501, Exemptions, Standard Deduction, and Filing Information, for more information.

References:
• Publication 501, Exemptions, Standard Deduction, and Filing Information
• Tax Topic 353, What is your filing status

Q. *For head of household filing status, do you have to claim a child as a dependent to qualify?*

A. In certain circumstances, you do not need to claim the child as a dependent to qualify for head of household filing status, such as when the qualifying child is unmarried child and is your grandchild, stepchild, or adopted child. Refer to Publication 501, *Exemptions, Standard Deduction, and Filing Information*, for more information.

References:
• Publication 501, Exemptions, Standard Deduction, and Filing Information

Q. *I am divorced with one dependent child. This year my ex-spouse will claim the child as an exemption. Does this mean I cannot qualify as head of household?*

A. You can file as head of household even though you do not claim your unmarried dependent child as an exemption if you meet all of the following requirements:
• You are unmarried or considered unmarried on the last day of the year.
• You paid more than half the cost of keeping up a home for the year.
• A qualifying person must live with you in the home for more than half the year (except for temporary absences such as school). Refer to Publication 501, *Exemptions, Standard Deduction, and Filing Information,* for more information.

References:
• Publication 501, Exemptions, Standard Deduction, and Filing Information
• Tax Topic 353, What is your filing status

Q. *If I moved out of my house on July 10, but was not divorced at the end of the year, can I file as head of household and take the earned income credit if I have a minor child? Can I also claim child care expenses?*
A. You do not qualify for the head of household filing status because you and your spouse have not lived apart for the last 6 months of the taxable year and are not considered unmarried. Your filing status for the year will either be married filing separately, or married filing jointly. If it is married filing separately, you will not qualify for the Earned Income Credit and cannot claim a credit based on child care expenses. If you file a joint return with your spouse, you may be eligible to claim these credits. Refer to Publication 503, *Child and Dependent Care Expenses* and Publication 596, *Earned Income Credit.*

References:
• Tax Topic 353, What is Your Filing Status?
• Publication 501, Exemptions, Standard Deduction, and Filing Information
• Publication 503, Child and Dependent Care Expenses
• Publication 596, Earned Income Credit

Q. *For head of household filing status, do you have to claim a child as a dependent to qualify?*

A. In certain circumstances, you do not need to claim the child as a dependent to qualify for head of household filing status, such as when the qualifying child is unmarried child and is your grandchild, stepchild, or adopted child. Refer to

Publication 501, *Exemptions, Standard Deduction, and Filing Information,* for more information.

References:
• Publication 501, Exemptions, Standard Deduction, and Filing Information

Keyword(s): Dependents, Exemptions; Keyword(s): Child Tax Credit; Keyword(s): Child Custody Tax Issues; Keyword(s): Joint Custody; Keyword(s): Foster Child; Keyword(s): Married Filing Separately

2.3 Dependents & Exemptions

Q. If I claim my daughter as a dependent because she is a full-time college student, can she claim herself as a dependent when she files her return?

A. If you claim your daughter as a dependent on your income tax return, she cannot also claim herself on her income tax return.

If an individual is filing his or her their own tax return, and if the individual can be claimed as a dependent on someone else's return, then the individual cannot claim their own personal exemption. In this case, your daughter should check the box on her return indicating that someone else can claim her as a dependent.

References:
• Publication 501, Exemptions, Standard Deduction and Filing Information
• Tax Topic 354, Dependents

Q. My son was born on December 31st. Can I claim him as a dependent? If so, will he be also qualified for the Child Tax Credit?

A. If your child was born alive during the year, and the exemption tests are met, you may take the full exemption. You may be entitled to a Child Tax Credit for him. Refer to Publication 501, *Exemptions, Standard Deduction and Filing Information.* Refer to the Instructions for Form 1040 for information about the Child Tax Credit.

References:
• Publication 501, Exemptions, Standard Deduction and Filing Information
• Instructions for Form 1040 (General Inst.)
• Tax Topic 354, Dependents
• Publication 17, Your Federal Income Tax

Q. *I am adopting a child and do not yet have a social security number for the child. How can I claim the exemption for the child?*

A. Parents in the process of a domestic U. S. adoption who do not have and/or are unable to obtain the child's Social Security Number (SSN) should request an Adoption Taxpayer Identification Number (ATIN) in order to claim the child as a dependent and (if eligible) to claim the child care credit. Form W-7A, Application for Taxpayer Identification Number for Pending U.S. Adoptions, is used by qualifying taxpayers to obtain an ATIN. To get Form W-7A, you may go to any IRS walk-in site or call 1-800-829-3676. You may also download the form. For more information about the ATIN, refer to the Form W-7A, instructions. If the child is not a U. S. citizen or resident, use Form W-7, Application for IRS Individual Taxpayer Identification Number, to obtain an ITIN. For more information, refer to Individual Taxpayer Identification Number.

References:
• Form W-7, Application for IRS Individual Taxpayer Identification Number
• Form W-7A, Application for Taxpayer Identification Number for Pending Adoptions
• Individual Taxpayer Identification Number
• Publication 501, Exemption, Standard Deductions, and Filing Information

Q. *My husband and I have provided a home for my niece and her son for the past seven months. She receives no child support from her ex-spouse, and she does not work or have any income of her own. Can I claim her and her son as dependents?*

A. Your niece doesn't need to live with you for the entire year in order to be claimed as a dependent. She meets the first of five dependency exemption tests, which is the relationship test. She must still meet the other four dependency exemption tests.
• Citizenship test.
• Joint return test.
• Gross income test.
• Support test. Your niece's son did not live with you for the entire year and does not meet the relationship test. Therefore, he cannot be claimed as a dependent. Refer to Publication 501, *Exemptions, Standard Deduction and Filing Information*, for more information.

References:
• Publication 501, Exemptions, Standard Deduction and Filing Information

Q. *How do you claim a child if you agree with your ex-spouse to claim him 6 months and he claims him the other 6 months of the year?*

A. The dependency exemption can not be split. Generally, the custodial parent is treated as the parent who provided more than half of the child's support. This parent is usually allowed to claim the exemption for the child if the other exemption tests are met. However, the noncustodial parent may be treated as the parent who provided more than half of the child's support if certain conditions are met.

The custodial parent signs a Form 8332, Release of Claim to Exemption for Child of Divorced or Separated Parents, or a substantially similar statement, and provides it to the noncustodial parent who attaches it to his or her return. Please beware that if the custodial parent releases the *exception, the custodial parent may not claim the Child Tax Credit. Refer to Publication 501, Exemption, Standard Deduction, and Filing Information* or Publication 504, *Divorced or Separated Individuals*, for more information on the special rule for children of divorced or separated parents.

References:
• Publication 501, Exemption, Standard Deduction
• Publication 504, Divorced or Separated Individuals
• Form 8332, Release of Claim to Exemption for Child of Divorced or Separated Parents
• Tax Topic 354, Dependents

Q. *My wife and I are married filing separately. We have one son and we meet all of the dependency exemption tests. We contributed an equal amount to our son's support and want to know if we both can claim him on our separate returns?*

A. Refer to Publication 501, *Exemptions, Standard Deduction and Filling Information*, for more information.

A dependency exemption may only be claimed on one return. Since neither you nor your wife contributed more than half of your son's support, one of you can still claim dependency exemption for your son only if the other spouse provides a written declaration that he or she will not claim the child as a dependent for that year. Form 2120, *Multiple Support Declaration*, can be used for this purpose.

References:
• Publication 501, Exemptions, Standard Deduction and Filing Information

• Form 2120, Multiple Support Declaration
• Tax Topic 354, Dependents

Q. *My husband and I were separated the last 11 months of the year and our two children lived with me. My husband provided all the financial support. Who can claim the children as dependents on the tax return?*

A. For children of divorced or separated parents, generally, the custodial parent is treated as the parent who provided more than half of the child's support. This parent is usually allowed to claim the exemption for the child if the other exemption tests are met. However, the non custodial parent may be treated as the parent who provided more than half of the child's support if certain conditions are met. This parent is usually allowed to claim the exemption for the child if the other exemption tests are met. However, the non custodial parent may be treated as the parent who provided more than half of the child's support if the custodial parent releases his or her claim to the exemption by completing Form 8332, *Release of Claim to Exemption for Child of Divorced or Separated Parents*, or signing a substantially similar statement. Please be aware that if you release your claim to the dependency exemption for a child, you may not claim a Child Tax Credit for that child.

Refer to Publication 501, *Exemption, Standard Deduction, and Filing Information* or Publication 504, *Divorced or Separated Individuals*, for more information on the special rule for children of divorced or separated parents.

References:
• Publication 501, Exemptions, Standard Deduction and Filing Information
• Publication 504, Divorced or Separated Individuals
• Form 8332, Release of Claim to Exemption for Child of Divorced or Separated Parents
• Tax Topic 354, Dependents

Q. *If you pay child support, are you allowed to deduct anything on your taxes or claim the child as an exemption?*

A. Nothing can be deducted for the child support payments. Child support payments are neither deductible by the payer nor taxable income to the payee. You may be able to claim the child as a dependent. Generally, the custodial parent generally is treated as the parent who provided more than half of the child's support. This parent is usually allowed to claim the exemption for the child if the other exemption tests are met. However, the non custodial parent may be treated as the parent who provided more than half of the child's support if the custodial parent signs a Form 8332, *Release of Claim to Exemption for Child of Divorced of Separated Parents*, or a substantially similar statement. Refer to Publication 501, *Exemptions, Standard Deduction and Filing Information*, and Publication 504, *Divorced or Separated Individuals*, for more information.

References:
• Publication 501, Exemptions, Standard Deduction and Filing Information
• Publication 504, Divorced or Separated Individuals
• Tax Topic 354, Dependents

Q. *Can a court order determine who takes a child for a deduction? Does the court order supersede the IRS requirements?*

A. Federal law determines who may claim a dependency exemption. Refer to Publication 504, *Divorced or Separated Individuals*, for more information on the special rule for children of divorced or separated parents.

References:
• Publication 501, Exemptions, Standard Deductions, and Filing Information
• Publication 504, Divorced or Separated Individuals
• Tax Topic 354, Dependents

Q. *My son was born on December 31st. Can I claim him as a dependent? If so, will he be also qualified for the Child Tax Credit?*

A. If your child was born alive during the year, and the exemption tests are met, you may take the full exemption. You may be entitled to a Child Tax Credit for him. Refer to Publication 501, *Exemptions, Standard Deduction and Filing Information*. Refer to the Instructions for Form 1040 for information about the Child Tax Credit.

References:
• Publication 501, Exemptions, Standard Deduction and Filing Information
• Instructions for Form 1040 (General Inst.)
• Tax Topic 354, Dependents
• Publication 17, Your Federal Income Tax

Q. *My daughter was born at the end of the year. We are still waiting for a social security number. Can I send in my return and later supply the social security number for her?*

A. If you file your return claiming your daughter as a dependent and do not provide her social security number on the return, the dependent exemption will be disallowed. You have two options. You could file your income tax return without claiming your daughter as a dependent. After you receive her social security number, you could then amend your return on Form 1040X, *Amended U.S. Individual Income Tax Return*. You have three years from the later of the due date of the return or from the date the return was filed to amend the return.

The other option is to file a Form 4868, *Application for Automatic Extension of Time to File U.S. Individual Income Tax Return*. This would give you an additional four months to file your return; by then you should have your daughter's social security number.

References:
• Form 1040X, Amended U.S. Individual Income Tax Return
• Form 4868, Application for Automatic Extension of Time to File U.S. Individual Income Tax Return
• Tax Topic 354, Dependents

Q. *My child was stillborn. He died right before he was delivered. Can I claim my child?*

A. You cannot claim a dependency exemption for a stillborn child. Refer to Publication 501, *Exemption, Standard Deduction, and Filing Information*, for more information.

References:
• Publication 501, Exemption, Standard Deduction, and Filing Information
• Tax Topic 354, Dependents

Chapter 3

Itemized Deductions/Standard Deductions

~~~~~

Keyword(s): Listed Property; Keyword(s): Educational Expenses

3.1 Autos, Computers, Electronic Devices (Listed Property)

Q. My university required each incoming freshman to come to school with their own computer. Is there any way to deduct the cost of the computer from my tax liability?

A. The cost of a personal computer is generally a personal expense that is not deductible. However, if the school bills everyone, as a condition of attendance or enrollment, for proprietary computer devices and/or software available no where else, then this may qualify as an expense towards either the Lifetime Learning Credit or Hope Credit. For more information, refer to Publication 970, *Tax Benefits for Education.*

References:
• Tax Topic 513, Educational expenses
• Publication 970 Tax Benefits for Education

Keyword(s): Student Loan Interest Deduction; Keyword(s): Reimbursements; Keyword(s): Interest Expense; Keyword(s): Employee Business Expenses; Keyword(s): Loans; Keyword(s): Coverdell Education Savings Account; Keyword(s): Educator expense deduction

3.2 Education & Work-Related Expenses

Q. What are the limits for deducting interest paid on a student loan?

A. The maximum deductible interest on a qualified student loan is $2,500 per return. If you are a taxpayer whose return status is married filing jointly, you are allowed to deduct the full $2,500 only when your Modified Adjusted Gross

Income (MAGI) is $100,000 or less. If your MAGI is between $100,000 and $130,000, the amount of your student loan interest deduction is gradually reduced. The instructions for Form 1040 show you how to compute the deduction. If your MAGI is $130,000 or more, you are not able to take any deduction.

For those whose filing status is single, head of household, or qualifying widow(er), the full $2,500 deduction is allowed for MAGI levels equal to or below $50,000. For MAGI between $50,000 and $65,000, the deduction amount is phased out, and computation instructions are provided in the Instructions for Form 1040. If your MAGI amount is $65,000 or more, there is no deduction.

There is no deduction if you file as married filing separately, if you are claimed as a dependent, or if the loan is from a related party or a qualified employer plan. For more information, refer to Publication 970, Tax Benefits for Education; Tax Topic 505, *Interest Expense*; and Tax Topic 513, *Educational Expenses*.

References:
• Publication 970, Tax Benefits for Education
• Tax Topic 505, Interest Expense
• Tax Topic 456
• Tax Topic 513, Educational Expenses

Q. Is the $2,500 maximum deduction for student loan interest per PERSON, or per RETURN? I am married filing jointly and have paid over $5,000 of qualified interest payments for my husband and me. Are we allowed to deduct up to $5,000 ($2,500/person) or only $2,500 total on our return?

A. The deduction is limited to $2,500 per return for tax year 2001 and beyond. If you file as "married filing separately, " there is no deduction. For more information, refer to Publication 970, *Tax Benefits for Education;* and Tax Topic 505, *Interest Expense.*

References:

• Publication 970, Tax Benefits for Education
• Tax Topic 505, Interest Expense
• Tax Topic 513, Educational Expenses

Q. Last year, my parents took out a student loan for me in their name and I also took out a student loan. My parents received Form 1098-E for their loan and I also received Form 1098-E for my loan. Can we both claim the interest from the loans on our tax returns? Last year, I was not their dependent.

A. In order for a taxpayer to claim a deduction for student loan interest, the loan must be incurred for the taxpayer, the taxpayer' spouse, or a person who was the taxpayer's dependent when the taxpayer took out the loan. Since you were not your parents' dependent when they took out the student loan, the interest they paid on the loan does not qualify for deduction. However, the student loan interest payments you made on the student loan you took out on your behalf are eligible for deduction, provided all the other requirements are met. For more information, refer to Publication 970, *Tax Benefits for Education;* Tax Topic 505, *Interest Expense*; and Tax Topic 513, *Educational Expenses.*

References:
• Publication 970, Tax Benefits for Education
• Tax Topic 505, Interest Expense
• Tax Topic 513, Educational Expenses

Q. *My employer is including my graduate school tuition reimbursements on my W-2 as wages. Where do I claim these education expenses on my Form 1040?*

A. If your graduate school tuition is deductible and the reimbursements are included in your income as wages, you may take the expense as a miscellaneous itemized deduction on Form 1040, Schedule A, *Itemized Deductions*, line 20. You may also need to attach Form 2106, *Employee Business Expenses.* For more information, refer to Publication 970 *Tax Benefits for Education*; Tax Topic 513, Educational Expenses; and Form 2106, *Employee Business Expenses.*

References:
• Publication 970, Tax Benefits for Education
• Form 1040, Schedule A, Itemized Deductions
• Tax Topic 513, Educational Expenses
• Form 2106, Employee Business Expenses

Q. *Can I deduct the cost of classes I need for work?*

A. In some cases, you may be able to deduct the cost of classes you need for work. This deduction, however, would be subject to the 2 percent of AGI limitation, along with most other miscellaneous itemized deductions you list on Form 1040, Schedule A, *Itemized Deductions.*

To be deductible, your expenses must be for education that:
(1) Maintains or improves skills required in your present job, or

(2) Serves a business purpose and is required by your employer, or by law, to keep your present salary, status, or job.

However, these same expenses are not deductible if:

(1) The education is required to meet the minimum educational requirements of your job, or

(2) The education is part of a program that will lead to qualifying you in a new trade or business.

Educational expenses, related to your present work, that are incurred during periods of temporary absence from your job may also be deductible provided you return to the same job or same type of work. Generally, absence from work for one year or less is considered temporary.

For more information, refer to Publication 970, *Tax Benefits for Education;* and Tax Topic 513, *Educational Expenses*

References:
Publication 970, Tax Benefits for Education
Tax Topic 513, Educational Expenses
Form 8863, Education Credits (Hope and Lifetime Learning Credits)

Q. I am an educator. Are there any special tax deductible expenses available to persons such as myself?

A. If you are an educator, you may be able to deduct up to $250 of expenses you paid for purchases of books and classroom supplies, even if you don't itemize your deductions, according to the IRS. These out-of-pocket expenses may lower your 2005 tax bill.

The Working Families Tax Relief Act of 2004 reinstated the educator expense deduction, which had expired at the end of last year, for both 2004 and 2005. Expenses incurred any time this year may qualify for the deduction, not just those since the Act was signed on Oct. 4.

The deduction is available if you are an eligible educator in a public or private elementary or secondary school. To be eligible, you must work at least 900 hours during a school year as a teacher, instructor, counselor, principal or aide.

You may subtract up to $250 of qualified expenses when figuring your adjusted gross income. Qualified expenses are unreimbursed expenses you paid or incurred for books, supplies, computer equipment (including related software and services), other equipment, and supplementary materials that you use in the classroom. For courses in health and physical education, expenses for supplies are qualified expenses only if they are related to athletics.

To be deductible, the qualified expenses must be more than the following amounts for the tax year:

- The interest on qualified U.S. savings bonds that you excluded from income because you paid qualified higher education expenses,
- Any distribution from a qualified tuition program that you excluded from income, or
- Any tax-free withdrawals from your Coverdell Education Savings Account.

For more information, call the IRS Tele-Tax system toll-free at 1-800-829-4477 and select Topic 458, or read it online.

References:
- Form 1040, U.S. Individual Income Tax Return
- Form 1040A, U.S. Individual Income Tax Return
- Tax Topic 458, Educator Expense Deduction

Keyword(s): Contributions (Charitable); Keyword(s): Deductible Contributions

3.3 Gifts & Charitable Contributions

Q. I donated a used car to a qualified charity. I itemize my deductions, and I would like to take a charitable contribution for the donation. Do I need to attach any special forms to my return? What records do I need to keep?

A. If you claim a deduction on your return of over $500 for all contributed property, you must attach a Form 8283, Noncash Charitable Contributions, to your return. If you claim a total deduction of $5,000 or less for all contributed property, you need only complete Section A of Form 8283. If you claim a deduction of more than $5,000 for an item or a group of similar items, you generally need to complete Section B of Form 8283 which requires, in most cases, a qualified appraisal by a qualified appraiser.

You will need to obtain and keep evidence of your car donation and be able to substantiate the fair market value of the car. If you are claiming a deduction of $250 or more for the car donation, you will also need a contemporaneous written acknowledgement from the charity that includes a description of the car and a statement of whether the charity provided any goods or services in return for the car and, if so, a description and estimate of the fair market value of the goods or services.

For more information on these requirements, refer to Publication 526, *Charitable Contributions*, Publication 561, *Determining the Value of Donated Property;* Form 8283, *Noncash Charitable Contributions*; and its instructions, and Tax Topic 506, *Contributions.*

References:
• Publication 526, Charitable Contributions
• Publication 561, Determining the Value of Donated Property
• Form 8283, Noncash Charitable Contributions
• Tax Topic 506, Contributions
• Form 1040, Schedule A , Itemized Deductions

Q. *How do I verify an organization's charitable status?*

A. You can:
• Check with the organization to which you made the donation. The organization should be able to provide you with verification of its charitable status. • Refer to Pub. 78 for a list of most qualified organizations. You can access Pub. 78 on the IRS website at www.irs.gov under Charities and Non-Profits. • Call our Tax Exempt/Government Entities Customer Account Services at 1-877-829-5500. Assistance is available Monday through Friday from 8:00 a.m. to 6:30 p.m. EST.

Keyword(s): Alimony; Keyword(s): Gambling income; Keyword(s): Gambling winnings

3.4 Interest, Investment, Money Transactions (Alimony, Bad Debts, Applicable Federal Interest Rate, Gambling, Legal Fees, Loans, etc.;

Q. *Can I deduct alimony paid to my former spouse?*

A. If you are divorced or separated, you may be able to deduct the alimony or separate maintenance payments that you are required to make to your spouse or former spouse, or on behalf of that spouse. For additional information, refer to Tax Topic 452, *Alimony Paid* (this topic covers alimony under decrees or agreements after 1984); and Publication 504, *Divorced or Separated Individuals.*

References:
• Publication 504, Divorced or Separated Individuals
• Tax Topic 452, Alimony Paid

Q. *Is the interest amount that we paid to the IRS deductible?*

A. Interest and penalties paid to the IRS on Federal taxes are not deductible. For more information, refer to Items You Cannot Deduct in Chapter 25, *Interest Expense*, in Publication 17, *Your Federal Income Tax for Individuals;* and Tax Topic 505, *Interest Expense.*

References:
• Publication 17, Your Federal Income Tax for Individuals
• Tax Topic 505, Interest Expense

Q. *I made some money gambling, but I also had some losses. What are the tax effects?*

A. Hit a big one in 2005? With more and more gambling establishments, the IRS reminds people that they must report all gambling winnings as income on their tax return.
Gambling income includes, but is not limited to, winnings from lotteries, raffles, horse and dog races and casinos, as well as the fair market value of prizes such as cars, houses, trips or other noncash prizes.

Generally, if you receive $600 ($1,200 from bingo and slot machines and $1,500 from keno) or more in gambling winnings and your winnings are at least 300 times the amount of the wager, the payer is required to issue you a Form W-2G. If you have won more than $5,000, the payer may be required to withhold 25 percent of the proceeds for Federal income tax. However, if you did not provide your Social Security number to the payer, the amount withheld will be 28 percent. The full amount of your gambling winnings for the year must be reported on line 21, Form 1040. If you itemize deductions, you can deduct your gambling losses for the year on line 27, Schedule A (Form 1040). You cannot deduct gambling losses that are more than your winnings. It is important to keep an accurate diary or similar record of your gambling winnings and losses. To deduct your losses, you must be able to provide receipts, tickets, statements or other records that show the amount of both your winnings and losses.

For more information on record keeping, see IRS Publication 529, *Miscellaneous Deductions,* or Publication 525, *Taxable and Nontaxable Income.* You may also want to check out Form W-2G and its instructions and Tax Topic 419, *Gambling Income and Expenses.* All are available on this Web site. You may also order free publications and forms by calling toll free 1-800-TAX-FORM (1-800-829-3676).

References:
- Form W-2G, Certain Gambling Winnings
- Publication 529, Miscellaneous Deductions
- Publication 525, Taxable and Nontaxable Income
- Tax Topic 419, Gambling Income and Expenses

Keyword(s): Medical Expenses

3.5 Medical, Nursing Home, Special Care Expenses

Q. My father is in a nursing home and I pay for the entire cost. Can I deduct the expenses on my tax return?

A. You may deduct qualified medical expenses you pay for yourself, your spouse, and your dependents, including a person you claim as a dependent under a Multiple Support Agreement. You can also deduct medical expenses you paid for someone who would have qualified as your dependent for the purpose of taking personal exemptions except that the person did not meet the gross income or joint return test.

Nursing home expenses are allowable as medical expenses in certain instances. If you, your spouse, or your dependent is in a nursing home, and the primary reason for being there is for medical care, the entire cost, including meals and lodging, is a medical expense. If the individual is in the home mainly for personal reasons, then only the cost of the actual medical care is a medical expense, and the cost of the meals and lodging is not deductible.

You deduct medical expenses on Form 1040, Schedule A, *Itemized Deductions.* The total of all allowable medical expenses must be reduced by 7.5% of your Adjusted Gross Income. For more information, refer to Publication 502, *Medical and Dental Expenses.*

References:
• Publication 502, Medical and Dental Expenses

Q. Whose medical and dental expenses can I include in my Tax Return?

A. You can include medical and dental bills you paid for: • Yourself and your spouse.
• All dependents you claim on your return. • Your child whom you do not claim as a dependent because of the rules explained in Pub. 501 for children of divorced or separated parents. • Any person you could have claimed as a dependent on your return if that person had not filed a joint return or received $3,200 or more of gross income. *(**Check 1040-INSTRUCTIONS for the current threshold amount**)*

Keyword(s): Home Mortgage Interest; Keyword(s): Refinancing Fees; Keyword(s): Closing Cost; Keyword(s): Loan Origination Fee; Keyword(s): Investment Interest; Keyword(s): Itemized Deductions; Keyword(s): Mortgage Interest Deduction; Keyword(s): Primary Residence

3.6   Real Estate (Taxes, Mortgage Interest, Points, Other Property Expenses)

Q. *I have a mortgage for my primary residence and a second mortgage for land that I intend to build a home on. Can the interest be deducted for the second mortgage?*

A. Unless you have begun construction of a home on the bare land that you can occupy within 24 months, the land would be considered an investment and the interest you paid on the second mortgage would not qualify as deductible mortgage interest. However, it would constitute investment interest if you itemize your deductions. For more information, refer to Publication 550, *Investment Income and Expenses,* and Publication 936, *Home Mortgage Interest Deduction.*

References:
* Publication 936, Home Mortgage Interest Deduction
* Publication 550, Investment Income and Expenses
* Tax Topic 505, Interest expense

Q. *Is interest on a home equity line of credit deductible as a second mortgage?*

A. You may deduct home equity debt interest, as an itemized deduction, if you are legally liable to pay the interest, pay the interest in the tax year, secure the debt with your home, and do not exceed certain limitations. For more information, refer to Publication 936, *Home Mortgage Interest Deduction;* and Tax Topic 505, *Interest Expense.*

References:
- Publication 936, Home Mortgage Interest Deduction
- Tax Topic 505, Interest Expense

Q. I refinanced my home last year and paid points. Are they all deductible this year?

A. Generally points paid to refinance your home are not deductible in their entirety in the year paid. They are "amortized" or deducted over the life of the loan. For more information, refer to Publication 936, *Home Mortgage Interest Deduction*, and Tax Topic 504, *Home Mortgage Points.*

References:
- Publication 936, Home Mortgage Interest Deduction
- Tax Topic 504, Home Mortgage Points

Q. I took out a home equity loan to pay off personal debts. Is this interest deductible? Where do I enter this amount on my tax return?

A. A loan taken out for reasons other than to buy, build, or substantially improve your home, such as to pay off personal debts may qualify as home equity debt. The interest would be deducted on line 10, Form 1040, Schedule A, Itemized Deductions. The amount you can deduct as interest on home equity debt is subject to certain limitations. For more information, refer to Publication 936, *Home Mortgage Interest Deduction;* and Tax Topic 505, *Interest Expense.*

References:
- Publication 936, Home Mortgage Interest Deduction
- Tax Topic 505, Interest Expense

Q. Is the mortgage interest and property tax on a second residence deductible?

A. The mortgage interest on a second home which you use as a residence for some portion of the taxable year, is generally deductible if the interest satisfies the same requirements for deductibility as interest on a primary residence. Real estate taxes paid on your primary and second residence are, generally, deductible. Deductible real estate taxes include any state, local, or foreign taxes on real property levied for the general public welfare. Deductible real estate taxes do not include taxes charged for local benefits and improvements that increase the value of the property. For more information, refer to Publication 17, *Your Federal Income Tax* for Individuals; Tax Topic 503, *Deductible Taxes; and Publication 530, Tax Information for First-Time Home Owners.*

43

References:
* Publication 936, Home Mortgage Interest Deduction
* Publication 530, Tax Information for First-Time Homeowners
* Publication 17, Your Federal Income Tax for Individuals
* Tax Topic 503, Deductible Taxes
* Tax Topic 505, Interest Expense

Q. If I must deduct points over the life of my mortgage, and I have a 30 year mortgage, does this mean that I divide the points paid by 30 and enter that amount on Schedule A?

A. No, you don't divide the points by 30. If you choose to use the straight-line method, you need to divide the points by the number of payments over the term of the loan and deduct points for a year according to the number of payments made in the year. If the loan ends prematurely, due to payoff or refinance with a different lender, for example, then the remaining points are deducted in that year. Points not included in Form 1098 (usually not included on a refinance) should be entered on line 12 of Form 1040, Schedule A, *Itemized Deductions.* For more information, refer to Publication 936, *Home Mortgage Interest Deduction*; and Tax Topic 504, *Home Mortgage Points.*

References:
* Publication 936, Home Mortgage Interest Deduction
* Tax Topic 504, Home Mortgage Points
* Form 1040, Schedule A, Itemized Deductions

Q. Our home was seriously damaged by flooding last year. Are there special provisions for claiming a loss since our home is located in a declared disaster area?

A. Casualty losses not compensated for by insurance or otherwise are generally deductible only in the year the casualty occurred. However, if you have a deductible loss from a disaster in an area that is officially designated by the President of the United States as eligible for federal disaster assistance, you can choose to deduct that loss on your return for the year immediately preceding the loss year. In other words, you may treat the loss as having occurred in either the current year or the previous year, whichever provides the best tax results for you. If you have already filed your return for the preceding year, the loss may be claimed by filing an amended return, Form 1040X, Amended U.S. Individual Income Tax Return. For more information on disaster area losses (including flood losses), refer to Tax Topic 515, *Disaster Area Losses* (Including Flood

Losses), or Publication 547, *Casualties, Disasters and Thefts*. Publication 584, *Casualty, Disaster, and Theft Loss Workbook*, can be used to help you catalog your property.

References:
• Publication 547, Casualties, Disasters, and Thefts (Business and Non-Business)
• Publication 584, Casualty, Disaster, and Theft Loss Workbook
• Form 1040X, Amended U.S. Individual Income Tax Return
• Tax Topic 515, Disaster Area Losses (Including Flood Losses)

Keyword(s): Itemize or not Itemize

3.7 Other Deduction Questions ✓

Q. How Do I determine if I should Itemize or not Itemize?

A. Whether to itemize deductions on your tax return depends on how much you spent on certain expenses last year. According to the IRS, money paid for medical care, mortgage interest, taxes, contributions, casualty losses, and miscellaneous deductions can reduce your taxes. If the total amount spent on those categories is more than the standard deduction, you can usually benefit by itemizing.

For tax year 2005 itemized returns, you still have a choice of claiming a state and local tax deduction for either sales or income taxes. The IRS will provide optional tables for use in determining the deduction amount, relieving taxpayers of the need to save receipts throughout the year. Sales taxes paid on motor vehicles and boats may be added to the table amount, but only up to the amount paid at the general sales tax rate. Check a box on Schedule A, Itemized Deductions, to indicate whether your deduction is for sales or income taxes.

The standard deduction amounts are based on your filing status and are subject to inflation adjustments each year. For 2005, they are:

Single — $5,000
Married Filing Jointly — $10,000
Head of Household — $7,300
Married Filing Separately — $5,000

The standard deduction amount is more for taxpayers age 65 or older and for those who are blind. It is generally less for those who can be claimed as a dependent on some other taxpayer's return. Your itemized deductions may be limited by your adjusted gross income. This limit applies to all itemized deductions except medical and dental expenses, casualty and theft losses, gambling losses, and investment interest. See IRS Publication 501, *Exemptions, Standard Deduction, and Filing Information* applicable to the 2005 tax year.

When a married couple files separate returns and one spouse itemizes deductions, the other spouse must also itemize and cannot claim the standard deduction.

There are some taxpayers who are not eligible for the standard deduction. They include nonresident aliens, dual-status aliens, and individuals who file returns for periods of less than 12 months.

For additional information, see Publication 501,*Exemptions, Standard Deduction, and Filing Information.* Use Form 1040, *U.S. Individual Income Tax Return*, and Schedule A, *Itemized Deductions*, to itemize your deductions. For more details on itemized deductions, see the instructions for Schedule A or Publication 17, *Your Federal Income Tax.* Download the publications and forms or order them by calling toll free 1-800-TAX-FORM (1-800-829-3676).

References:
> Publication 17, Your Federal Income Tax
> Instructions for Schedule A, Itemized Deductions

Q. *My spouse and I are filing separate returns. How can we split our itemized deductions?*

A. If you and your spouse file separate returns and one of you itemizes deductions, the other spouse will have a standard deduction of zero. Therefore, the other spouse should also itemize deductions.

You may be able to claim itemized deductions on a separate return for certain expenses that you paid separately or jointly with your spouse. Deductible expenses that are paid out of separate funds, such as medical expenses, are deductible by the spouse who pays them. If these expenses are paid from community funds, the deduction may depend on whether or not you live in a community property state. In a community property state, the deduction is, generally, divided equally between you and your spouse. For more information refer to Publication 504, *Divorced or Separated Individuals;* and Publication 555, *Community Property.*

References:
• Publication 504, Divorced or Separated Individuals
• Publication 555, Community Property

Q. *I am in a disaster area and heard the IRS could help me. What can the IRS do?*

A. If you have been affected by a Presidentially declared disaster, the IRS may help you by allowing additional time for filing returns and making payments, and in some circumstances, waiving penalties if the disaster has caused you to file or pay late. The IRS may also, provide copies or transcripts of previously filed returns, free of charge. You may be eligible to file for a casualty loss deduction on the prior year's tax return, or if you have already filed, by amended return (Form 1040X). For additional information on this subject, refer to Tax Topic 515, *Casualty, Disaster, and Theft Losses*, and Publication 547, *Casualties, Disasters, and Theft*.

References:
• Publication 547, Casualties, Disasters, and Thefts
• Tax Topic 515, Casualty, Disaster, and Theft Losses

Q. *I pay various types of taxes. Which of them are deductible?*

A. Did you know that you may be able to deduct certain taxes on your federal income tax return? The IRS says you can if you file Form 1040 and itemize deductions on Schedule A. Deductions decrease the amount of income subject to taxation. There are four types of deductible non-business taxes:
1. State, local and local income taxes;
2. Real estate taxes;
3. Personal property taxes; and
4. Foreign income taxes.

This year, people will have a chance of claiming a state and local tax deduction for either income or sales taxes on their returns.

You can deduct any estimated taxes paid to state or local governments and any prior year's state or local income tax as long as they were paid during the tax year. If deducting sales taxes instead, you may deduct actual expenses or use optional tables provided by the IRS to determine your deduction amount, relieving you of the need to save receipts. Sales taxes paid on motor vehicles and boats may be added to the table amount, but only up to the mount paid to the general sales tax rate.

Taxpayers will check a box on Schedule A, Itemized Deductions, to indicate whether their deduction is for income or sales tax Deductible real estate taxes are usually any state, local, or foreign taxes on real property. If a portion of your monthly mortgage payment goes into an escrow account and your lender periodically pays your real estate taxes to local governments out of this account, you can deduct only the amount actually paid during the year to the taxing authorities. Your lender will normally send you a Form 1098, Mortgage Interest Statement, at the end of the tax year with this information.

Personal property taxes are deductible when they are based on the value of personal property, such as a boat or car. To be deductible, the tax must be charged to you on a yearly basis, even if it is collected more than once a year or less than once a year. Generally, you can take either a deduction or a tax credit for foreign income taxes but not for taxes paid on income that is excluded for U. S. tax.

You can find more information on non-business deductions for taxes in Publication 17, *Your Federal Income Tax*. Taxes. You may download Pub. 17 or order it by calling toll free 1-800-TAX-FORM (1-800-829-3676).

References:
- Schedules A&B, Itemized Deductions and Interest & Dividend Income
- Publication 17, Your Federal Income Tax

Q. What is a Coverdell Education Savings Account? How much can I contribute? Are the distributions taxable?

A. A Coverdell Education Savings Account (ESA) is a savings account created as an incentive to help parents and students save for education expenses. The total contributions for the beneficiary (who is under age 18 or is a special needs beneficiary) of this account in any year cannot be more than $2,000, no matter how many accounts have been established. The beneficiary will not owe tax on the distributions if, for a year, the distributions from an account are not more than a beneficiary's qualified education expenses at an eligible education institution. This benefit applies to higher education expenses as well as to elementary and secondary education expenses. Generally, any individual (including the beneficiary) can contribute to a Coverdell ESA if the individual's modified adjusted gross (MAGI) income is less than $110,000 ($220,000 if the individual is filing a joint return). The $2,000 maximum contribution per beneficiary is gradually reduced if the contributor's MAGI is between $95,000 and $110,000 ($190,000 and $220,000 if the contributor is filing a joint return).

Usually, MAGI for the purpose of determining your maximum contribution limit is the adjusted gross income (AGI) shown on your tax return increased by the following exclusion from your income: foreign earned income of U.S. citizens or residents living abroad, housing costs of U.S. citizens or residents living abroad, and income from sources within Puerto Rico or American Samoa. Contributions to a Coverdell ESA may be made until the due date of the contributor's return, without extensions. Distributions are tax-free as long as they are used for qualified education expenses, such as tuition, books, fees, etc., at an eligible educational institution. This includes any public, private or religious school that provides elementary or secondary education as determined under state law.

The Hope and lifetime learning credits can be claimed in the same year the beneficiary takes a tax-free distribution from a Coverdell ESA, as long as the same expenses are not used for both benefits. Refer to Publication 970 for more details. If the distribution exceeds education expenses, a portion will be taxable to the beneficiary and will be subject to an additional 10 percent tax. Exceptions to the additional 10 percent tax include the death or disability of the beneficiary or if the beneficiary receives a qualified scholarship.

If there is a balance in the Coverdell ESA at the time the beneficiary reaches age 30, it must be distributed within 30 days. A portion representing earnings on the account will be taxable and subject to the additional 10 percent tax. The beneficiary may avoid these taxes by rolling over the full balance to another Coverdell ESA for another family member.

For more information, please see Publication 970, *Tax Benefits for Higher Education.* Download the publication or order it by calling toll free 1-800-TAX-FORM (1-800-829-3676).

References:
* Publication 970, Tax Benefits for Higher Education
* Tax Topic 310 — Coverdell Education Savings Accounts

Remember, the Hope and lifetime learning credits can be claimed in the same year the beneficiary takes a tax-free distribution from a Coverdell ESA, as long as the same expenses are not used for both benefits. Refer to Publication 970 for more details.

Chapter 4

Interest/Dividends/Other Types of Income
~~~~~

Keyword(s): 1099 Information Returns; Keyword(s): Interest Income; Keyword(s): Dividends; Keyword(s): Mutual Fund

4.1 1099–DIV Dividend Income

Q. How do I report this 1099-DIV from my mutual fund?

A. Enter the ordinary dividends from Form 1099-DIV, box 1a, on line 9a of Form 1040, U.S. Individual Income Tax Return. Enter any qualified dividends from Form 1099-DIV, box 1b, on line 9b of Form 1040. Enter the total capital gain distributions from box 2a on line 13, column (f) of Form 1040, Schedule D. Enter the 28% rate gain portion of your capital gain distributions from box 2b on line 13, column (g) of Schedule D. If you have an amount in box 2c or box 2d, refer to Instructions for Form 1040, Schedule D. Nontaxable distributions, box 3, that are return of capital distributions, reduce your cost basis and are not taxable until your basis is reduced to zero. If no amount is shown in boxes 2b through 2d, and your only capital gains and losses are capital gain distributions, refer to Instructions for Form 1040 for line 13.

References:
• Form 1040, Schedule D, Capital Gains and Losses
• Instructions for Form 1040
• Instructions for Form 1040, Schedule D

Q. I received dividends from my credit union. How do I report this income?

A. Certain distributions commonly referred to as dividends are actually interest. They include "dividends " on deposits or share accounts in cooperative banks, credit unions, domestic savings and loan associations, and mutual savings banks.

Report interest income on line 8a of Form 1040 or Form 1040A, or line 2 of Form 1040EZ. If your taxable interest income is more than $1,500, be sure to show that income on Schedule B of Form 1040, or on Schedule 1 of Form 1040A. You cannot file Form 1040EZ if your interest income is more than

$1,500. Refer to Tax Topic 403, *Interest Received*, for additional information on interest income.

References:
• Form 1040, U.S. Individual Income Tax Return
• Form 1040A, U.S. Individual Income Tax Return
• Form 1040EZ, U.S. Individual Income Tax Return for Single and Joint Filers with No Dependents
• Tax Topic 403, Interest Received

Keyword(s): Installment Proceeds; Keyword(s): Investment income; Keyword(s): Interest Received

4.2 1099–INT Interest Income

Q. How do I report interest received on an installment sale?

A. If you receive interest on an installment sale, report the entire amount on line 8a of Form 1040 or Form 1040A, or line 2 of Form 1040EZ. If your taxable interest income is more than $1,500, be sure to show that income on Schedule B of Form 1040, or on Schedule 1 of Form 1040A. You cannot file Form 1040EZ if your interest income is more than $1,500. Refer to Tax Topic 403, *Interest Received*, for additional information on interest income Form 1040, Schedule B. For additional information on installment sales, refer to Tax Topic 705, or Publication 537, *Installment Sales.*

References:
• Publication 537, Installment Sales
• Form 1040, Schedule B. Interest and Dividend Income
• Tax Topic 705, Installment sales
• Form 1040, U.S. Individual Income Tax Return
• Form 1040A, U.S. Individual Income Tax Return
• Form 1040EZ, U.S. Individual Income Tax Return for Single and Joint Filers with No Dependents
• Tax Topic 403, Interest Received

Q. My dependent child had an investment income of $2000. Is it taxable?, If so on him or me the parent?

A. Part or all of a child's investment income may be taxed at the parent's rate rather than the child's rate, according to the IRS. Because a parent's taxable income is usually higher than a child's income, the parent's top tax rate will often be higher as well. This special method of figuring the federal income tax only applies to children who are under the age of 14. For 2004, it applies if the child's total investment income for the year was more than $1,600. Investment income includes interest, dividends, capital gains and other unearned income. *(**Check Pub. 929 for the current threshold amount**)*

To figure the child's tax using this method, fill out Form 8615, *Tax for Children Under Age 14 With Investment Income of More Than $1,600,* and attach it to the child's federal income tax return. Alternatively, a parent can, in many cases, choose to report the child's investment income on the parent's own tax return. Generally speaking, this option is available if the child's income consists entirely of interest and dividends (including capital gain distributions) and the amount received is less than $8,000. Eligible parents can choose this option by filling out Form 8814, *Parent's Election to Report Child's Interest and Dividends,* and including it with their tax return. However, choosing this option may reduce certain credits or deductions that parents may claim.

These special tax rules do not apply to investment income received by children who are age 14 and over. In addition, wages and other earned income received by a child of any age are taxed at the child's normal rate.

More information can be found in IRS Publication 929, *Tax Rules for Children and Dependents.* This and the forms are available for downloading or by calling the IRS toll free at 1-800-TAX-FORM (1-800-829-3676).

References:
- Form 8615, Tax for Children Under Age 14 With Investment Income of More Than $1,500
- Form 8615, Instructions
- Form 8814, Parent's Election to Report Child's Interest and Dividends
- Publication 929, Tax Rules for Children and Dependents

Keyword(s): 1099-MISC; Keyword(s): Schedule C or C-EZ; Keyword(s): Nonemployee Compensation; Keyword(s): Self-employed

4.3 1099–MISC, Independent Contractors, and Self-employed

Q. I received a Form 1099-MISC instead of a Form W-2. I'm not self-employed, I do not have a business. How do I report this income?

A. If payment for services you provided is listed in box 7 of Form 1099-MISC, you are being treated as a self-employed worker, also referred to as an independent contractor. You do not necessarily have to "have a business, " but simply perform services as a nonemployee to have your compensation treated this way. The payer has determined that an employer-employee relationship does not exist in your case. That determination is complex, but is essentially made by examining the right to control how, when, and where you perform those services. It is not based on how you are paid, how often you are paid, nor whether you work part-time or full-time. There are three basic areas that are relevant to determine employment status:

- behavioral control,
- financial control, and
- relationship of the parties

For more information on employer-employee relationships, refer to Chapter 2 of Publication 15, Circular E, Employer's Tax Guide and Chapter 2 of Publication 15-A, Employer's Supplemental Tax Guide. If you think that you were, or are, an employee and you would like the IRS to issue a determination, you may submit Form SS-8, Determination of Worker Status for Purposes of Federal Employment Taxes and Income Tax Withholding.

Unless you think you were an employee, you report your nonemployee compensation on Form 1040, Schedule C, *Profit or Loss from Business* (Sole Proprietorship), or Form 1040, Schedule C-EZ, *Net Profit from Business.* You also need to complete Form 1040, Schedule SE, *Self-Employment Tax,* and pay self-employment tax on your net earnings from self-employment, if you had net earnings from self-employment of $400 or more. This is the manner by which self-employed persons pay into the social security and Medicare trust funds. Employees pay these payroll taxes, as well as income tax withholding, through deductions from their paychecks. Generally, there are no tax withholdings on self-employment income. However, you may be subject to the requirement to make quarterly estimated tax payments. If you did not make estimated tax payments, you may be charged an underpayment of estimated tax penalty.

References:
- Publication 15, Circular E, Employer's Tax Guide
- Publication 17, Your Federal Income Tax
- Publication 533, Self-Employment Tax
- Publication 505, Tax Withholding and Estimated Tax
- Publication 15-A , Employer's Supplemental Tax Guide
- Tax Topic 762, Independent contractor vs. employee
- Tax Topic 407, Business Income

• Tax Topic 355, Estimated tax

Q. *I am self-employed. How do I report my income and how do I pay Medicare and social security taxes?*

A. You are a sole proprietor if you are the sole owner of a business that is not a corporation. Report your income and expenses from your sole proprietorship on Form 1040, Schedule C, *Profit or Loss from Business* (Sole Proprietorship), or on Form 1040, Schedule C-EZ, *Net Profit from Business.*

If the total of your net profit from all businesses is $400 or more, you must pay into the Social Security and Medicare systems by filing Form 1040, Schedule SE, *Self-Employment Tax.* Self-Employment tax consists of the Old-Age, Survivors, and Disability Insurance (social security) and the Hospital Insurance (Medicare) taxes. For more information on this, refer to Publication 533, *Self-Employment Tax.*

The Federal tax system is based on a pay-as-you-go plan. Tax is generally withheld from your wages or salary before you get it. However, tax is generally not withheld from self-employment income. Thus, you may be required to make estimated tax payments. Publication 505, *Tax Withholding and Estimated Tax,* provides information on making estimated tax payments.

References:
• Form 1040, Schedule C, Profit or Loss from Business (Sole Proprietorship)
• Form 1040, Schedule C-EZ, Net Profit from Business (Sole Proprietorship)
• Form 1040, Schedule SE, Self-Employment Tax
• Publication 533, Self-Employment Tax
• Publication 505, Tax Withholding and Estimated Tax

Q. *I received a Form 1099-MISC with an amount in box 7, (nonemployee compensation). What forms and schedules should be used to report income earned as an independent contractor?*

A. Independent contractors report their income on Form 1040, Schedule C, *Profit or Loss from Business* (Sole Proprietorship), or you may qualify to use Form 1040, Schedule C-EZ, *Net Profit from Business* (Sole Proprietorship). You should also be aware of Form 1040, Schedule SE, *Self-Employment Tax,* which must be filed if net earnings from self-employment are $400 or more. This form is used to figure your social security and Medicare tax which is based on your net self-employment income. You may also need to file Form 2210, *Underpayment*

54

of Estimated Tax by Individuals, Estates & Trusts, if you do not make estimated tax payments.

References:
- Form 1040, Schedule C, Profit or Loss from Business (Sole Proprietorship)
- Form 1040, Schedule C-EZ, Net Profit from Business
- Instructions for Form 1040, Schedule C
- Form 1040, Schedule SE, Self-Employment Tax
- Instructions for Form 1040, Schedule SE
- Publication 533, Self-employment Tax
- Publication 334, Tax Guide for Small Business
- Tax information for Business
- Form 2210 Underpayment of Estimated Tax

Q. *My son is a newspaper carrier. I would like to know if this income is subject to Social Security and Medicare tax and if I must file a Schedule C for him?*

A. Your son may be liable to pay into the Social Security and Medicare system by paying self-employment tax. However, if your son is under the age of 18, he is exempt from self-employment tax. His employer should complete box 3, other income, on Form 1099-MISC, *Miscellaneous Income.* Persons engaged in the trade or business of delivering or distributing newspapers or shopping news (including any services directly related to such delivery or distribution) are considered by statute as nonemployees and are treated as self-employed for all Federal tax purposes, including income and employment taxes. Only if they receive income based on number of sales or distribution volume and work under a written contract that says the carrier will not be treated as an employee for federal employment tax purposes.

Independent contractors report their income on Form 1040, Schedule C, *Profit or Loss from Business* (Sole Proprietorship), or you may qualify to use Form 1040, Schedule C-EZ, *Net Profit from Business.* Refer to Form 1040, Schedule SE, *Self-Employment Tax*, which must be filed if net earnings from self-employment are $400 or more.

References:
- Publication 15, Circular E, Employer's Tax Guide
- Form 1040, Schedule C, Profit or Loss from Business (Sole Proprietorship)
- Form 1040, Schedule C-EZ, Net Profit from Business
- Instructions for Form 1040, Schedule C
- Form 1040, Schedule SE, Self-Employment Tax
- Instructions for Form 1040, Schedule SE
- Publication 334, Tax Guide for Small Business

- Tax information for Business
- Form 1099-MISC, Miscellaneous Income
- Publication 15-A, Employer's Supplemental Tax Guide

Q. *What, if any, quarterly forms must I file to report income as an independent contractor?*

A. There are no quarterly income reporting requirements for Federal income tax purposes. However, because you will have no withholding taken from your income, you may need to make quarterly estimated tax payments. You use Form 1040-ES, *Estimated Tax for Individuals.*
You need to be aware that there may be state and local requirements for estimated tax payments. You can start looking for information at How to Contact Us. You may want to go to your state's individual Website for additional information. To access the state you need go to IRS website (www.IRS.gov). Click on Alphabetical State Index.

References:
- Form 1040-ES, Estimated Tax for Individuals
- Publication 505, Tax Withholding and Estimated Tax
- Tax Topic 355, Estimated Tax
- Publication 334, Tax Guide for Small Business
- Alphabetical State Index
- Tax Information for Business

Keyword(s): State Taxes; Keyword(s): I haven't received a Form 1099

4.4 1099 Information Returns (All Other)

Q. *I received a Form 1099-G, for my state tax refund. Do I have to include this amount as income on my return?*

A. If you did not itemize your deductions on your Federal tax return for the same year as the state or local tax refund applies to, do not report any of the refund as income. If you itemized deductions on your Federal tax return for 2004, and received a refund of state or local taxes in 2005, you may have to include all or part of the refund as income on your 2005 tax return. Report your taxable State or Local Refunds on Form 1040, Line 10. You cannot use Form 1040A or 1040EZ. Refer to Tax Topic 405, *Refund of State and Local Taxes, and Publication 525, Taxable and Nontaxable Income*, for further information.

References:

• Publication 525, Taxable and Nontaxable Income
• Tax Topic 405, Refund of State and Local Taxes
• Instructions for Form 1040

Q. What Do I do if I Haven't Received a Form 1099?

A. If you received certain types of income, you may receive a Form 1099 for use with your federal tax return. You should receive these forms from the payer by January 31, 2006, according to the IRS. If you have not received an expected 1099 by a few days after that, contact the payer. If you still do not get the form by February 15, call the IRS for help at 1-800-829-1040.

In some cases, you may obtain the information that would be on the 1099 from other sources. For example, your bank may put a summary of the interest paid during the year on the December or January statement for your savings or checking account, or, it may make the interest figure available through its customer service line or web site. Some payers include cumulative figures for the year with their quarterly dividend statements. If you are able to get the accurate information needed to complete your tax return, you do not have to wait for the 1099 to arrive. If you file your return and later receive a Form 1099 for income that you did not fully include on that return, you should report the income and take credit for any income tax withheld by filing Form 1040X, *"Amended U.S. Individual Income Tax Return"*. You will not usually attach a 1099 series form to your return, except when you receive a Form 1099-R that shows income tax withheld. You should keep all other 1099s for your records. There are several different forms in this series, including:
•   Form 1099–B, Proceeds From Broker and Barter Exchange Transactions
•   Form 1099–DIV, Dividends and Distributions
•   Form 1099–G, Certain Government and Qualified State Tuition Program Payments
•   Form 1099–INT, Interest Income
•   Form 1099–MISC, Miscellaneous Income
•   Form 1099–OID, Original Issue Discount
•   Form 1099–R, Distributions From Pensions, Annuities, Retirement or Profit-Sharing Plans, IRAs, Insurance Contracts, etc.
•   Form SSA–1099, Social Security Benefit Statement
•   Form RRB–1099, Payments by the Railroad Retirement Board

References:
•   Form 1040X, Amended U.S. Individual Income Tax Return
•   Instructions for Form 1040X
•   Forms and Publications Subscribe to Tax Tips

4.5 Alimony, Child Support, Court Awards, Damages

Q. Are child support payments considered taxable income?

A. No. Child support payments are neither deductible by the payor nor taxable to the payee. When you total your gross income to Refer to if you are required to file a tax return, do not include child support payments received. For additional information, refer to Tax Topic 422, *Nontaxable Income,* or Publication 504, *Divorced or Separated Individuals.*

References:
• Publication 504, Divorced or Separated Individuals
• Tax Topic 422, Nontaxable Income

Keyword(s): Employee Benefits; Keyword(s): Dependent Care Benefits

4.6 Employee Reimbursements, Form W–2, Wage Inquiries

Q. Should Line 10, Dependent Care Benefits, of my Form W-2 be included when calculating my income?

A. A portion of the amount in Box 10 of the Form W-2 may be includable in your income. Refer to the Instructions for Form 2441, *Child and Dependent Care Expenses,* 1040A filers refer to Form 1040A, Schedule 2, Child and Dependent Care Expenses for 1040A Filers to determine how much, if any, of the dependent care benefits may be excluded.

If you meet the requirements described in Form 2441, *Child and Dependent Care Expenses,* you can exclude up to $5,000 of dependent care benefits provided under a qualified employer plan. However, this amount is reduced or eliminated if your earned income (or your spouse's earned income) is less than $5,000, or if your child is not under age 13. Any benefits that exceed the exclusion limit ($5,000) are also includable in your income, and your employer should have included these amounts in Boxes 1, 3, and 5 of your Form W-2 in addition to reporting these amounts in Box 10. The amount you can exclude is figured and claimed by completing Part III of Form 2441 or Schedule 2 of Form 1040A.

References:
• Publication 503, Child and Dependent Care Expenses
• Form 2441, Child and Dependent Care Expenses
• Instructions for Form 2441, Child and Dependent Care Expenses

• Form 1040A, Schedule 2, Child and Dependent Care Expenses for 1040A Filers

Q. What box on the Form W-2 do I use to determine my income to go on my tax return? What are all of these other boxes for? Does the amount from any other box go anywhere on my tax return?

A. For most people, only the amount in box 1 (wages, tips, other compensation) needs to be reported as income on your tax return. If you are an employee who receives tips, you may have to include the amount from box 8 (allocated tips) as income on your return.

Any employer-provided dependent care benefits listed in box 10 that are not excludable from income must be reported as wages on line 7 of the Form 1040. Any credit taken for child and dependent care expenses must be reported on line 44 of the Form 1040. Refer to Form 2441, *Child and Dependent Care Expenses,* to determine the amount, if any, of the exclusion or credit.

Employer-provided adoption benefits that must be used to complete Form 8839, *Qualified Adoption Expenses,* appear in box 12 with a code T. *Employer contributions to a medical savings account* (MSA), which you report on line 3b of Form 8853, *Medical Savings Accounts and Long-Term Care Insurance* Contracts, also appear in box 12 with a code R. Employer-provided benefits may be taxable as compensation under certain conditions. Refer to the relevant form instructions.

If you received advanced earned income credit payments from your employer (box 9), you must include the amount on your individual income tax return Form 1040 or 1040A.
The other boxes either display information that the employer wanted to provide to you, or contain information that must be reported to the Social Security Administration or to the IRS.

References:
• Instructions for Form W-2 and W-3
• Instructions for Form 1040 (General Inst.)
• Instructions for Form 1040A

Keyword(s): Inheritance; Keyword(s): Gift of money; Keyword(s): Gift of property

4.7 Gifts & Inheritances

Q. *Is the money received from the sale of inherited property considered taxable income?*

A. To determine if the sale of inherited property is taxable, you must first determine your basis in the property. The basis of inherited property is generally one of the following:

(1) The fair market value (FMV) of the property on the date of the decedent's death.

(2) The FMV of the property on the alternate valuation date if the executor of the estate chooses to use alternate valuation. Refer to Form 706, *United States Estate (and Generation-Skipping Transfer) Tax Return.*

(3) The special use valuation for estate tax purposes of qualified real property used for farming purposes or in a trade or business other than farming. However, if an interest in such property is disposed of or ceases to be used in a qualified use during the 10 year period following the decedent's death, additional estate tax is imposed. If the qualified heir elects to pay interest on the additional estate tax, the adjusted basis of the property will be deemed to have been increased, immediately before disposition, by an amount equal to the excess of its fair market value on the date of the decedent's death over its special use value. Refer to Form 706, *U.S. Estate (and Generation-Skipping Transfer) Tax Return* and section 2032A of Internal Revenue Code.

(4) If an election is made to exclude a portion of the value of land from a decedent's gross estate section 2031 (c) (regarding the transfer of qualified conservation easement), the decedent's adjusted basis in the land to the extent the value of the land was excluded from the decedent's gross estate under 2031(c) by reason of the transfer of a qualified conservation easement plus the fair market value of the land to the extent the value of the land was included in the gross estate.

For more information on qualified conservation easement Refer to the Instructions for Form 706, U. S. Estate (and Generation-Skipping Transfer) Tax Return and section 2031(c) of the Internal Revenue Code.

If you or your spouse gave the property to the descendent within one year of their death, refer to Publication 551, *Basis of Assets.*

Report the sale on Form 1040, Schedule D, Capital Gain and Losses. If you sell the property for more than your basis, you have a taxable gain. For information on how to report the sale on Schedule D, Refer to Publication 550, *Investment Income and Expenses.*

References:
- Publication 551, Basis of Assets
- Tax Topic 703, Basis of assets
- Tax Topic 422, Nontaxable income

Q. I gave my spouse a $20,000 gift of money. I also gave my brother a gift of one of my property valued at $50,000. Do I or the recipients have to pay tax on the gifts?

A. If you gave any one person gifts valued at more than $11,000, it is necessary to report the total gift to the Internal Revenue Service. You may even have to pay tax on the gift.

The person who received your gift does not have to report the gift to the IRS or pay either gift or income tax on its value.

You make a gift when you give property, including money, or the use of or income from property, without expecting to receive something of equal value in return. If you sell something at less than its value or make an interest-free or reduced-interest loan, you may be making a gift.

There are some exceptions to the tax rules on gifts. The following gifts do not count against the annual limit:
- Tuition or medical expenses that you pay directly to an educational or medical institution for someone's benefit
- Gifts to your spouse
- Gifts to a political organization for its use
- Gifts to charities.

If you are married, both you and your spouse can give separate gifts of up to the annual limit to the same person without making a taxable gift.

For more information, get IRS Publication 950, *Introduction to Estate and Gift Taxes*, IRS Form 709 or 709-A, *United States Gift Tax Return,* and the instructions for Form 709. They are available for downloading or by calling toll free 1-800-TAX-FORM (1-800-829-3676).

References:
- Publication 950, Introduction to Estate and Gift Taxes
- Form 709, United States Gift (And Generation-Skipping Transfer) Tax Return
- Form 709, Instructions

Keyword(s): Scholarships; Keyword(s): Fellowships; Keyword(s): Grants

4.8 Grants, Scholarships, Student Loans, Work Study

Q. I received an academic scholarship that is designated to be used for tuition and books. Is this taxable?

A. Qualified scholarships and fellowships are treated as tax-free amounts if all of the following conditions are met:
• You are a candidate for a degree at an educational institution,
• Amounts you receive as a scholarship or fellowship are used for tuition and fees required for enrollment or attendance at the educational institution, or for books, supplies, and equipment required for courses of instruction, and
• The amounts received are not a payment for your services.
For additional information on Scholarship and Fellowship Grants, refer to Tax Topic 421, and Publication 970, Tax Benefits for Education.

References:
• Publication 970, Tax Benefits for Education
• Tax Topic 421, Scholarship and fellowship grants

Keyword(s): Insurance Proceeds; Keyword(s): Disability Income

4.9 Life Insurance & Disability Insurance Proceeds

Q. Are proceeds paid under a life insurance contract taxable and do they have to be reported as income?

A. Generally, if you receive the proceeds under a life insurance contract because of the death of the insured person the benefits are not taxable income and do not have to be reported. Any interest you receive would be taxable and would need to be reported just like any other interest received.

However, if the policy was transferred to you for valuable consideration, the exclusion for the proceeds is limited to the sum of the consideration you paid, additional premiums you paid, and certain other amounts. There are some exceptions to this rule. For additional information, call 1 800-829-1040.

References:

62

- Publication 525, Taxable and Nontaxable Income
- Tax Topic 422, Nontaxable Income

Q. *I am receiving long-term disability. Is it considered taxable?*

A. Generally, you must report as income any amount you receive for your disability through an accident or health insurance plan paid for by your employer.

If both you and your employer have paid the premiums for the plan, only the amount you receive for your disability that is due to your employer's payments is reported as income. If you pay the entire cost of a health or accident insurance plan, do not include any amounts you receive for your disability as income on your tax return. If you pay the premiums of a health or accident insurance plan through a cafeteria plan, and the amount of the premium was not included as taxable income to you; the premiums are considered paid by your employer, and the disability benefits are fully taxable.

Refer to Publication 525, *Taxable and Nontaxable Income*, for more details. If the amounts are taxable, you can submit a Form W-4S, *Request for Federal Income Tax Withholding*, to the insurance company, or make estimated tax payments by filing Form 1040-ES, *Estimated Tax for Individuals.*

Amounts you receive from your employer while you are sick or injured are part of your salary or wages. Report the amount you receive on line 7, Form 1040 ; line 7, Form 1040A ; or line 1, Form 1040EZ. You must include in your income sick pay from any of the following:
- A welfare fund.
- A state sickness or disability fund.
- An association of employers or employees.
- An insurance company, if your employer paid for the plan.

Payments you receive from qualified long-term care insurance contracts will generally be excluded from income as reimbursement of medical expenses received for personal injury or sickness under an accident and health insurance contract. Also, certain payments received under a life insurance contract on the life of a terminally or chronically ill individual (accelerated death benefits) can be excluded from income. Refer to the chapter on "Other Income" in Publication 17, *Your Federal Income Tax.*

You may be able to deduct your out of pocket expenses for medical care above any reimbursements, if you are eligible to itemize your deductions. You will need to review Publication 502, *Medical and Dental Expenses.*

For more information, refer to Publication 907, *Tax Highlights for Persons with Disabilities.*

References:
• Publication 502, Medical and Dental Expenses
• Publication 525, Taxable and Nontaxable Income
• Publication 907, Tax Highlights for Persons with Disabilities
• Tax Topic 422, Nontaxable Income
• Form 1040, U.S. Individual Income Tax Return
• Form 1040A, U.S. Individual Income Tax Return
• Form 1040EZ, U.S. Individual Income Tax Return for Single and Joint Filers with No Dependents
• Form W-4S, Request for Federal Income Tax Withholding

Keyword(s): Salaries; Keyword(s): Self-employed; Keyword(s): Housing Allowance

4.10 Ministers' Compensation & Housing Allowance

Q. Are all ministers treated as self-employed for social security purposes?

A. Services that a duly ordained, commissioned or licensed minister performs in the exercise of his or her ministry are covered under the Self-Employment Contributions Act (SECA). That means they are exempt from Social Security and Medicare withholding, but they are responsible for paying self-employment tax on their net earnings from self-employment. There are some members of religious orders, ministers, and Christian Science practitioners who have requested and been granted exemption from self-employment tax. There are also members of religious orders who have taken a vow of poverty and ministers who are covered solely by the social security laws of another country under a social security agreement between the United States and that other country.

References:
•   Publication 517, Social Security and Other Information for the Members of the Clergy and Religious Workers
•   Tax Topic 417, Earnings for clergy

Q. A minister receives a salary plus a housing allowance. Is the housing allowance income? Where do the minister report it?

A. A minister's housing allowance, sometimes called a parsonage allowance or a rental allowance, is excludable from gross income for income tax purposes, but not for self-employment tax purposes.

If you are a minister and receive as part of your salary (as a minister) an amount officially designated as a rental allowance, you can exclude from gross income the amount that is used to provide or rent a home. However, the exclusion is limited to the lesser of the fair market rental value (including furnishing, utilities, garage, etc.), the amount officially designated (in advance of payment) as a rental or housing allowance, or the actual amount used to provide a home, and cannot exceed what is reasonable pay for your services. The payments must be used in the year received.

If housing is furnished to you by your congregation as pay for your services as a minister, the exclusion cannot be more than what is reasonable pay for your services, and is limited to the fair market rental value (including furnishings, utilities, garage, etc.) of the home.

If you own your home and you receive a housing allowance as part of your pay, for your services as a minister, the exclusion cannot be more than the smaller of the following:

- the amount actually used to provide a home,
- the amount officially designated (in advance of payment) as a rental or housing allowance, or
- the fair market rental value of the home, including furnishings, utilities, garage, etc.

An amount which represents reasonable pay for your services as a minister.

For additional information on housing allowance, refer to Publication 517, *Social Security and Other Information for the Members of the Clergy and Religious Workers*. For information on earnings for clergy and reporting of self-employment tax, refer to Tax Topic 417, *Earnings for clergy.*

References:
- Publication 517, Social Security and Other Information for the Members of the Clergy and Religious Workers
- Tax Topic 417, Earnings for clergy

Keyword(s): Series E, Series EE; Series I Savings bonds

4.11 Savings Bonds

Q. I cashed some Series E, Series EE and Series I savings bonds, how do I report the interest?

A. If your total taxable interest for the year is more than $1500, you report (and separately identify) the interest on Schedule B of Form 1040 or Schedule 1 of Form 1040A. If your total interest is not more than $1500 for the year, report the savings bond interest with your other interest on the "Interest " line of your tax return. If you do not report the increase in the redemption value of the bonds as interest each year, you must report all of the interest in the year they are cashed or otherwise disposed of.

References:
• Publication 550, Investment Income and Expenses

Keyword(s): Allocated Tips; Keyword(s): Tips/Allocated Tips

4.12 Tips

Q. Of my allocated tips, I tip-out 15% to the busboy and 5% to the bar. Where do I deduct this on my tax return?

A. You cannot deduct tip-outs (the tips you split with other employees) on your tax return. Nor can you deduct them from your allocated tips. The practice of tipping-out is one of the reasons you should keep a detailed daily log of your tips. If you document that you tip-out, and you reported all your tips to your employer, then you do not include in your income the allocated tips in box 8 of Form W-2.

Tipping-out, by itself, should not cause an allocated tip situation. First, when you report the cash tips you receive, you should report the total tips, then the amount tipped-out. Publication 1244, *Employee's Daily Record of Tips and Report to Employer*, includes Forms 4070 and 4070A, *Employee's Report of Tips to Employer* that provides the following lines:
• Cash tips received, line 1
• Credit card tips received, line 2
• Tips paid out, line 3
• Net tips (lines 1 + 2 - 3), line 4

The detail of the information provided should enable your employer to develop a reasonable, fair, and accurate method for determining whether tips need to be allocated, and, if so, how much. Employers who operate large food and beverage establishments are only required to allocate tips if the total tips reported by all the employees who customarily receive tips are less than 8% of gross sales. Thus, when there is a tip-splitting arrangement, it is important that all tips, including those received through tip-splitting, be reported to the employer by each employee who receives $20 or more in a month.

For more information, refer to Publication 531, Reporting Tip Income.

References:
• Publication 1872, Tips on Tips - A Guide to Tip Income Reporting for Employees in the Food and Beverage Industry
• Publication 531, Reporting Tip Income
• Publication 1244, Employee's Daily Record of Tips and Report to Employer
• Tax Topic 402, Tips

Chapter 5

Pensions and Annuities

~~~~~

Keyword(s): 1099-R; Keyword(s): Pension Plan; Keyword(s): Minimum Distribution; Keyword(s): Minimum Distribution; Keyword(s): Nonedeductible Contributions (IRA); Keyword(s): Deductible Contributions (IRA); Keyword(s): Contributions (IRAs & Pension Plans); Keyword(s): 401(K) Pension Plan; Keyword(s): 403(b) Pension Plan; Keyword(s): Traditional IRA; Keyword(s): Qualified Plan; Keyword(s): Retirement Plan; Keyword(s): Maximum Contribution; Keyword(s): IRA Account; Keyword(s): Distributions; Keyword(s): Profit Sharing Plan.

5.1 General

Q. This is the first year that I received retirement benefits. Are any of my benefits taxable?

A. If you receive retirement benefits in the form of pension or annuity payments, the amounts you receive may be fully taxable, or partly taxable in the year received. Refer to Tax Topic 410, *Pensions and Annuities*, for detailed information, or Publication 575, *Pension and Annuity Income.* For social security and equivalent railroad retirement benefits, refer to Tax Topic 423 or Publication 915, *Social Security and Equivalent Railroad Retirement Benefits.*

References:
• Publication 575, Pension and Annuity Income
• Publication 915, Social Security and Equivalent Railroad Retirement Benefits
• Tax Topic 410, Pensions and Annuities
• Tax Topic 423, Social Security and Equivalent Railroad Retirement Benefits

Q. Am I considered covered by an employer sponsored retirement plan for the year if I do not participate in the plan or if I did not work long enough to be vested?

A. The answer to this question depends on your type of retirement plan. If your employer's plan has a separate account for each employee, this is called a defined contribution plan. If any amount was contributed or allocated by you or your employer to your account, you are considered covered. It does not matter if you have worked long enough to be vested.

In the other type of plan, the plan employer must make enough contributions (together with earnings) to provide the retirement benefit promised in the retirement plan. This is called a defined benefit plan. In this type of plan, if you meet the minimum age and years of service requirements to participate in your employer's plan, you are considered covered. It does not matter if you are vested.

The Form W-2 you receive from your employer has a box used to indicate whether you were covered for the year. The "Pension Plan" box should have a mark in it if you were covered.

References:
• Publication 575, Pensions and Annuity Income
• Tax Topic 510, Pensions and Annuities

Q. This is the first year that I received retirement benefits. Are any of my benefits taxable?

A. If you receive retirement benefits in the form of pension or annuity payments, the amounts you receive may be fully taxable, or partly taxable in the year received. Refer to Tax Topic 410, *Pensions and Annuities*, for detailed information, or Publication 575, *Pension and Annuity Income.* For social security and equivalent railroad retirement benefits, refer to Tax Topic 423 or Publication 915, *Social Security and Equivalent Railroad Retirement Benefits.*

References:
• Publication 575, Pension and Annuity Income
• Publication 915, Social Security and Equivalent Railroad Retirement Benefits
• Tax Topic 410, Pensions and Annuities
• Tax Topic 423, Social Security and Equivalent Railroad Retirement Benefits

5.2 Contributions

Q. What is the maximum amount that I can contribute to my 401(k) plan?

A. For 2005, the maximum amount an employee can contribute to a 401(k) plan is $14,000 except for catch-up contributions for employees age 50 or over who can contribute up to $18,000. The maximum amount applies to an employee's aggregate pre-tax contributions to a 401 (k) plan and 403 (b) plan. There are several different limits that apply to a 401(k) plan in addition to the overall contribution limit. These limits, your salary and the type of 401(k) plan to which you are contributing may limit your 401 (k) contributions to a lesser amount. The rules for retirement plans are complex. Your plan administrator should have written information about your particular plan that explains these limitations as well as other regulations that apply.

For further information, refer to Tax Topic 424, *401(k) plans.*

References:
- Publication 575, Pension and Annuity Income
- Publication 560, Retirement Plans for Small Business
- Tax Topic 424, 401(k) plans

Keyword(s): 10% Additional Tax (Penalty); Keyword(s): Lump-sum Distribution; Keyword(s): First-time Home Buyer; Keyword(s): Rollover; Keyword(s): Early Withdrawals/Distributions

5.3 Distributions, Early Withdrawals, 10% Additional Tax

Q. I received a lump-sum distribution when I retired. Is there any special tax treatment on a lump-sum distribution?

A. You may be able to elect optional methods of figuring the tax on lump-sum distributions you received from a qualified retirement plan.

A lump-sum distribution is the distribution or payment, within a single tax year, of an employee's entire balance from all of the employer's qualified pension, profit-sharing, or stock bonus plans. The distribution must have been made under specific conditions. For details, refer to Tax Topic 412 which discusses Lump-Sum Distributions or Publication 575, *Pension and Annuity Income.*

References:
- Publication 575, Pension and Annuity Income
- Tax Topic 412, Lump-Sum distributions

Q. Since money was withheld from my 401(k) distribution, do I have to include that money as income and do I pay the 10% early withdrawal fee as well?

A. Yes, you need to include in income the total amount of your 401(k) distribution reported on Form 1099-R, *Distributions From Pensions, Annuities, Retirement on Profit-Sharing Plans, IRAs Insurance Contracts, etc.* In addition,

70

if you took the distribution before age 59 1/2, you may need to pay a 10 percent additional tax on early distributions from qualified retirement plans unless you meet one of the exceptions in Publication 575, *Pension and Annuity Income.* You will include the federal income tax withheld on the appropriate line of your federal tax return along with any other federal income tax.

References:
• Publication 575, Pension and Annuity Income
• Form 5329, Additional Taxes on Qualified Plans (including IRA's), and Other Tax-Favored Accounts
• Instructions for Form 5329, Additional Taxes on Qualified Plans (including IRA's), and Other Tax-Favored Accounts
• Tax Topic 558, Tax on Early Distributions from Retirement Plans
• Tax Topic 412, Lump-Sum Distributions

Q. *Can I withdraw funds penalty free from my 401(k) plan to purchase my first home?*

A. If you are under the age of 59 1/2, you cannot withdraw funds from your 401(k) plan to purchase your first home without being subject to a 10 percent additional tax on early distributions from qualified retirement plans. However, depending on the rules for your 401(k) plan, you may be able to borrow money from your 401(k) plan to purchase your first home. Your plan administrator should have written information about your particular plan that explains when you can borrow funds from your 401(k) plan as well as other plan rules.

References:
• Publication 575, Pension and Annuity Income
• Publication 560, Retirement Plans for Small Business
• Tax Topic 424, 401(k) Plans
• Tax Topic 558, Tax on Early Distributions From Retirement Plans

Q. *I changed jobs and my old employer sent me a check for my 401(k) money withholding 20% for Federal Income Tax. I rolled over the distribution to my 401(k) plan at my current employer within 60 days. Since money was withheld from the 401(k) distribution, do I have to include that money as income?*

A. If the amount rolled over was the net amount, that is, the amount of the distribution less the tax withheld, then the 20% withholding amount not rolled over is included in gross taxable income and may be subject to a 10 percent additional tax on early distributions from qualified retirement plans. Use Form

5329, *Additional Taxes on Other Qualified Plans* (including IRA's), and Other Tax-Favored Accounts, to report the penalty.

If the amount rolled over was the gross amount, that is, you added an amount equal to the withholding to the amount that was rolled over, you would not add any of that amount to gross taxable income this year or owe a 10 percent additional tax on early distributions from qualified retirement plans.

References:
• Publication 575, Pension and Annuity Income
• Publication 590, Individual Retirement Arrangements (IRAs)
• Form 5329, Additional Taxes on Other Qualified Plan (including IRA's), and OtherTax-Favored Accounts
• Instructions for Form 5329, Additional Taxes on Other Qualified Plan (including IRA's), and Other Tax-Favored Accounts
• Tax Topic 558, Tax on Early Distributions From Retirement Plans
• Tax Topic 412, Lump-Sum Distributions

Q. *If I retire or am laid off before I am 59 1/2, can I withdraw the funds accumulated in a 401(k) plan, without having to pay a 10% penalty?*

A. In most cases, if you withdraw funds from your 401(k) plan before you are 59 1/2, you must pay the 10 percent additional tax on early distributions from qualified retirement plans on any amounts that are not rolled into an IRA. However, there are some exceptions listed in Publication 560, *Retirement Plans for Small Business* and Publication 575, *Pension and Annuity Income.*

References:
• Publication 575, Pension and Annuity Income
• Publication 560, Retirement Plans for Small Business
• Tax Topic 558, Tax on Early Distributions From Retirement Plans
• Tax Topic 412, Lump-Sum Distributions

5.4 Loans & Other Retirement Account Transactions

Q. *My understanding is that if I am over age 55 and default on a loan through my 401(k) plan when leaving the company, the 10% penalty is forgiven. Can you confirm that for me?*

A. If you default on a loan from your 401(k) plan, you are considered to have received a distribution from your 401(k) plan. Whether or not you will have to

72

pay the 10 percent additional tax on early distributions from 401(k) plan depends on a number of factors, including your age.

In order to avoid the 10 percent additional tax on early distributions from qualified retirement plans, the following all must be true:

- you received the distribution after you left the company; and
- you left the company during or after the calendar year in which you reached age 55; and
- your departure from the company qualifies as a separation from service. In addition, you may avoid the 10 percent additional tax if you meet one of the other exceptions shown in Publication 560, *Retirement Plans for Small Business* and Publication 575, *Pension and Annuity Income*.

References:
- Publication 560, Retirement Plans for Small Business
- Publication 575, Pension and Annuity Income
- Tax Topic 558, Tax on Early Distributions From Retirement Plans

5.5 Rollovers ✓

Q. *How long do I have to roll over a retirement distribution?*

A. You must complete the rollover by the 60th day following the day on which you receive the distribution. (This 60-day period is extended for the period during which the distribution is in a frozen deposit in a financial institution). The IRS may waive the 60 day requirement where failure to do so would be against equity or good conscience, such as in the event of a casualty, disaster, or other event beyond your reasonable control. To obtain the waiver in most cases, a request for a letter ruling must be made. A user fee of $90.00 will apply Refer to Revenue Procedure 2003-16 (within IRS Bulletin 2003-4). A written explanation of rollover must be given to you by the issuer making the distribution. For information on distributions which qualify for rollover treatment, refer to Tax Topic 413, *Rollovers from Retirement Plans*. For information on the Direct Rollover Option, refer to Chapter 1 of Publication 590, *Individual Retirement Arrangements (IRA's)*.

References:
- Publication 17, Your Federal Income Tax
- Publication 575, Pensions and Annuity
- Tax Topic 413, Rollovers from Retirement Plans

Chapter 6

Social Security Income

~~~~~

Keyword(s): Social Security Benefits/Income; Keyword(s): Considered taxable Income (SSA); Keyword(s): Social Security Benefits/Income

6.1 Back Payments

Q. We received social security benefits this year that were back pay for prior years. Do we refile our returns for prior years? Are the back benefits paid in this year for past years taxable for this year?

A. You must include the taxable part of a lump-sum (retroactive) payment of benefits received in the current year in your current year's income, even if the payment includes benefits for an earlier year.

Generally, you use your current year's income to figure the taxable part of the total benefits received in the current year. However, you may be able to figure the taxable part of a lump-sum payment for an earlier year separately, using your income for the earlier year. You can elect this method if it lowers the taxable portion of your benefits. Refer to Publication 915, *Social Security and Equivalent Railroad Retirement Benefits,* for a detailed explanation of the election and worksheets.

References:
• Tax Topic 423, Social Security and Equivalent Railroad Retirement Benefits
• Publication 915, Social Security and Equivalent Railroad Retirement Benefits

Keyword(s): Tax Treaty; Keyword(s): Canada/Canada Issues

6.2 Canadian & Foreign Treaties

Q. For an American citizen residing in Canada using Form 1040A, should the taxable amount of U.S. social security benefits shown on line 14b be $0.00 due to the Canada-U.S. tax treaty?

A. Under the 1997 protocol to the Canada - U.S. tax treaty, the Canadian and U.S. governments agreed to return to a residence-based system under which social security benefits are taxable exclusively in the country where the recipient resides. As a result, the entry for line 14b would be $0.00.

References:
• Tax Topic 423, Social Security and Equivalent Railroad Retirement Benefits
• Publication 597, Information on the United States-Canada Income Tax Treaty
• Publication 915, Social Security and Equivalent Railroad Retirement Benefits

Q. *In addition to U.S. Social Security, I also receive British Social Security. How should I report the British Social Security income?*

A. Under the U.S. United Kingdom income tax treaty that entered into force during 2003, social security income is taxable only by the country of residence. If you are a resident of the U.S. for tax purposes, the income would be reported and taxed in the U.S. You would not treat the income as U.S. social security benefits. The entire amount would be taxable as pension and annuity income on your U.S. tax return. Your "investment in the contract " for purposes of determining the portion of each payment that is taxable would be $0. Under the prior treaty with the UK, social security benefits were treated the same way.

References:
• Tax Topic 410, Pensions and Annuities

Keyword(s): Social Security Benefits

6.3 Regular & Disability Benefits

Q. *I retired last year, and started receiving social security payments. Do I have to pay taxes on my social security benefits?*

A. To determine whether any of your benefits are taxable, compare the base amount for your filing status with the total of one half of your social security payments plus all your income from other sources, including tax exempt interest. If you are married and file a joint return, you must combine your incomes and your social security and equivalent tier 1 railroad retirement benefits when figuring the taxable portion of the benefits.

The taxable amount of the benefits is figured on a worksheet in the Form 1040 or 1040A instruction book, or in Publication 915, *Social Security and Equivalent Railroad Retirement Benefits.* Refer to Tax Topic 423, Social *Security and Equivalent Railroad Retirement Benefits,* for base amounts, and additional information regarding taxability and reporting requirements.

75

References:
- Publication 915, Social Security and Equivalent Railroad Retirement Benefits
- Tax Topic 423, Social Security and Equivalent Railroad Retirement Benefits

Keyword(s): Social Security Survivor (Death) Benefits

6.4 Survivors' Benefits

Q. Are social security survivor benefits for children considered taxable income?

A. The person who has the legal right to receive the benefits must determine whether the benefits are taxable. For example, if you and your child receive benefits, but the check for your child is made out in your name, you must use only your part of the benefits to Refer to whether any benefits are taxable to you. One half of the part that belongs to your child must be added to your child's other income to Refer to whether any of those benefits are taxable to the child.

References:
- Publication 915, Social Security and Equivalent Railroad Retirement Benefits
- Tax Topic 423, Social Security and Equivalent Railroad Retirement Benefits

Chapter 7

Child Care Credit/Other Credits

~~~~~

Keyword(s): Flexible Spending Account

7.1 Child and Dependent Care Credit & Flexible Benefit Plans

Q. My spouse and I both work and are eligible for the Child and Dependent Care Credit. May I include my 5 year old son's parochial school kindergarten tuition cost as a qualified expense in Form 2441, Child Care Expenses?

A. The expenses for kindergarten do not qualify for the dependent care credit if the kindergarten is primarily educational in nature. Expenses for school in the first grade or higher do not qualify for the credit. However, you can count the part of the expenses of sending your child to school that is for your child's care if it can be separated from the expenses of education. For example, you may count the cost of an after school care program even though the school tuition does not qualify.

References:
*   Publication 503, Child and Dependent Care Expenses
*   Tax Topic 602, Child and Dependent Care Credit

Q. I was under the impression that a Dependent Care Benefit Plan would benefit me, not penalize me with an increase in taxes. How can my employer say they provided a benefit in the total amount of $3,000 in W-2, Block 10 when I had $3,000 in wages set aside for dependent care benefits?

A. The actual mechanism for this type of plan is an agreement to voluntarily reduce your salary in return for an employer-provided fringe benefit. These plans must be set up this way because you have a choice of whether to receive the cash wages or the benefits, which would make the benefit taxable to you. Therefore, the benefits are actually employer provided or funded. You are receiving a tax benefit because you are not paying taxes on the money that is set aside.

References:
*   Publication 503, Child and Dependent Care Expenses
*   Tax Topic 602, Child and dependent care credit

- Publication 17, Your Federal Income Tax

Q. *How do I complete Form 2441 if I have flexible Spending Account?*

A. You must complete Part III of Form 2441, *Child and Dependent Care Expenses*, (or Form 1040A, Schedule 2, Child and Dependent Care Expenses for Form 1040A Filers) to claim the exclusion of the benefits from income even if you cannot claim the credit. Enter your total employer-provided dependent care benefits on line 14 (this amount should appear in box 10 of your Form W-2) and your qualified expenses on line 17. The last six lines of Part III will determine whether you can also take the credit and what your dollar limit is on qualified expenses. Also complete Part I, Persons or Organizations Who Provided the Care.

References:
- Form 2441, Child and Dependent Care Expenses
- Instructions for Form 2441, Child and Dependent Care Expenses
- Publication 503, Child and Dependent Care Expenses
- Tax Topic 602, Child and Dependent Care Credits

Q. *My babysitter refused to provide me with her social security number. Can I still claim what I paid for child care on my taxes while I worked? If so, how?*

A. Yes, assuming that you already meet the other requirements to claim the child care credit, but are missing the required ID number of the provider, you can still claim the credit by demonstrating "due diligence" in attempting to secure the needed information. When the care provider refuses to give the identifying information, the taxpayer can still claim the credit and is instructed to provide whatever information is available about the provider (such as name and address) on the form used to claim the credit Form 2441, *Child and Dependent Care Expenses*, or Form 1040A, Schedule 2, *Child and Dependent Care Expenses* for Form 1040A Filers). The taxpayer should write "Refer to page 2" in the columns calling for the missing information. He/she would write at the bottom of page 2 that the provider refused to give the requested information. This statement will show that the taxpayer used due diligence in trying to secure and furnish the necessary information.

References:
- Form W-10, Dependent Care Provider's Identification and Certification
- Form 2441, Child and Dependent Care Expenses
- Instructions for Form 2441, Child and Dependent Care Expenses
- Publication 503, Child and Dependent Care Expenses

•   Tax Topic 602, Child and dependent care credit

Q. I am thinking of having a family member baby-sit for my child full time in their own home while I work. Are either of us responsible for taxes on the money I would pay? Can I claim this money as a child care expense even though my family member is not a registered day care provider?

A. You may have qualified child care expenses if the family member baby-sitting is not your dependent or your child under age 19 and you meet all the tests to claim the Child and Dependent Care Credit. Who is responsible for taxes depends on whether your family member is your employee or is self-employed. Refer to Publication 15-A, *Employer's Supplemental Tax Guide*, for a discussion of how to tell whether someone who is performing services for you is an employee or an independent contractor. If your family member is not your employee, then the family member will be responsible for paying income taxes and self-employment taxes on the money earned. These rules are explained in Pub. 533, *Self-Employment Tax*. If your family member is your employee, then you are generally responsible for withholding and paying the taxes. However, special rules apply to family employees. Refer to Publication 15, Circular E, *Employer's Tax Guide,* for these rules.

References:
•   Form 2441, Child and Dependent Care Expenses
•   Instructions for Form 2441, Child and Dependent Car Expenses
•   Publication 15, Circular E, Employer's Tax Guide
•   Publication 15-A, Employer's Supplemental Tax Guide

Q. What is new with the child and dependent care tax credits?

Child and Dependent Care Credit

A. If you paid someone to care for a child or a dependent so you could work, you may be able to reduce your tax by claiming the credit for child and dependent care expenses on your federal income tax return, according to the IRS. This credit is available to people who, in order to work or to look for work, have to pay for child care services for dependents under age 13. The credit is also available if you paid for care of a spouse or a dependent of any age who is physically or mentally incapable of self-care.

79

The credit is a percentage, based on your adjusted gross income, of the amount of work-related child and dependent care expenses you paid to a care provider. The credit can range from 20 to 35 percent of your qualifying expenses, depending upon your income. For 2004, you may use up to $3,000 of the expenses paid in a year for one qualifying individual, or $6,000 for two or more qualifying individuals. These dollar limits must be reduced by the amount of any dependent care benefits provided by your employer that you exclude from your income. *(**Check Pub.503 for the current threshold amount**)*

To claim the credit for child and dependent care expenses, you must meet the following conditions:
• You must have earned income from wages, salaries, tips or other taxable employee compensation, or net earnings from self-employment. If you are married, both you and your spouse must have earned income, unless one spouse was either a full-time student or was physically or mentally incapable of self-care. If you chose to include nontaxable combat pay in earned income when figuring the Earned Income Tax Credit for 2005, also include it in earned income when you figure the amount of dependent care benefits you exclude or deduct from income.

• The payments for care cannot be paid to someone you can claim as your dependent on your return or to your child who is under age 19.

• Your filing status must be single, head of household, qualifying widow(er) with a dependent child, or married filing jointly.

• The care must have been provided for one or more qualifying persons identified on the form you use to claim the credit.

• You (and, if you're married, your spouse) must maintain a home that you live in with the qualifying child or dependent.

***Q**. What is a "qualifying" child or dependent?*

A. The child must have been under age 13 when care was provided and you must be able to claim the child as an exemption on your tax return. (For an exception to this rule, Refer to *Child of Divorced or Separated Parents* in IRS Publication 503.) A spouse who is mentally or physically unable to care for himself or herself also qualifies. A dependent of any age who is physically or mentally incapable of self-care also qualifies if the person can be claimed as an exemption on your tax return (or could have been claimed, except for the fact that the person had $3,200 or more of gross income).

To claim the credit, you'll need to provide the name, address and taxpayer identification number of the care provider. If the provider is an individual, you need the Social Security number. If it's a business, you need the provider's employer identification number. You can use Form W-10, *Dependent Care Provider's Identification and Certification*, to request this information from the care provider. If you're filing Form 1040, write the care provider information on Form 2441 and attach it to the tax return. If you're filing Form 1040A, the care provider information goes on Schedule 2. You cannot use Form 1040EZ if you claim the child and dependent care credit.

As with all good things, there are some limitations on the amount of credit you can claim. If you received dependent care benefits from your employer, other rules apply. For more information on the Child and Dependent Care Credit, Refer to Publication 503, *Child and Dependent Care Expenses*, or Publication 17, *Your Federal Income Tax*. You may download these free publications from this Website or order them by calling toll free 1-800-TAX-FORM (1-800-829-3676).

References:
- Publication 503, Child and Dependent Care
- Form W-10, Dependent Care Provider's Identification and Certification
- Form 2441, Child and Dependent Care Expenses
- Form 2441 Instructions
- Publication 17, Your Federal Income Tax
- Tax Topic 602

Keyword(s) Noncustodial Parent

7.2 Child Tax Credit

Q. *Does the Form 8332 (used to release the exemption to the noncustodial parent) affect the Child Tax Credit?*

A. Yes. The Child Tax Credit can only be claimed by the parent claiming the exemption. In this case the noncustodial parent would qualify for the dependency exemption and therefore the child tax credit. Refer to the Instructions for Form 1040 or the Instructions for Form 1040A index for Child Tax Credit. The referenced pages will explain who qualifies for this credit, and how to calculate it.

References:
- Instructions for Form 1040 (General Inst.)
- Instructions for Form 1040A
- Publication 17, Your Federal Income Tax

- Publication 972, Child Tax Credit
- Tax Topic 606, Child Tax Credits

Q. *Can I get the Child Tax Credit for a child with an ITIN, not a social security number?*

A. Yes, with an individual tax identification number (ITIN), you can claim the Child Tax Credit if you otherwise qualify. The Child Tax Credit can only be claimed by the parent claiming the child as a dependent.

Refer to the Instructions for Form 1040 or the Instructions for Form 1040A index for the Child Tax Credit. The referenced pages will explain who qualifies for the Child Tax Credit, and how to calculate it.

References:
• Instructions for Form 1040 (General Inst.)
• Instructions for Form 1040A
• Tax Topic 606, Child Tax Credits

Q. *Can you file for the Child Tax Credit and the Child Care Credit, too?*

A. The Child Tax Credit and the Child and Dependent Care Credit can both be claimed on the same return. They can be claimed on either Form 1040 U.S. Individual Income Tax Return, or Form 1040A, U.S. Individual Income Tax Return. Refer to the Instructions for Form 1040 or the Instructions for Form 1040A index for the Child Tax Credit. The referenced pages will explain who qualifies for the Child Tax Credit, and how to calculate it. Publication 503, *Child and Dependent Care Expenses*, has more information for the Child Care Credit.

References:
- Instructions for Form 1040 (General Inst.)
- Instructions for Form 1040A
- Tax Topic 606, Child Tax Credits

Q. *What is new with regard to the Child tax credit?*

Child Tax Credit

A. With the Child Tax Credit, you may be able to reduce the federal income tax you owe by up to $1,000 for each qualifying child under age 17. A qualifying child for this credit is someone who:

1. Is claimed as your dependent,
2. Was under age 17 at the end of 2005,
3. Is your son, daughter, adopted child, grandchild, stepchild or eligible foster child, your sibling, stepsibling or their descendant, and
4. Is a U.S. citizen or resident alien.

The credit is limited if your modified adjusted gross income is above a certain amount. The amount at which this phase-out begins varies depending on your filing status:
• Married Filing Jointly $110,000
• Married Filing Separately $55,000
• All others $75,000
In addition, the Child Tax Credit is limited by the amount of the income tax you owe as well as any alternative minimum tax you owe. For example, if the amount of the credit you can claim is $1,000, but the amount of your income tax is $500, the credit ordinarily will be limited to $500.
However, there are two exceptions to this general rule. If the amount of your Child Tax Credit is greater than the amount of income tax you owe, you may be able to claim some or all of the difference as an "additional " Child Tax Credit. First, you may claim up to 15 percent of the amount by which your earned income exceeds $10,750 (for members of the Armed Forces who served in a combat zone, nontaxable combat pay counts as earned income when figuring this credit limit). Second, if you have three or more qualifying children, you may claim up to the amount of Social Security taxes you paid during the year, minus any Earned Income Tax Credit you receive. If you qualify under both these exceptions, you receive the greater of the two amounts, up to the difference between your tax liability and your regular Child Tax Credit. Use Form 8812 to figure the additional Child Tax Credit.

For 2004, the total amount of the Child Tax Credit and any additional Child Tax Credit cannot exceed the maximum of $1,000 for each qualifying child. *(**Check Pub. 972 for the current threshold amount**)*

Individuals entitled to receive the Child Tax Credit and additional child tax credit may also be eligible to receive the Child and Dependent Care Credit and the Earned Income Tax Credit.

You may claim the Child Tax Credit on Form 1040 or 1040A. Details on how to compute the credit can be found in the forms' instructions and in Publication 972, *Child Tax Credit*. Download the forms and publications or order them by calling toll free 1-800-TAX-FORM (1-800-829-3676).

References:
• Form 8812, Additional Child Tax Credit
• Publication 972, Child Tax Credit
• Form 1040
• Form 1040 Instructions

7.3 Credit for the Elderly or the Disabled

Q. *Can I get the Credit for the Elderly or the Disabled?*

A. Generally, if you were age 65 or older or disabled and your income and nontaxable social security and other nontaxable pension are below specified amounts, you may be able to take this credit. For more details, refer to Tax Topic 603, *Credit for the Elderly or the Disabled,* or Publication 524, *Credit for the Elderly or the Disabled.*

References:
•   Publication 524, Credit for the Elderly or the Disabled
•   Tax Topic 603, Credit for the Elderly or the Disabled

Keyword(s): Lifetime Learning Credit; Keyword(s): Hope Credit; Keyword(s): Education Tax Credit; Keyword(s): Post Secondary Education

7.4 Hope & Life Time Learning Educational Credits

Q. *If I pay college tuition and fees with a scholarship, can I claim an education credit on Form 8863 for those payments?*

A. No. You cannot claim a credit for the amount of higher education expenses paid for by tax-free scholarships.

References:
• Publication 970, Tax Benefits for Education
• Tax Topic 605, Education Credits
• Tax Topic 421, Scholarship and Fellowship Grants
• Form 8863, Education Credits (Hope and Lifetime Learning Credits)

Q. *If the amount of qualified tuition and fees I pay is greater than the amount of my scholarship, should I fill out Form 8863? If I cannot use Form 8863 because I received a scholarship, what can I do?*

A. You must reduce the qualified expenses by the amount of any tax-free educational assistance. Do not reduce the qualified expenses by amounts paid with the student's earnings, loans, gifts, inheritances, and personal savings. Also, do not reduce the qualified expenses by any scholarship reported as income on the student's return or any scholarship which, by its terms, cannot be applied to qualified tuition and related expenses.

References:
• Publication 970, Tax Benefits for Education
• Tax Topic 605, Education Credits
• Tax Topic 513, Educational Expenses
• Form 8863, Education Credits (Hope and Lifetime Learning Credits)
References:
• Form 1040, Schedule C, Profit or Loss from Business (Sole Proprietorship)
• Form 1040, Schedule C-EZ, Net Profit from Business
• Instructions for Form 1040, Schedule C
• Form 1040, Schedule SE, Self-Employment Tax
• Instructions for Form 1040, Schedule SE
• Publication 533, Self-employment Tax
• Publication 334, Tax Guide for Small Business
• Tax information for Business
• Form 2210 Underpayment of Estimated Tax

Q. *Can I claim an education credit if I am married but file separately?*

A. No. Neither the Hope Credit nor the Lifetime Learning Credit can be claimed if the individual is married but filed a separate return.

References:
• Publication 970, Tax Benefits for Education
• Tax Topic 605, Education Credits
• Form 8863, Education Credits (Hope and Lifetime Learning Credits)

Q. *How is the amount of the Hope or Lifetime Learning Credit determined?*

A. The amount of the credit is determined by the amount you pay for qualified tuition and related expenses paid for each eligible student and the amount of your modified adjusted gross income (AGI).

References:
• Publication 970, Tax Benefits for Education
• Tax Topic 605, Education Credits
• Form 8863, Education Credits (Hope and Lifetime Learning Credits)

Q. *If tuition was paid by a government subsidized loan, can I still take the Hope or Lifetime Learning Credit?*

A. If you take out a loan to pay higher education expenses, those expenses may qualify for the credit if you will be required to pay back the loan. The credit is claimed in the year in which the expenses are paid, not in the year in which the loan is repaid.

References:
• Publication 970, Tax Benefits for Education
• Tax Topic 605, Education Credits
• Form 8863, Education Credits (Hope and Lifetime Learning Credits)

Q. *What is a Lifetime Learning Credit?*

A. A nonrefundable tax credit up to $2,000 per family for all undergraduate and graduate level education. Figured by taking 20% of the first $10,000 of qualified educational expenses paid.

References:
• Publication 970, Tax Benefits for Education
• Tax Topic 605, Education Credits
• Form 8863, Education Credits (Hope and Lifetime Learning Credits)

Q. *Who is eligible for the Lifetime Learning Credit?*

A. Generally, you can claim the Lifetime Learning Credit if all three of the following requirements are met.
• You pay qualified tuition and related expenses of higher education.
• You pay the tuition and related expenses for an eligible student.
• The eligible student is either yourself, your spouse, or a dependent for who you claim an exemption on your tax return.

The Lifetime Learning Credit is based on qualified tuition and related expenses you pay for yourself, your spouse, or a dependent for who you can claim an exemption on your tax return. Generally, the credit is allowed for qualified tuition and related expenses paid in 2005 for an academic period beginning in 2005 or in the first 3 months of 2006.

For purposes of the Lifetime Learning Credit, an eligible student is a student who is enrolled in one or more courses at an eligible educational institution.

An eligible educational institution is an college, university, vocational school, or other post-secondary educational institution eligible to participate in a student aid program administered by the Department of Education. It includes virtually all accredited, public, nonprofit, and proprietary (privately owned profit-making) post-secondary institutions. The educational institution should be able to tell you if it is an eligible educational institution.

You cannot claim the Lifetime Learning Credit if any of the following apply.
• Your filing status is married filing separately.
• You are listed as a dependent in the Exemptions section on another person's tax return (such as your parent's).
• Your modified adjusted gross income is $52,000 or more ($105,000 or more in the case of a joint return).
• You (or your spouse) were a nonresident alien for any part of 2005 and the nonresident alien did not elect to be treated as a resident for tax purposes. More information on resident aliens can be found in Publication 519, *U.S. Tax Guide for Aliens*.
• You claim the Hope credit for the same student in 2005.

References:
• Publication 970, Tax Benefits for Education
• Tax Topic 605, Education credits
• Form 8863, Education Credits (Hope and Lifetime Learning Credits)

Q. Can the Lifetime Learning Credit be used for a high school student taking classes at an approved college prior to graduation from high school?

A. College courses taken while attending high school may qualify for the Hope Scholarship Credit or for the Lifetime Learning Credit if the student meets the qualifications for claiming either of the credits.

References:
• Publication 970, Tax Benefits for Education
• Tax Topic 605, Education Credits

• Form 8863, Education Credits (Hope and Lifetime Learning Credits)

Q. *Who can claim the Hope Credit?*

A. Generally, you can claim the Hope Credit if all three of the following requirements are met.
• You pay qualified tuition and related expenses of higher education.
• You pay the tuition and related expenses for an eligible student.
• The eligible student is either yourself, your spouse, or a dependent for whom you claim an exemption on your tax return.
You cannot claim the Hope Credit if any of the following apply.
• Your filing status is married separately.
• You are listed as a dependent in the Exemptions section on another person's tax return (such as your parents').
• Your modified adjusted gross income is $52,000 or more ($105,000 or more in the case of a joint return).
• You (or your spouse) were a nonresident alien for any part of 2005 and the nonresident alien did not elect to be treated as a resident alien for tax purposes. More information on nonresident alien can be found in Publication 519, U.S. Tax Guide for Aliens.
• You claim the Lifetime Learning Credit for the same student in 2003.
In general, qualified tuition and related expenses are tuition and fees required for enrollment or attendance at an eligible educational institution

An eligible educational institution is a college, university, vocational school, or other post-secondary educational institution eligible to participate in a student aid program administered by the Department of Education. It includes virtually all accredited, public, nonprofit, and proprietary (privately owned profit-making) postsecondary institutions. The educational institution should be able to tell you if it is an eligible educational institution.

To claim the Hope Credit, the student for whom you pay qualified tuition and related expenses must be an eligible student. This is a student who meets all of the following requirements.
• Did not have expenses that were used to figure a Hope Credit in any 2 earlier tax years.
• Had not completed the first 2 years of postsecondary education (generally, the freshman and sophomore years of college) before 2006.
• Was enrolled at least half-time in a program that leads to a degree, certificate, or other recognized educational credential for at least one academic period beginning in 2006.
• Was free of any federal or state felony conviction for possessing or distributing a controlled substance as of the end of 2006.

References:
• Publication 970, Tax Benefits for Education
• Tax Topic 605, Education Credits
• Form 8863, Education Credits (Hope and Lifetime Learning Credits)

Q. *What expenses qualify for the education credits?*

A. Expenses that qualify are tuition and fees required for enrollment or attendance at any college, vocational school, or other post-secondary educational institution eligible to participate in the student aid programs administered by the Department of Education. Qualified expenses do not include books, room and board, student activities, athletics (unless the course is part of the student's degree program), insurance, equipment, transportation, or other similar personal, living, or family expenses. The cost of books and equipment are generally not qualified expenses because eligible educational institutions usually do not require that fees for such books or equipment be paid to the institution as a condition of the student's enrollment or attendance at the institution.

References:
• Publication 970, Tax Benefits for Education
• Tax Topic 605, Education Credits
• Form 8863, Education Credits (Hope and Lifetime Learning Credits)

Q. *Are expenses to attend private high schools eligible for the education credits?*

A. No. Expenses paid to attend high school do not qualify for the education credits because a high school is not an eligible educational institution. An eligible educational institution is any college, university, vocational school, or other post-secondary educational institution eligible to participate in a student aid program administered by the Department of Education. It includes virtually all accredited, public, nonprofit, and proprietary (privately owned profit making) post-secondary institutions.

References:
• Publication 970, Tax Benefits for Education
• Tax Topic 605, Education Credits
• Form 8863, Education Credits (Hope and Lifetime Learning Credits)

Q. *Are expenses to attend private high schools eligible for the education credits?*

A. No. Expenses paid to attend high school do not qualify for the education credits because a high school is not an eligible educational institution. An eligible educational institution is any college, university, vocational school, or other post-secondary educational institution eligible to participate in a student aid program administered by the Department of Education. It includes virtually all accredited, public, nonprofit, and proprietary (privately owned profit making) post-secondary institutions.

References:
- Publication 970, Tax Benefits for Education
- Tax Topic 605, Education Credits
- Form 8863, Education Credits (Hope and Lifetime Learning Credits)

Keyword(s): Work Opportunity Tax Credit; Keyword(s): Custodian Parent; Keyword(s): Qualifying Child (EITC)

7.5 Other Credits

Q. *I heard there is a credit for hiring certain groups of workers, such as veterans or ex-felons. Is that the same thing as the Work Opportunity Tax Credit?*

A. The Work Opportunity Credit provides an incentive to hire individuals from targeted groups that have a particularly high unemployment rate or other special employment needs. The credit can be as much as 40% of the "qualified first year wages" you pay to individuals who begin work for you before January 1, 2006. The credit can be claimed by filing Form 5884, Work Opportunity Credit.
An individual is a member of a targeted group if he or she is a:
- Qualified recipient of assistance under temporary assistance for needy families (TANF).
- Qualified veteran.
- Qualified ex-felon.
- High-risk youth.
- Vocational rehabilitation referral.
- Qualified summer youth employee.
- Qualified food stamp recipient.
- Qualified SSI recipient.

An individual is not considered a member of a targeted group unless your state employment security agency certifies him or her as a member. This certification requirement can be satisfied in either of two ways:

1) On or before the day on which the individual begins work for you, you have received a certification from your state employment security agency that the individual is a member of a targeted group, or

2) On or before the day you offer employment to an individual, you complete Form 8850, *Pre-Screening Notice and Certification Request for the Work Opportunity and Welfare-to-Work Credits*, and send it to your state employment security agency no later than the 21st day after the individual begins work.

You must receive the certification before claiming the credit.

Refer to Tax Topic 750, *Employer Tax Information, and Tax Info for Business* for other employer information.

References:
- Form 5884, Work Opportunity Credit
- Form 8850, Pre-Screening Notice and Certification Request for the Work Opportunity and Welfare-to-Work Credits
- Tax Topic 750, Employer Tax Information

Chapter 8

Earned Income Tax Credit

~~~~~

8.1 Qualifying Child Rules

Q. *My child was born and only lived 40 minutes. Can she be used as a qualifying child when figuring the Earned Income Credit and the Child Tax Credit?*

A. If your child was born alive and died during the same year, and the exemption tests are met, you can take the full exemption. This is true even if the child lived only for a moment. Whether your child was born alive depends on state or local law. There must be proof of a live birth shown by an official document such as a birth certificate. Under these circumstances, if you do not have a social security number for the child, you may attach a copy of the child's birth certificate instead and enter "DIED" in column 2 of line 6c of the Form 1040 or 1040A.

If you have determined that you are eligible to claim your child's exemption, you may also be eligible to claim the Child Tax Credit. Refer to the Instructions for Form 1040 (General Inst.) or Instructions for Form 1040A for the Child Tax Credit. The referenced pages will explain who qualifies for this credit and how to calculate it.

The Earned Income Credit generally requires that you provide a valid social security number for your qualifying child. However, if you meet all the other requirements to claim this credit and your child was born and died in the same year, you will not be required to provide a social security number for that child. Instead, you may enter "DIED" on line 4 of Form 1040, Schedule EIC, Earned Income Credit, and attach a copy of the child's birth certificate.

References:
- Publication 501, Exemptions, Standard Deduction, and Filing Information
- Publication 596, Earned Income Credit
- Instructions for Form 1040 (General Inst.)
- Instructions for Form 1040A

- Tax Topic 601, Earned Income Credit (EIC)
- Tax Topic 606, Child Tax Credits

Q. *In order to claim the Earned Income Credit, does the child have to be claimed as a dependent?*

A. A qualifying child for the Earned Income Credit does not need to qualify as a dependent unless he or she is married.
Refer to Publication 596, Earned Income Credit, for a full discussion of the Earned Income Credit rules.

References:
• Publication 596, Earned Income Credit
• Tax Topic 601, Earned IncomeTax Credit (EITC)

Q. *If the noncustodial parent receives permission from the custodial parent to claim a child on his or her tax return, is the noncustodial parent eligible for the Earned Income Credit?*

A. The noncustodial parent cannot claim the Earned Income Credit on the basis of that child because the child did not live with that parent and does not meet the residency test. The custodial parent may be able to claim the Earned Income Credit. Refer to Publication 596, *Earned Income Credit,* for the Earned Income Credit rules.

8.2 Taxable & Nontaxable Income

Q. *Is child support considered income when calculating the Earned Income Credit?*

A. No, for purposes of calculating the Earned Income Credit, child support is not considered earned income. Refer to Publication 596, *Earned Income Credit,* for a complete discussion of the Earned Income Credit.

References:
• Publication 596, Earned Income Credit
• Tax Topic 601, Earned Income Tax Credit (EIC)

8.3 Other EITC Issues

Q. *If both parents want to claim the Earned Income Credit, who is entitled to it if there was no marriage?*

A. If the child is a qualifying child of both parents, they may choose which one will claim the credit. If there are two qualifying children, each parent may claim the credit on the basis of one of the children or one parent may claim the credit with both children. If both actually claim the credit on the basis of the same child or children, the parent who is entitled to the credit is the parent with whom the child lived for the longest period of time during the tax year, or the parent with the higher Adjusted Gross Income (AGI) if the child lived with each parent for the same amount of time during the year. Refer to Publication 596, *Earned Income Credit*, for full discussion of the Earned Income Credit rules.

References:
• Publication 596, Earned Income Credit
• Tax Topic 601, Earned Income Tax Credit (EIC)

Chapter 9

Estimated Tax

~~~~~

Keyword(s): S Corporation; Keyword(s): Partnership

9.1 Businesses

Q. Is an S-Corporation required to pay quarterly estimated tax?

A. Generally, the corporation must make estimated tax payments for the following taxes if the total of these taxes is $500 or more:
• the tax on certain capital gains,
• the tax on built-in gains,
• the excess net passive income tax, and
• the investment credit recapture tax.
For more information regarding estimated tax, refer to Instructions for Form 1120S, *U.S. Income Tax Return for an S Corporation* and Publication 542, *Corporations*.

References:
• Publication 542, Corporations
• Instructions for Form 1120S

Q. How do partnerships file and pay quarterly estimated tax payments?

A. Partnerships file Form 1065, U.S. *Partnership Return of Income*, to report income and expenses. The partnership passes the information to the individual partners on Schedule K-1, Form 1065. The partners report the information and pay any taxes due on Form 1040. Because partners are not employees of the partnership, no withholding is taken out of their distributions to pay the income and self-employment taxes on their Forms 1040. The partners may need to pay Estimated Tax Payments using Form 1040-ES.

Refer to Instructions for Form 1065, *U.S. Partnership Return of Income* and Publication 505, *Tax Withholding and Estimated Tax* for additional information.

References:
• Publication 505, Tax Withholding and Estimated Tax

- Form 1065, U.S. Partnership Return of Income
- Instructions for Form 1065, U.S. Partnership Return of Income

Keyword(s): Farming

9.2 Farmers & Fishermen

Q. Most of my income is from farming. Are there any special provisions related to estimated tax payments for farmers?

A. If you have income from farming, you may be able to avoid making estimated tax payments by filing your return and paying the entire tax due on or before March 1 of the year your return is due. If March 1 falls on a weekend or legal holiday, you have until the next business day to file and pay tax. This estimated tax rule generally applies if at least 2/3 of your total gross income is from farming this year or previous year. Refer to Publication 225, *Farmer's Tax Guide*, and Tax Topic 416, *Farming and Fishing Income*, for additional information.

References:
- Publication 225, Farmer's Tax Guide
- Tax Topic 416, Farming and Fishing Income

Keyword(s): Self-employment Tax

9.3 Individuals

Q. Do self-employment taxes need to be paid quarterly or yearly?

A. Self-employment tax is paid by making quarterly estimated tax payments which include both income tax and social security tax.

References:
- Publication 334, Tax Guide for Small Business
- Publication 505, Tax Withholding and Estimated Tax
- Publication 533, Self-Employment Tax

Q. How do I know if I have to file quarterly individual estimated tax payments?

A. Estimated tax payments can be used to pay Federal income tax, self-employment tax, and household employment tax. To estimate if you need to pay tax on income not subject to withholding or on other income from which not enough tax is withheld, you need to calculate if the total tax you'll owe on your annual income tax return will be covered by the amount of tax you have already had either:
- withheld from wages and other payments, or
- paid in earlier estimated payments for the year, or
- credited to your account from adjustments or overpayments to previously filed returns.

Generally, you should make estimated tax payments if you will owe tax of $1,000 or more, after withholding and credits, and the total amount of tax withheld and your credits will be less than the smaller of:
- 90% of the tax to be shown on your current tax return, or
- 100% of the tax shown on your prior year's tax return, if your prior year's tax return covered all 12 months of the year. However, if your prior year's adjusted gross income exceeded $150,000, or $75,000 if you filed a separate return from your spouse, then you must pay 110% instead of 100% of last year's tax. (*Note:* the percentages change depending on the tax year. Refer to Publication 505, *Tax Withholding and Estimated Tax.*)

Estimated tax requirements are different for farmers and fishermen. Publication 505, *Tax Withholding and Estimated Tax, provides* more information about these special estimated tax rules and about estimated tax in general. Get Form 1040-ES, *Estimated Tax for Individuals*, to help you figure your estimated tax liability for 2005.

References:
- Publication 505, Tax Withholding and Estimated Tax
- Form 1040-ES, Estimated Tax for Individuals

Q. *When are the quarterly estimated tax returns due?*

A. Your first estimated tax payment is usually due the 15th of April. You may pay the entire year's estimated tax at that time, or you may pay your estimated tax in four payments. The four payments are due April 15th, June 15th, September 15, and January 15th of the following year.

If the due date for making an estimated tax payment falls on a Saturday, Sunday, or legal holiday, the payment will be on time if you make it on the next day that is not a Saturday, Sunday, or legal holiday.

References:
- Publication 505, Tax Withholding and Estimated Tax

Keyword(s): Capital Gains

9.4 Large Gains, Lump-sum Distributions, etc.

Q. If I anticipate a sizable capital gain on the sale of an investment during the year, do I need to make a quarterly estimated tax payment during the tax year?

A. If you first receive income subject to estimated tax during a period other than the first quarter, you must make your first payment by the due date for the period the income is received. You can pay your entire estimated tax by the due date for the period the income is received, or you can pay it in installments by the due date for that period and the due dates for the remaining periods. If you are making estimated tax payments you can increase your quarterly estimated tax payments or increase your Federal income tax withholding to cover the tax liability.

If you have the proper amount withheld you may not be required to make estimated tax payments nor have to file Form 2210, *Underpayment of Estimated Tax by Individuals, Estates and Trusts,* with your tax return (as you would if you just increased the remaining estimated tax payments). If you wait and make increased estimated tax payments in the later quarters, you would have to file Form 2210 with your tax return because we do not know when you received the income. Since you really did not receive the income evenly throughout the year, you have to tell us when the income was received by filing Form 2210.

References:
• Publication 505, Tax Withholding and Estimated Tax
• Form 1040-ES, Estimated Tax for Individuals
• Form 2210, Underpayment of Estimated Tax by Individuals, Estates and Trusts
• Tax Topic 306, Penalty for Underpayment of Estimated Tax

9.5 Penalty Questions
Q. What is meant by "no tax liability" in the exceptions to the estimated tax penalty?

A. You do not have to pay estimated tax for 2006 if you meet all three of the following conditions.

1. You had no tax liability for 2005.
2. You were a U.S. citizen or resident for the whole year.
3. Your 2005 tax year covered a 12-month period.
You had no tax liability for 2005 if your total tax was zero or you did not have to file an income tax return.

For additional information on this topic refer to Form 1040-ES, Estimated Tax for Individuals, and Publication 505, *Tax Withholding and Estimated Tax.*

References:
* Form 1040-ES, Estimated Tax for Individuals
* Publication 505, Tax Withholding and Estimated Tax

Q. *If I believe I owe some Interest and Penalties do I have to figure them myself?*

A. You do not have to figure the amount of any interest or penalties you may owe. Because figuring these amounts can be complicated, the IRS will do it for you if you want. The IRS will send you a bill for any amount due.

However, if you include interest or penalties (other than the estimated tax penalty) with your payment, identify and enter the amount in the bottom margin of Form 1040, page 2. Do not include interest or penalties (other than the estimated tax penalty) in the amount you owe on line 74.

Q. *If I am granted an extension of time to file my Tax Return will I still pay or be charged interest?*

A. The IRS will charge you interest on <u>taxes not paid by their due date</u>, even if an extension of time to file is granted. The IRS will also charge you interest on penalties imposed for failure to file, negligence, fraud, substantial valuation misstatements, and substantial understatements of tax. Interest is charged on the penalty from the due date of the return (including extensions).

Q. *What are some of the penalties a tax payer should expect from the IRS?*

A. The IRS imposes a variety of penalties. They range from penalties for late filing, penalties for late payment of tax, penalties for frivolous return and some others.

Q. *What is the penalty for late filing?*

A. If you do not file your return by the due date (including extensions), the penalty is usually 5% of the amount due for each month or part of a month your return is late, unless you have a reasonable explanation. If you do, attach it to your return. The penalty can be as much as 25% (more in some cases) of the tax due. If your return is more than 60 days late, the minimum penalty will be $100 or the amount of any tax you owe, whichever is smaller.

Q. *What is the penalty for Late payment of tax?*

A. If you pay your taxes late, the penalty is usually 1~2 of 1% of the unpaid amount for each month or part of a month the tax is not paid. The penalty can be as much as 25% of the unpaid amount. It applies to any unpaid tax on the return. This penalty is in addition to interest charges on late payments.

Q. *What is the penalty for filing a Frivolous Return?*

In addition to any other penalties, the law imposes a penalty of $500 for filing a frivolous return. A frivolous return is one that does not contain information needed to figure the correct tax or shows a substantially incorrect tax because you take a frivolous position or desire to delay or interfere with the tax laws. This includes altering or striking out the preprinted language above the space where you sign.

A. *What are some of the other types of penalties that the IRS may impose?*

Other penalties can be imposed for negligence, substantial understatement of tax, and fraud. Criminal penalties may be imposed for willful failure to file, tax evasion, or making a false statement. Refer to Pub. 17 for details on some of these penalties

Chapter 10

Capital Gains, Losses/Sale of Home
~~~~~

Keyword(s): Vacation Home; Keyword(s): Cost Basis; Keyword(s): Depreciation Deduction; Keyword(s): Sale or Trade of Business Property; Keyword(s): Main Home Sale; Keyword(s):Rental Property; Keyword(s): Holding Period; Keyword(s): Vacation Home

10.1 Property (Basis, Sale of Home, etc.)

Q. How do you report the sale of a second residence?

A. Your second home is considered a capital asset. Use Form 1040, Schedule D to report sales, exchanges, and other dispositions of capital assets.

References:
• Publication 544, Sales and Other Dispositions of Assets
• Tax Topic 703, Basis of Assets
• Tax Topic 409, Capital Gains and Losses

Q. I sold my principal residence this year. What form do I need to file?

A. If you meet the ownership and use tests, you will generally only need to report the sale of your home if your gain is more than $250,000 ($500,000 if married filing a joint return). This means that during the 5-year period ending on the date of the sale, you must have:
• Owned the home for at least 2 years (the ownership test), and
• Lived in the home as your main home for at least 2 years (the use test). If you owned and lived in the property as your main home for less than 2 years, you may still be able to claim an exclusion in some cases. The maximum amount you can exclude will be reduced. If you are required or choose to report a gain, it is reported on Form 1040, Schedule D, *Capital Gains and Losses.*
If you were on qualified extended duty in the U.S. Armed Services or the Foreign Service you may suspend the five-year test period for up to 10 years. You are on qualified extended duty when:
• At a duty station that is at least 50 miles from the residence sold, or
• When residing under orders in government housing, for more than 90 days or for an indefinite period.

This change applies to home sales after May 6, 1997. You may use this provision for only one property at a time and one sale every two years.

For additional information on selling your home, refer to Publication 523, *Selling Your Home*.

References:
• Publication 523, Selling Your Home
• Tax Topic 701, Sale of your Home - after May 6, 1997
• Tax Topic 703, Basis of Assets

Q. *If I sell my home and use the money I receive to pay off the mortgage, do I have to pay taxes on that money?*

A. It is not the money you receive for the sale of your home, but the amount of gain on the sale over your cost, or basis, that determines whether you will have to include any proceeds as taxable income on your return. You may be able to exclude any gain from income up to a limit of $250,000 ($500,000 on a joint return in most cases). If you can exclude all of the gain, you do not need to report the sale on your tax return. For additional information on selling your home, refer to Publication 523, *Selling Your Home*.

References:
• Publication 523, Selling Your Home
• Tax Topic 701, Sale of your Home - after May 6, 1997
• Tax Topic 703, Basis of Assets

Q. *If I take the exclusion of capital gain tax on the sale of my old home this year, can I also take the exclusion again if I sell my new home in the future?*

A. With the exception of the 2-year waiting period, there is no limit on the number of times you can exclude the gain on the sale of your principle residence so long as you meet the ownership and use tests.

References:
• Publication 523, Selling Your Home
• Tax Topic 701, Sale of Your Home - after May 6, 1997
• Tax Topic 703, Basis of Assets

Q. *I lived in a home as my principal residence for the first 2 of the last 5 years. For the last 3 years, the home was a rental property before selling it. Can I still avoid the capital gains tax and, if so, how should I deal with the depreciation I took while it was rented out?*

A. If, during the 5-year period ending on the date of sale, you owned the home for at least 2 years and lived in it as your main home for at least 2 years, you can exclude up to $250,000 of the gain ($500,000 on a joint return in most cases). However, you cannot exclude the portion of the gain equal to depreciation allowed or allowable for periods after May 6, 1997. This gain is reported on Form 4797. If you can show by adequate records or other evidence that the depreciation allowed was less than the amount allowable, the amount you cannot exclude is the amount allowed. Refer to Publication 523, *Selling Your Main Home* and Form 4797, *Sale of Business Property* for specifics on calculating and reporting the amount of the eligible exclusion.

References:
• Publication 523, Selling Your Home
• Publication 527, Residential Rental Property
• Publication 587, Business Use of Your Home
• Form 4797, Sale of Business Property

Q. *What is the basis of property received as a gift?*

A. To figure the basis of property you get as a gift, you must know its adjusted basis to the donor just before it was given to you. You also must know its fair market value (FMV) at the time it was given to you. If the FMV of the property at the time of the gift is less than the donor's adjusted basis, your basis depends on whether you have a gain or loss when you dispose of the property. Your basis for figuring gain is the same as the donor's adjusted basis, plus or minus any required adjustments to basis while you held the property. Your basis for figuring a loss is the FMV of the property when you received the gift, plus or minus any required adjustments to basis while you held the property. Refer to Adjusted Basis in Publication 551, *Basis of Assets.*
If you use the donor's adjusted basis for figuring a gain and get a loss, and then use the FMV for figuring a loss and get a gain, you have neither a gain or loss on the sale or disposition of the property.

If the FMV is equal to or greater than the donor's adjusted basis, your basis is the donor's adjusted basis at the time you received the gift. Increase your basis by all or part of any gift tax paid, depending on the date of the gift. Also, for figuring gain or loss, you must increase or decrease your basis by any required adjustments to basis while you held the property. Refer to Adjusted Basis in Publication 551, *Basis of Assets.*

If you received a gift before 1977, increase your basis in the gift (the donor's adjusted basis) by any gift tax paid on it. However, do not increase your basis above the FMV of the gift at the time it was given to you.

If you received a gift after 1976, increase your basis by the part of the gift tax paid on it that is due to the net increase in value of the gift. Figure the increase to basis by multiplying the gift tax paid by the following fraction. The numerator of the fraction is the net increase in value of the gift and the denominator is the amount of the gift.

The net increase in value of the gift is the FMV of the gift less the donor's adjusted basis. The amount of the gift is its value for gift tax purposes, after reduction by any annual exclusion and any marital or charitable deduction that applies to the gift. For more information on the gift tax, Refer to Publication 950, Introduction to Estate and Gift taxes.
For additional information on this subject Refer to Gifts.

References:
• Publication 551, Basis of Assets
• Publication 950, Introduction to Estate and Taxes

Q. *What is the basis of property received as a gift?*

A. To figure the basis of property you get as a gift, you must know its adjusted basis to the donor just before it was given to you. You also must know its fair market value (FMV) at the time it was given to you. If the FMV of the property at the time of the gift is less than the donor's adjusted basis, your basis depends on whether you have a gain or loss when you dispose of the property. Your basis for figuring gain is the same as the donor's adjusted basis, plus or minus any required adjustments to basis while you held the property. Your basis for figuring a loss is the FMV of the property when you received the gift, plus or minus any required adjustments to basis while you held the property. Refer to Adjusted Basis in Publication 551, *Basis of Assets.*
If you use the donor's adjusted basis for figuring a gain and get a loss, and then use the FMV for figuring a loss and get a gain, you have neither a gain or loss on the sale or disposition of the property.

If the FMV is equal to or greater than the donor's adjusted basis, your basis is the donor's adjusted basis at the time you received the gift. Increase your basis by all or part of any gift tax paid, depending on the date of the gift. Also, for figuring gain or loss, you must increase or decrease your basis by any required adjustments to basis while you held the property. Refer to Adjusted Basis in Publication 551, *Basis of Assets.*

104

If you received a gift before 1977, increase your basis in the gift (the donor's adjusted basis) by any gift tax paid on it. However, do not increase your basis above the FMV of the gift at the time it was given to you.

If you received a gift after 1976, increase your basis by the part of the gift tax paid on it that is due to the net increase in value of the gift. Figure the increase to basis by multiplying the gift tax paid by the following fraction. The numerator of the fraction is the net increase in value of the gift and the denominator is the amount of the gift.

The net increase in value of the gift is the FMV of the gift less the donor's adjusted basis. The amount of the gift is its value for gift tax purposes, after reduction by any annual exclusion and any marital or charitable deduction that applies to the gift. For more information on the gift tax, Refer to Publication 950, Introduction to Estate and Gift taxes.

For additional information on this subject Refer to Gifts.

References:
• Publication 551, Basis of Assets
• Publication 950, Introduction to Estate and Taxes

Keyword(s): Stock Options; Keyword(s): Stock Sale; Keyword(s):Stock Split; Keyword(s):Stock Options; Keyword(s): Short Sale; Keyword(s): Schedule D; Keyword(s): Employee Stock Purchase Plan; Keyword(s): Dividend Reinvestment; Keyword(s): Average Costs

10.2 Stocks (Options, Splits, Traders)

Q. I purchased stock from my employer under an employee stock purchase plan. Now I have received a Form 1099-B from selling it. How do I report this?

A. If the special holding period requirements are met, generally treat gain or loss from the sale of the stock as capital gain or loss. However, you may have compensation income if:
• The option price of the stock was below the stock's fair market value at the time the option was granted, or
• You did not meet the holding period requirement.

The holding period requirement is that you must hold the stock for more than 2 years from the time the option is granted to you and for more than 1 year from when the stock was transferred to you. If you do not meet these holding period requirements, there is a disqualifying disposition of the stock. The compensation income that you should report in the year of the disposition is the excess of the fair market value of the stock on the date the stock was transferred to you less the amount paid for the shares.

If the holding period requirement are met, but the option price is below the fair market value of the stock at the time the option was granted, you report the difference as compensation income (wages) when you sell the stock. Generally, this compensation income is the lesser of the excess of the fair market value of the stock on the date of the disposition less the exercise price OR the excess of the fair market value of the stock at the time the option was granted less the exercise price.

If your gain is more than the amount you report as compensation income, the remainder is a capital gain reported on Form 1040, Schedule D. If you sell the stock for less than the amount you paid for it, your loss is a capital loss, and you do not have ordinary income.

For more information, refer to Publication 525, *Taxable and Nontaxable Income*, and Publication 551, *Basis of Assets*.

References:
• Publication 525, Taxable and Nontaxable Income
• Publication 551, Basis of Assets
• Form 1040, Schedule D, Capital Gains and Losses

Q. How do I figure the cost basis of stock that has split, giving me more of the same stock, so I can figure my capital gain (or loss) on the sale of the stock?

A. When the old stock and the new stock are identical the basis of the old shares must be allocated to the old and new shares. Thus, you generally divide the adjusted basis of the old stock by the number of shares of old and new stock. The result is your new basis per share of stock. If the old shares were purchased in separate lots for differing amounts of money, the adjusted basis of the old stock must be allocated between the old and new stock on a lot by lot basis.

References:
• Publication 550, Investment Income and Expenses
• Tax Topic 409, Capital Gains and Losses

Q. How do I compute the basis for stock I sold, when I received the stock over several years through a dividend reinvestment plan?

A. The basis of the stock you sold is the cost of the shares plus any adjustments, such as sales commissions. If you have not kept detailed records of your dividend reinvestments, you may be able to reconstruct those records with the help of public records from sources such as the media, your broker, or the company that issued the dividends.

If you cannot specifically identify which shares were sold, you must use the first-in first-out rule. This means that you deem that you sold the oldest shares first, then the next oldest, then the next-to-the-next oldest, until you have accounted for the number of shares in the sale. In order to establish the basis of these shares, you need to have kept adequate documentation of all your purchases, including those that were through the dividend reinvestment plan. You may not use an average cost basis. Only mutual fund shares may have an average cost basis.

Refer to Publication 550, *Investment Income and Expenses, and Publication 551, Basis of Assets.*

References:
- Publication 550, Investment Income and Expenses
- Publication 551, Basis of Assets
- Tax Topic 404, Dividends

Q. *Do I need to pay taxes on that portion of stock I gained as a result of a split?*

A. No, you generally do not need to pay tax on the additional shares of stock you received due to the stock split. You will need to adjust your per share cost of the stock. Your overall cost basis has not changed, but your per share cost has changed.

You will have to pay taxes if you have gain when you sell the stock. Gain is the amount of the proceeds from the sale, minus sales commissions, that exceeds the adjusted basis of the stock sold.

References:
- Publication 550, Investment Income and Expenses
- Tax Topic 409, Capital gains and losses

Q. *Should I advise the IRS why amounts reported on Form 1099-B do not agree with my Schedule D for proceeds from short sales of stock not closed by the end of year that I did not include?*

107

A. If you are able to defer the reporting of gain or loss until the year the short sale closes, the following will allow you to reconcile your Forms 1099-B to your Schedule D and still not recognize the gain or loss from the short sale:
• Your total of lines 3 and 10, column (d), on your Schedule D should equal your total gross proceeds reported to you on all Forms 1099-B.
• In columns (b) and (c) write "SHORT SALE," and
• in column (f) write "Refer to attached statement."
• In your statement, explain the details of your short sale and that it has not closed as of the end of the year. Include your name as it appears on the return and your social security number.
For more on these rules and exceptions that may apply, refer to Chapter 4 of Publication 550, Investment Income and Expenses.

References:
• Publication 550, Investment Income and Expenses
• Tax Topic 409, Capital gains and losses

Q. *How do I report an employee stock purchase plan on my tax return?*

A. If your stock option is granted under an employee stock purchase plan, you do not include any amount in your gross income as a result of the grant or exercise of your option. When you sell the stock that you purchased by exercising the option, you may have to report compensation and capital gain or capital loss. For additional information on tax treatment and holding period requirements, refer to Publication 525, *Taxable and Nontaxable Income*.

References:
• Publication 525, Taxable and Nontaxable Income

Q. *How do we show on our tax form where dividends are reinvested?*

A. Some corporations allow investors to choose to use their dividends to buy more shares of stock in the corporation instead of receiving the dividends in cash. If you are a member of this type of plan, you must report the fair market value on the dividend payment date of the dividends that are reinvested as income on your tax return. You do not actually show that the dividends were reinvested on your return. Keep good records of the dollar amount of the reinvested dividends, the number of additional shares purchased, and the purchase dates. You will need this information when you sell the shares.

Report the dividends that were reinvested with your other dividends, if any, on line 9 of Form 1040 or Form 1040A. If your total income from ordinary dividends is over $1,500.00, you also must file either Form 1040, Schedule B or Form 1040A, Schedule 1. For more information on this and other types of dividend reinvestment plans, refer to Ordinary Dividends in Chapter 1 of Publication 550, *Investment Income and Expenses.*

References:
• Publication 550, Investment Income and Expenses
• Form 1040, Schedule B
• Tax Topic 404, Dividends

Q. How do I calculate the average cost method of a mutual fund if the fund price splits?

A. If your mutual fund splits, or adjusts its price, it is treated like a stock split. Your total basis doesn't change after the split, but since you now own more shares without paying any more money, your per-share basis will decrease. To calculate your per-share basis, divide the total cost that you have invested in the fund (minus any shares previously sold) by the current number of shares that you hold.

References:
• Publication 564, Mutual Fund Distributions

10.3 Mutual Funds (Costs, Distributions, etc.)
Q. How do I calculate the average basis for the sale of mutual fund shares?

A. In order to figure your gain or loss using an average basis, you must have acquired the shares at various times and prices and have left them on deposit in a managed account.

There are two average basis methods:
• Single-category method, and
• Double-category method.
Single-category method. First, add up the cost of all the shares you own in the mutual fund. Divide that result by the total number of shares you own. This gives you your average per share. Multiply that number by the number of shares sold.

Double-category method. First, divide your shares into two categories, long-term and short-term. Then use the steps above to get an average basis for each category. The average basis for that category is then the basis of each share in the sale from that category.

Once you elect to use an average basis method, you must continue to use it for all accounts in the same fund. You must clearly identify on your tax return the average basis method that you have elected to use. You do this identification by including "AVGB " in column (a) of Form 1040, Schedule D .

Refer to Publication 564, *Mutual Fund Distributions, Sales, Exchanges and Redemptions*.

References:
• Publication 564, Mutual Fund Distributions
• Instructions for Form 1040, Schedule D

Q. *If I used an average basis method for shares of one mutual fund I sold, do I have to use it for all mutual funds I sell?*

A. No, you may use a different method, as long as you have not used an average basis method for that fund previously. Once you have elected to use an average basis method to compute the gain or loss on shares in a mutual fund, you must use that same method for the sale of shares from any account in that same fund.

References:
• Publication 564, Mutual Fund Distributions

Q. *I have both purchased and sold shares in a money-market mutual fund. The fund is managed so the share price is constant. All gain is reported as dividends. Do I have to report the sale of these shares?*

A. Yes, you report the sale of your shares on Form 1040, Schedule D, Capital Gains and Losses. Generally, whenever you sell, exchange, or otherwise dispose of a capital asset, you report it on Schedule D.

If the share price were constant, you would have neither a gain nor a loss when you sell shares because you are selling the shares for the same price you purchased them. If you actually owned shares that were later sold, the fund or the broker should have issued a Form 1099-B There is no requirement with that form that there be gain or loss on the sale, only a sale or exchange of an investment asset and sales proceeds.

References:
• Publication 564, Mutual Fund Distributions

Q. *I received a 1099-DIV showing a capital gain. Why do I have to report capital gains from my mutual funds if I never sold any shares?*

A. A mutual fund is a regulated investment company that pools funds of investors allowing them to take advantage of a diversity of investments and professional asset management. You own shares in the fund, but the fund owns assets such as shares of stock, corporate bonds, government obligations, etc. One of the ways the fund makes money for its investors is to sell these assets at a gain. If the asset was held by the mutual fund for more than one year, the nature of the income is capital gain, which gets passed on to you. These are called capital gain distributions, which are distinguished on Form 1099-DIV, from income that is from other profits, called ordinary dividends.

Capital gains distribution are taxed as long term capital gains regardless of how long you have owned the shares in the mutual fund. If your capital gains distribution is automatically reinvested, the reinvested amount is the basis of the additional shares purchased.

References:
• Publication 564, Mutual Fund Distributions

Q. *How do return of principal payments affect my cost basis when I sell mutual funds?*

A. A return of principal (or return of capital) reduces your basis in your mutual fund shares. Unlike a dividend or a capital gain distribution, a return of capital is a return of part of your investment (cost). However, basis cannot be reduced below zero. Once your basis reaches zero, any return of principal is capital gain and must be reported on Form 1040 Schedule D, Capital Gains and Losses.

References:
• Publication 564, Mutual Fund Distributions

Keyword(s): Capital Loss; Keyword(s): Worthless Securities

10.4 Losses (Homes, Stocks, Other Property)

Q. *Is the loss on the sale of your home deductible?*

A. The loss on the sale of a personal residence is a nondeductible personal loss.

References:

• Publication 523, Selling Your Home
• Tax Topic 409, Capital gains and losses

Q. *I own stock which became worthless last year. Can I take a bad debt deduction on my tax return?*

A. If you own securities and they become totally worthless, you can take a deduction for a loss, but not for a bad debt.

The worthless securities are treated as though they were capital assets sold on the last day of the tax year if they were capital assets in your hands. Report worthless securities on line 1 or line 8 of Form 1040, Schedule D, whichever applies. In columns (c) and (d), write "Worthless. " For additional information, refer to Publication 550, *Investment Income and Expenses* (Including Capital Gains and Losses). For more information on bad debts, refer to Tax Topic 453, *Bad Debt Deduction.*

References:
• Publication 550, Investment Income and Expenses (Including Capital Gains and Losses)
• Form 1040, Schedule D, Capital Gains and Losses
• Tax Topic 453, Bad Debt Deduction

Chapter 11

Sale or Trade of Business, Depreciation, Rentals
~~~~~

Keyword(s): Apartment Building; Keyword(s): Mileage Rate; Keyword(s): Travel Expenses; Keyword(s): Home Office; Keyword(s): Business Use/Expense; Keyword(s): Home Based Business; Keyword(s): Computer; Keyword(s): Day Trader

11.1 Depreciation & Recapture

Q. We have incurred substantial repairs to our rental property: new roof, gutters, windows, furnace, and outside paint. What are the IRS rules concerning depreciation?

A. Replacements of roof, rain gutters, windows, and furnace on a residential rental property are capital improvements to the structure because they materially add to the value of your property or substantially prolong its life. The items would be in the same class of property as the rental property to which they are attached. Since the property is residential rental property, the items are generally depreciated over a recovery period of 27.5 years using the straight line method of depreciation and a mid-month convention.

Repairs, such as repainting the residential rental property, are currently deductible expenses. A repair keeps your property in good operating condition. It does not materially add to the value of your property or substantially prolong its life. Repainting your property inside or out, fixing gutters or floors, fixing leaks, plastering, and replacing broken windows are examples of repairs. If you make repairs as part of an extensive remodeling or restoration of your property, the whole job is an improvement. In that case, you should capitalize and depreciate the repair costs as the same class of property that you have restored or remodeled as discussed above. For more information, refer to Publication 527, *Residential Rental Property, and Publication 946, How to Depreciate Property.*

References:
• Publication 527, Residential Rental Property
• Publication 946, How to Depreciate Property

Q. *I purchased a computer last year to do online day trading part-time from home for additional income. Can I deduct or depreciate the cost of the computer or internet connection from my investment income?*

A. You may deduct investment expenses (other than interest expenses) as miscellaneous itemized deductions on Form 1040, Schedule A, line 22, Itemized Deductions. This would include depreciation on the portion of your computer used for investment purposes, and the portion of your internet access charges used for investment purposes.

The entire acquisition cost of a computer purchased for business use can be expensed under Code section 179 in the first year if qualified, or depreciated over a 5-year recovery period. Under section 179, you can elect to recover all or part of the cost of certain qualifying property, up to a dollar limit, by deducting it in the year you place the property in service. You can elect to expense the cost of qualifying property instead of recovering the cost by taking depreciation. To claim the expense in the first year, the property must be used more than 50% for business use (as opposed to investment use), and meet the other requirements for expensing. One of those requirements is that the total cost of qualifying property you can deduct after you apply the dollar limit is limited to the taxable income from the active conduct of any trade or business during the year. Any cost not deductible in one year under section 179 because of the business income limit can be carried to the next year.

The 2003 Jobs and Growth Act raised the aggregate cost that can be expensed for any tax year beginning after 2002 and before 2006 to $100,000. The new law also expanded the definition of Code Section 179 property to include off-the-shelf computer software. Refer to Code Section 179 for the expanded definition. If the business use falls to 50% or less in a later year, these tax benefits may be subject to recapture. Refer to Publication 946, *How to Depreciate Property* for additional information on the section 179 deduction.

Because these deductions are for investment expenses rather than for business expenses, these deductions must be reduced by 2% of your adjusted gross income. Use Form 4562, Depreciation and Amortization, to compute the depreciation for the portion of your computer used for investment purposes.

Note: Unless the computer is used more than 50% for business purpose (as opposed to investment purposes), you cannot claim section 179 expensing of the computer or claim accelerated depreciation (including the special depreciation) for it. For more information, refer to "Listed Property" in Publication 946, *How to Depreciate Property.*

References:
- Form 1040, Schedule A, Itemized Deductions
- Form 4562, Depreciation and Amortization
- Publication 946, How to Depreciate Property
- Publication 535, Business Expenses

Q. *I have a home office. Can I deduct expenses like mortgage, utilities, etc., but not deduct depreciation so that when I sell this house, the basis won't be affected?*

A. If you qualify to deduct expenses for the business use of your home, you can claim depreciation for the part of your home that is a home office. Generally, the part of your home that is a home office is depreciated over a recovery period of 39 years using the straight line method of depreciation and a mid-month convention. If you do not claim depreciation on that part of your home that is a home office, you are still required to reduce the basis of your home for the allowable depreciation of that part of your home that is a home office when reporting the sale of your home. For more information, refer to Publication 587, *Business Use of Your Home.*

References:
- Publication 946, How to Depreciate Property
- Publication 544, Sales and Other Dispositions of Assets
- Publication 587, Business Use of Your Home

Q. *What form and line do I deduct the 40.5 cents per mile on for my business travel and do I need to figure depreciation of the vehicle, too?*

A. A Sole Proprietor's business use of a car or truck is claimed on line 9 of Form 1040, Schedule C, Schedule C, Profit or Loss from Business or, if eligible, line 2 of Form 1040, Schedule C-EZ, Net Profit from Business. You may use either the actual expense method in calculating your car or truck expense or, if eligible, the 2005 standard mileage rate of 40.5 cents per mile. Depreciation expense is already included in this standard mileage rate.

Depreciation is only calculated as a separate expense when using the actual expense method. Deductible employee business use of a car or truck may be taken on Form 2106, Employee Business Expenses, or if, eligible, line 1 of Form 2106-EZ, *Unreimbursed Employee Business Expenses.* The car and truck expenses are then taken with other employee business expenses on line 20, Form 1040, Schedule A&B *Itemized Deductions.* For more information, refer to

Publication 463, *Travel, Entertainment, Gift, and Car Expenses*, and Publication 535, *Business Expenses.*

References:
• Publication 535, Business Expenses
• Publication 463, Travel, Entertainment, Gift, and Car Expenses
• Form 1040, Schedule C, Profit or Loss from Business (Sole Proprietorship)
• Form 1040, Schedule C-EZ, Unreimbursed Employee Business Expenses.
• Form 2106, Employee Business Expenses
• Form 2106EZ, Unreimbursed Employee Business Expenses

Q. *I have a home office. Can I deduct expenses like mortgage, utilities, etc., but not deduct depreciation so that when I sell this house, the basis won't be affected?*

A. If you qualify to deduct expenses for the business use of your home, you can claim depreciation for the part of your home that is a home office. Generally, the part of your home that is a home office is depreciated over a recovery period of 39 years using the straight line method of depreciation and a mid-month convention. If you do not claim depreciation on that part of your home that is a home office, you are still required to reduce the basis of your home for the allowable depreciation of that part of your home that is a home office when reporting the sale of your home. For more information, refer to Publication 587, *Business Use of Your Home.*

References:
• Publication 946, How to Depreciate Property
• Publication 544, Sales and Other Dispositions of Assets
• Publication 587, Business Use of Your Home

Q. *Can the entire acquisition cost of a computer that I purchased for my business be deducted as a business expense or do I have to use depreciation?*

A. The entire acquisition cost of a computer purchased for business use can be expensed under Code section 179 in the first year if qualified, or depreciated over a 5-year recovery period. Under section 179, you can elect to recover all or part of the cost of certain qualifying property, up to a dollar limit, by deducting it in the year you place the property in service. You can elect to expense the cost of qualifying property instead of recovering the cost by taking depreciation. To claim the expense in the first year, the property must be used more than 50% for business use, and meet the other requirements for expensing. One of those requirements is that the total cost of qualifying property you can deduct after you apply the dollar limit is limited to the taxable income from the active conduct of any trade or business during the year. Any cost not deductible in one year under section 179 because of the business income limit can be carried to the next year.

For any taxable year beginning after 2002 and before 2006, a new law raised the aggregate cost that can be expensed under section 179 to $100,000 and also expanded the definition of Code section 179 property to include off-the-shelf computer software. Refer to Code Section 179 for the expanded definition.

If you make a choice to depreciate the property you can claim in the placed-in service year of the property a special depreciation allowance for eligible property you acquired after September 10, 2001 and before January 1, 2005. The special depreciation is figured before you calculate your regular depreciation. To qualify for the special depreciation the property must:

• Be property that is depreciated generally under MACRS (Modified Accelerated Cost Recovery System) and that has a recovery period of 20 years or less. Property required to be depreciated under the straight-line method of the alternative depreciation system of MACRS generally is not eligible.
• Be property that is acquired by you after September 10, 2001 and before January 1, 2005.
• Be property that is placed in service by you before January 1, 2005.
• Be property the original use of which began with you after September 10, 2001. This means that the property is new property.

For eligible property acquired after September 10, 2001, and before May 6, 2003, the special depreciation deduction is equal to 30% of the property's depreciable basis. For eligible property acquired after May 5, 2003 and before January 1, 2005, the special depreciation deduction is equal to 50% of the property's depreciable basis. If the property is acquired after May 5, 2003, but there was a written binding contract to acquire the property in effect before May 6, 2003, the property is not eligible for the 50% special depreciation. Also, if the property is acquired after May 5, 2003, but the original use of the property began before May 6, 2003, the property is not eligible for the 50% special depreciation. And, if you acquired the property before May 6, 2003, but placed the property in service after May 5, 2003, the property is not eligible for the 50% special depreciation.

If the property is eligible for the 50% special depreciation deduction and you claim this 50% depreciation, you cannot claim the 30% special depreciation deduction for the property. However, you can elect to deduct the 30% (instead of 50%) special depreciation for property eligible for the 50% special depreciation deduction. These elections are made for an entire class of property (for example, 5-year property) instead of for each property.

If your property is located within the New York Liberty Zone, there are different rules for special depreciation deduction. Refer to Publication 946, *How to Depreciate Property for additional information on the special deduction.*

References:
• Publication 946, How to Depreciate Property
• Publication 535, Business Expenses

Q. *What kinds of property can be depreciated for tax purposes?*

A. Only property used in a trade or business or in an income producing activity can be depreciated. Additionally, the property must be something that wears out or becomes obsolete and it must have a determinable useful life substantially beyond the tax year. The kinds of property that can be depreciated include, but are not limited to, machinery, equipment, buildings, vehicles, and furniture. Some intangible property may also be depreciable (e.g. patents). Depreciation is a complex topic. For more information, refer to Tax Topic 704, *Depreciation,* or Publication 946, *How to Depreciate Property,* or Publication 534, *Depreciating Property Placed in Service Before 1987.*

References:
• Publication 534, Depreciating Property Placed in Service Before 1987
• Publication 946, How to Depreciate Property
• Tax Topic 704, Depreciation

11.2 Rental Expenses v Passive Activity Losses (PALs)

Q. *I purchased a rental property last year. What closing costs can I deduct?*

A. The only deductible closing costs are those for interest, and deductible real estate taxes. Other settlement fees and closing costs for buying the property become additions to your basis in the property. These basis adjustments include:
• Abstract fees,
• Charges for installing utility services,
• Legal fees,
• Recording fees,
• Surveys,
• Transfer taxes,
• Title insurance, and

• Any amounts the seller owes that you agree to pay, such as back taxes or interest, recording or mortgage fees, charges for improvements or repairs, and sales commissions.
• Fees related to obtaining a loan are capital expenses and should be amortized over the life of the loan. For additional information, refer to Publication 527, *Residential Rental Property*, Publication 17, *Your Individual Income Tax Guide*, and Publication 535, *Business Expenses*.

References:
• Publication 527, Residential Rental Property
• Publication 17, Your Individual Income Tax Guide
• Publication 535, Business Expenses

Q. Can you deduct Private Mortgage Insurance (PMI) premiums on rental property? If so, which line item on Schedule E?

A. Yes. You can deduct Private Mortgage Insurance premium on line 9 of Form 1040, Schedule E, Supplemental Income and Loss. Write "PMI " on the dotted line.

References:
• Publication 527, Residential Rental Property
• Form 1040, Schedule E, Supplemental Income and Loss
• Instructions for Form 1040, Schedule E, Supplemental Income and Loss

11.3 Personal Use of Business Property (Condo, Timeshare, etc.)

Q. I rent my home out for two weeks each year. Do I have to show the income on my return?

A. You must first consider if you use your dwelling as a home. You are considered to use a dwelling as a home if you use it for personal purposes during the tax year for more than the greater of 14 days or 10% of the total days it is rented to others at a fair rental price. It is possible that you will use more than one dwelling unit as a home during the year. For example, if you live in your main home for 11 months and in your vacation home for 30 days, your home is a dwelling unit and your vacation home is also a dwelling unit, unless you rent your vacation home to others at a fair rental value for more than 300 days during the year.

There is a special rule if you use a dwelling as a home and rent it for fewer than 15 days. In this case, do not report any of the rental income and do not deduct any expenses as rental expenses. If you itemize your deduction on Form 1040, Schedule A, Itemized Deductions, you may be able to deduct mortgage interest, property taxes, and any casualty losses. For additional information, refer to Tax Topic 415, *Renting Vacation Property/Renting to Relatives* and Publication 527, *Residential Rental Property* (including Rental of Vacation Homes).

References:
• Form 1040, Schedule A, Itemized Deductions
• Tax Topic 415, Renting Vacation Property/Renting to Relatives
• Publication 527, Residential Rental Property (Including Rental of Vacation Homes).

Q. *I am renting a house to my son and daughter-in-law. Can I claim rental expenses?*

A. In general, if you receive income from the rental of a dwelling unit, such as a house, apartment, or duplex, there are certain expenses you may deduct. Besides knowing which expenses may be deductible, it is important to understand potential limitations on the amounts of rental expenses that may be deducted in a tax year.

There are several types of limitations that may apply.
• Passive Activity losses: In general, you can deduct passive activity losses only from passive activity income (a limit on loss deductions). You carry any excess loss forward to the following year or years until used, or until deducted in the year you dispose of your entire interest in the activity in a fully taxable transaction. There are several exceptions that may apply to the passive activity limitations. Refer to Publication 527, *Residential Rental Property* and Publication 925, *Passive Activity and At-Risk Rules*.

• At risk rules: The at-risk rules limit your losses from most activities to your amount at risk in the activity. You treat any loss that is disallowed because of the at-risk limits as a deduction from the same activity in the next tax year. If your losses from an at-risk activity are allowed, they are subject to recapture in later years if your amount at risk is reduced below zero. Refer to Publication 925, *Passive Activity and At-Risk Rules*.
• Not for profit activities: If you do not rent your property to make a profit, you can deduct your rental expenses only up to the amount of your rental income. Any rental expenses in excess of rental income cannot be carried forward to the next year. Refer to Publication 527, *Residential Rental Property* and Publication 535, *Business Expenses*.
• Rental of a dwelling unit: The tax treatment of rental income and expenses for a dwelling unit that you also use for personal purposes (renting to a relative may

be considered personal use even if they are paying you rent) depends on whether you use it as a home. Refer to Publication 527, *Residential Rental Property.*
• Expenses in connection with rental of a dwelling unit for less than 15 days per year. Refer to Publication 527, *Residential Rental Property.*

References:
• Publication 527, Residential Rental Property
• Tax Topic 414, Rental Income and Expenses
• Tax Topic 415, Renting Vacation Property/Renting to Relatives

11.4 Sales, Trades, Exchanges

Q. What form(s) do we need to fill out to report the sale of rental property?

A. The gain or loss on the sale of rental property is reported on Form 4797, *Sale of Business Property.* Form 1040, Schedule D, *Capital Gains and Losses,* is often used in conjunction with Form 4797. For further information, refer to Publication 544, *Sales on Other Disposition of Assets,* Publication 550, *Investment Income and Expense,* the Instructions to Form 4797, *Sale of Business Property,* and the Instructions to Form 1040, Schedule D, *Capital Gain and Losses.*

References:
• Form 4797, Sale of Business Property
• Instructions for Form 4797
• Publication 544, Sales and Other Dispositions of Assets
• Publication 550,Investment Income and Expense
• Form 1040 Schedule D, Capital Gains and Losses

Q. We are selling rental property and have never claimed depreciation. What do we do about this when we file our taxes?

A. When reporting the sale of or computing gain or loss on rental property, you are required to make an adjustment to your basis for allowable depreciation regardless of whether the deduction was taken. For more information refer to Publication 544, *Sales or Other Dispositions of Assets,* and the Instructions for Form 4797, *Sales of Business Property.*

You can claim the depreciation not taken for the rental property in the years before the year of sale. How to do this depends on when you placed in service the rental property. If you placed in service the rental property before calendar year 2003, you may amend your income tax returns for the years before the year of the sale by using Form 1040X, Amended U.S. Individual Income Tax Return, to take the depreciation deductions for the rental property that should have been taken. Or, you may file a Form 3115, Application for Change in Accounting Method, to claim the depreciation for the rental property that should have been taken for the years before the year of the sale. The Form 3115 must be timely filed for the same tax year in which you sell the rental property.

If you placed in service the rental property after calendar year 2002 and you have unclaimed depreciation for two or more years before the year of sale, you must use Form 3115, Application for Change in Accounting Method, to claim the depreciation for the rental property that should have been taken for the years before the year of the sale. The Form 3115 must be timely filed for the same tax year in which you sell the rental property.

If you placed in service the rental property after calendar year 2002 and you have unclaimed depreciation for only the year immediately preceding the year of sale, you may amend your income tax return for that prior year by using Form 1040X, *Amended U.S. Individual Income Tax Return*, to take the depreciation deduction for the rental property that should have been taken. Or, you may file a Form 3115, Application for Change in Accounting Method, to claim the depreciation for the rental property that should have been taken for the prior year. The Form 3115 must be timely filed for the same tax year in which you sell the rental property.

References:
• Publication 544, Sales or Other Dispositions of Assets
• Form 1040X, Amended U.S. Individual Income Tax Return
• Form 3115, Application for Change in Accounting Method
• Instructions for Form 3115, Application for Accounting Method
• Instructions for Form 4797, Sales of Business Property
• Publication 527, Residential Rental Property (including Vacation Homes)

Q. What forms do we file to report a loss on the sale of a rental property?

A. The loss on the sale of rental property is reported on Form 4797, (*Sale of Business Property*) as ordinary loss.

References:
• Form 4797, Sale of Business Property
• Publication 544, Sales and Other Dispositions of Assets

Chapter 12

Small Business/Self-Employed/Other Business Entities
~~~~~

Keyword(s): Tax Identification Number; Keyword(s): Sole Proprietor; Keyword(s): Limited Liability Company (LLC); Keyword(s): ID Number; Keyword(s): Federal tax ID Number; Keyword(s): Employee Identification Tax Number (EIN); Keyword(s):Corporation; Keyword(s):New business

12.1 Sole Proprietor, Partnership, Limited Liability Company/Partnership (LLC/LLP), Corporation, Subchapter S Corporation

Q. I recently formed a limited liability company (LLC). The LLC has no employees. Do I need a separate Federal Tax ID number for the LLC?

A. No, you will not need a separate Federal Tax ID number for the LLC if you are the sole owner of the LLC and the LLC has no employees. If you are the sole owner of the LLC and the LLC has employees, you will need to get a separate Federal Tax ID number, if you choose to have the LLC report and pay employment taxes with respect to employees of the LLC. If you are not the sole owner of the LLC, you will need a separate Federal Tax ID number for the LLC. Refer to Notice 99-6, 1999-1 CB 321.

References:
• Publication 1635, Understanding your EIN - Employer identification Number - IRS
• Form SS-4, Application for Employer Identification Number
• Form 8832, Entity Classification Election

Q. Can a husband and wife run a business as a sole proprietor or do they need to be a partnership?

A. It is possible for either the husband or the wife to be the owner of the sole proprietor business. When only one spouse is the owner, the other spouse can work in the business as an employee. If the spouses intend to carry on the business together and share in the profits and losses, then they have formed a partnership. Refer to Rev. Proc. 2002-69 for Special Rules for Spouses in Community States.

References:
• Publication 334, Tax Guide for Small Business
• Publication 541, Partnerships

Q. *For IRS purposes, how do I classify a limited liability company? Is it a sole proprietorship, partnership or a corporation?*

A. A limited liability company (LLC) is an entity formed under state law by filing articles of organization as an LLC. Unlike a partnership, none of the members of an LLC are personally liable for its debts. An LLC may be classified for Federal income tax purposes as if it were a sole proprietorship (referred to as an entity to be disregarded as separate from its owner), a partnership or a corporation. If the LLC has only one owner, it will automatically be treated as if it were a sole proprietorship (referred to as an entity to be disregarded as separate from its owner), unless an election is made to be treated as a corporation. If the LLC has two or more owners, it will automatically be considered to be a partnership unless an election is made to be treated as a corporation. If the LLC does not elect its classification, a default classification of partnership (multi-member LLC) or disregarded entity (taxed as if it were a sole proprietorship) will apply. The election referred to is made using the Form 8832, Entity Classification Election. If a taxpayer does not file Form 8832, a default classification will apply.

References:
• Publication 334, Tax Guide for Small Business
• Tax Topic 103, Small Business Tax Education Program
• Publication 542, Corporations
• Publication 541, Partnerships
• Form 8832, Entity Classification Election

Q. *Are partners considered employees of a partnership or are they self-employed?*

A. Partners are considered to be self-employed. If you are a member of a partnership that carries on a trade or business, your distributive share of its income or loss from that trade or business is net earnings from self-employment. Limited partners are subject to self-employment tax only on guaranteed payments, such as salary and professional fees for services rendered.

References:
• Instructions for Form 1065, U.S. Partnership Return of Income

124

• Publication 533, Self-Employment Tax
• Revenue Ruling 69-184
• Publication 541, Partnerships

Keyword(s): Employee – Independent Contractor

12.2 Form 1099–MISC & Independent Contractors

Q. What is the difference between a Form W-2 and a Form 1099-MISC?

A. Both of these forms are called information returns. The Form W-2 is used by employers to report wages, tips and other compensation paid to an employee. The form also reports the employee's income tax and Social Security taxes withheld and any advanced earned income credit payments. The Form W-2 is provided by the employer to the employee and the Social Security Administration. A Form 1099-MISC is used to report payments made in the course of a trade or business to another person or business who is not an employee. The form is required among other things, when payments of $10 or more in gross royalties or $600 or more in rents or compensation are paid. The form is provided by the payor to the IRS and the person or business that received the payment.

References:
•   Tax Topic 752, Form W-2 - Where, When, and How to File
•   Instructions for Form W-2 and W-3
•   Instructions for Form 1099-MISC

Q. How do you determine if a person is an employee or an independent contractor?

A. The determination is complex, but is essentially made by examining the right to control how, when, and where the person performs services. It is not based on how the person is paid, how often the person is paid, nor whether the person works part-time or full-time. There are three basic areas which determine employment status:
•   behavioral control
•   financial control and
•   relationship of the parties
For more information on employer-employee relationships, refer to Publication 15, Circular E, *Employer's Tax Guide* and Publication 15-A, *Employer's Supplemental Tax Guide.* If you would like the IRS to determine whether services are performed as an employee or independent contractor, you may

submit Form SS-8, Determination of Worker Status for Purposes of Federal Employment Taxes and Income Tax Withholding.

Unless you think you were an employee, you should report your nonemployee compensation on Form 1040, Schedule C, Profit or Loss from Business (Sole Proprietorship), or Form 1040, Schedule C-EZ, Net Profit From Business. You also need to complete Form 1040, Schedule SE, Self Employment Tax, and pay self employment tax on your net earnings from self employment, if you had net earnings from self employment of $400 or more. This is the method by which self employed persons pay into the social security and Medicare trust funds.

Generally, there are no tax withholdings on this income. Thus, you may have been subject to the requirement to make quarterly estimated tax payments. If you did not make timely estimated tax payments, you may be assessed a penalty for an underpayment of estimated tax. Employees pay into the social security and Medicare trust funds, as well as income tax withholding, through payroll deductions.

If you are not sure whether you are an independent contractor or an employee, complete Form SS-8, Determination of Employee Work Status for Purposes of Federal Employment Taxes and Income Tax Withholding. For more information on employer-employee relationships, refer to Publication 15, Circular E, *Employer's Tax Guide* and Publication 15-A, *Employer's Supplemental Tax Guide* and Publication 1779, *Employee Independent Contractor Brochure*. For information on the tax responsibilities of self-employed persons, refer to Publication 505, *Tax Withholding and Estimated Tax*, and Publication 533, *Self-Employment Tax*.

References:
- Publication 15 Circular E, Employer's Tax Guide
- Publication 15-A, Employer's Supplemental Tax Guide
- Form SS-8, Determination of Worker Status for Purposes of Federal Employment Taxes and Income Tax Withholding
- Publication 533, Self-Employment Tax
- Publication 505, Tax Withholding and Estimated Tax
- Tax Topic 762, Independent Contractor vs. Employee
- Tax Topic 407, Business Income
- Tax Topic 355, Estimated Tax
- Publication 1779, Employee Independent Contractor Brochure

Q. I made some money repairing radios and television sets last year. How do I report this income?

A. This is self employment income. A person with income from Self-Employment files Form 1040, Schedule C, *Profit or Loss from Business*, or in some cases, files Form 1040, Schedule C-EZ, *Net Profit from Business* to report the profit or loss from the business, and files Form 1040, Schedule SE, *Self-Employment Tax* to figure Social Security and Medicare Tax. Refer to Tax Topic 407, Business Income, Publication 533, *Self-Employment Tax*, and Publication 334, *Tax Guide for Small Business*, for additional information. Since there is no withholding on your self-employment income, you may need to make quarterly estimated tax payments. This is done using a Form 1040-ES, Estimated Tax for Individuals.

References:
- Publication 334, Tax Guide for Small Business
- Publication 533, Self-Employment Tax
- Form 1040, Schedule C, Profit or Loss from Business (Sole Proprietorship)
- Form 1040, Schedule C-EZ, Net Profit from Business (Sole Proprietorship)
- Form 1040, Schedule SE, Self-Employment Tax
- Tax Topic 407, Business Income
- Form 1040-ES Estimated Tax for Individuals

12.3 Form W–2, FICA, Medicare, Tips, Employee Benefits

Q. *As an employer, do I have any liability if my employees receive tips but don't report them to me?*

A. Employees who customarily receive tips are required to report their cash tips to their employers at least monthly, if they receive $20 or more in the month. Cash tips are tips received directly in cash or by check, and charged tips. You have a liability to withhold and pay Social Security and Medicare tax on your employees' reported tips, to the extent that wages or other employee funds are available. If the employee does not report tips to you, it places you at risk of possible assessment of the employer's share of the Social Security and Medicare taxes on the unreported tips. If you are a large food or beverage establishment (more than 10 employees on a typical day and food or beverages consumed on the premises), you are required to allocate tips if the total tips reported to you are less than 8% of gross sales. Report the allocated amount on the employee's W-2 at the end of the year.

References:
- Publication 15, Circular E, Employer's Tax Guide
- Publication 531, Reporting Tip Income
- Publication 1872, Tips on Tips - A Guide to Tip Income Reporting for Employees in the Food and Beverage Industry

• Tax Topic 761, Tips - Withholding & Reporting

Q. *If the reported tips from employees are more than 8% of sales, must an employer still allocate tips to the employees?*

A. No. Tip allocation is required when the amount of tips reported by employees of a large food or beverage establishment is less than 8% (or an approved lower rate) of the gross receipts, other than nonallocable receipts, for the given period. If the employees are reporting more than the 8%, there would be no allocated tip amount. However, the employer must still file Form 8027, *Employer's Annual Information Return of Tip Income and Allocated Tips.*

References:
• Form 8027, Employer's Annual Information Return of Tip Income and Allocated Tips
• Instructions for Form 8027, Employer's Annual Information Return of Tip Income and Allocated Tips
• Publication 15, Circular E, Employer's Tax Guide
• Publication 1872, Tips on Tips - A Guide to Tip Income Reporting for Employees in the Food and Beverage Industry
• Tax Topic 402, Tips

Q. *When an employer provides day care assistance, should the employer's contribution be reported in box 10 of Form W-2?*

A. Yes. An employer reports dependent care assistance payments in box 10 on Form W-2.

References:
• Publication 15-A, Employer's Supplemental Tax Guide
• Publication 15-B, Employer's Tax Guide to Fringe Benefits
• Publication 535, Business Expenses
• Form W-2, Wage and Tax Statement

Q. *Can an employer take out taxes if a Form W-4 was never filed?*

A. Yes, the employer is required to withhold income taxes. Publication 15, Circular E, *Employer's Tax Guide,* states that if an employee does not give you a completed Form W-4, *Employee's Withholding Allowance Certificate*, withhold tax as if he or she is single, with no withholding allowances.
The employer is also required to withhold social security and Medicare taxes.

References:
• Publication 4081 Employee Income Tax Withholding
• Publication 15, Circular E, Employer's Tax Guide
• Form W-4, Employee's Withholding Allowance Certificate
• Tax Topic 753, Form W-4 - employee's withholding allowance certificate

Q. If an employee claims more than 10 exemptions on their Form W-4, does the employer have to report this to the IRS?

A. Yes, if you receive a Form W-4, *Employee's Withholding Allowance Certificate*, on which the employee claims more than 10 withholding allowances, you must send a copy of that Form W-4 to the IRS service center with your next Form 941, *Employer's Quarterly Federal Tax Return employment tax return.*

Also, if an employee claims exemption from withholding and his or her wages would normally be expected to exceed $200 or more a week, you must also send a copy of that Form W-4 to the service center with your next employment tax return.

If you want to submit the Form W-4 earlier, you can send a copy of the Form W-4 to the IRS with a cover letter, including your name, address, employer identification number, and the number of forms included. The service center will send you further instructions if it determines that you should not honor the Form W-4. Follow the W-4 unless you hear back from the IRS.

References:
• Form W-4, Employee's Withholding Allowance Certificate
• Tax Topic 753, Form W-4 - employee's withholding allowance certificate

12.4 Form W–4 & Wage Withholding

Q. Can an employer take out taxes if a Form W-4 was never filed?

A. Yes, the employer is required to withhold income taxes. Publication 15, Circular E, *Employer's Tax Guide*, states that if an employee does not give you a completed Form W-4, *Employee's Withholding Allowance Certificate*, withhold tax as if he or she is single, with no withholding allowances. The employer is also required to withhold social security and Medicare taxes.

References:
• Publication 4081 Employee Income Tax Withholding

129

- Publication 15, Circular E, Employer's Tax Guide
- Form W-4, Employee's Withholding Allowance Certificate
- Tax Topic 753, Form W-4 - employee's withholding allowance certificate

Q. *If an employee claims more than 10 exemptions on their Form W-4, does the employer have to report this to the IRS?*

A. Yes, if you receive a Form W-4, *Employee's Withholding Allowance Certificate*, on which the employee claims more than 10 withholding allowances, you must send a copy of that Form W-4 to the IRS service center with your next Form 941, *Employer's Quarterly Federal Tax Return employment tax return*.

Also, if an employee claims exemption from withholding and his or her wages would normally be expected to exceed $200 or more a week, you must also send a copy of that Form W-4 to the service center with your next employment tax return.

If you want to submit the Form W-4 earlier, you can send a copy of the Form W-4 to the IRS with a cover letter, including your name, address, employer identification number, and the number of forms included. The service center will send you further instructions if it determines that you should not honor the Form W-4. Follow the W-4 unless you hear back from the IRS.

References:
- Form W-4, Employee's Withholding Allowance Certificate
- Tax Topic 753, Form W-4 - employee's withholding allowance certificate

12.5 Form SS–4 & Employer Identification Number (EIN)

Q. *Is an employer ID number the same as a tax ID number?*

A. Yes, an employer identification number, or EIN, is also known as a taxpayer identification number, or TIN. A sole proprietorship that has no employees and files no excise or pension tax returns and a LLC with a single owner (where the owner will file employment tax returns) are the only businesses that do not need an employer identification number. In these instances, the sole proprietor uses his or her social security number as the taxpayer identification number.

References:
- Publication 334, Tax Guide for Small Business
- Publication 1635, Understanding Your EIN

Q. *Does a small company need a tax ID number?*

A. A sole proprietor who does not have any employees and who does not file any excise or pension plan tax returns is the only business person who does not need an employer identification number. In this instance, the sole proprietor uses his or her social security number as the taxpayer identification number.

References:
• Publication 334, Tax Guide for Small Business
• Publication 1635, Understanding Your EIN
• Tax Information for Business.

Q. *Under what circumstances am I required to change my employer identification number (EIN)?*

A. If you already have an EIN, and the organization or ownership of your business changes, you may need to apply for a new number. Some of the circumstances under which a new number is required are as follows:
•   An existing business is purchased or inherited by an individual who will operate it as a sole proprietorship
• A sole proprietorship changes to a corporation or a partnership,
• A partnership changes to a corporation or a sole proprietorship,
• A corporation changes to a partnership or a sole proprietorship, or
• An individual owner dies, and the estate takes over the business.
This list is not all inclusive. Refer to the website www.irs.gov under Business, then Employer ID Numbers.

References:
• Publication 1635, Understanding Your EIN
• Tax Information for Business

Q. *Do businesses have to obtain the taxpayer identification number (TIN) from vendors and keep it somewhere on file?*

A. In general, businesses are required to obtain the TIN from vendors if they are required to file any return, document or other statement that calls for the taxpayer identification numbers (TINs) of other taxpayers. Form W-9, *Request for Taxpayer Identification Number and Certification*, can be used to make the request. The business should also maintain the verification of these numbers in their records.

References:
• Form W-9, Request for Taxpayer Identification Number and Certification
• Instructions for Form 1099 General

12.6 Forms 941, 940, Employment Taxes

Q. We are about to hire employees and need to know how much tax to take out and where to send this money?

A. You will need to secure a completed Form W-4, *Employee's Withholding Allowance Certificate,* from each employee. You will need Publication 15, Circular E, *Employer's Tax Guide*, and Publication 15-A, *Employer's Supplemental Tax Guide*, to determine the amount of withholding and for directions on depositing the withholding amounts and other employment taxes. Publication 15T, *New Withholding Tables* contains the revised withholding tables. The change is a result of the Jobs and Growth Tax Relief Reconciliation Act of 2003. This publication is a supplement to Publication 15.

Generally, employers will quarterly file Form 941, *Employer's Quarterly Federal Tax Return*, and annually file Form 940, *Employer's Annual Federal Unemployment Tax Return* (FUTA), and Form W-2, *Wage and Tax Statement*, with Form W-3, *Transmittal of Income and Tax Statements.*

References:
• Publication 15, Circular E, Employer's Tax Guide
• Publication 15-A, Employer's Supplemental Tax Guide
• Form 940, Employer's Annual Federal Unemployment Tax Return
• Form 941, Employer's Quarterly Federal Tax Return
• Form W-2, Wage and Tax Statement
• Form W-3, Transmittal of Income and Tax Statements
• Form W-4, Employee's Withholding Allowance Certificate
• Publication 15-T, New Withholding Tables (For Wages Paid Through December 2005)

Q. If a new employee has reached the limit for social security wage base with a previous employer in the same year, does the new employer need to withhold FICA taxes on wages paid for both the company and employee?

A. Yes, the social security wages base limit is applied to each separate employer. The individual employee is subject to social security taxes up to the maximum amount from each employer. As a result of an employee working for two or more employers in the same year, social security tax in excess of the

132

maximum wage base may be withheld from his or her pay. An employee can claim the excess of social security tax withheld from pay resulting from working for two or more employers as a credit against the employee's income tax when filing Form 1040, *U.S. Individual Income Tax Return*. However, there is no provision for an employer to get a credit for the employer portion of social security tax paid in this situation. There is no wage limit on the Hospital Insurance tax.

References:
• Publication 15, Circular E, Employer's Tax Guide

Q. We hired a nanny to look after our baby while we work. How do we pay her social security taxes and properly report her income?

A. A nanny is considered a household employee. A household employer only has to pay social security and Medicare tax only for the employee(s) that receive $1,400 or more in cash wages for the year 2005. If the amount paid is less than $1,400, no social security or Medicare tax is owed. If social security and Medicare tax must be paid, you will need to file Form 1040, Schedule H, *Household Employment Taxes.* You must withhold the employee's portion of the social security and Medicare unless the employer chooses to pay both the employee's share and the employer's share.

The taxes are 15.3% of cash wages. Your share is 7.65% and the employee's share is 7.65%. You may also be responsible for paying federal unemployment taxes. For directions on household employees, refer to Publication 926, *Household Employer's Tax Guide.*

References:
• Publication 926, Household Employer's Tax Guide
• Form 1040, Schedule H, Household Employment Taxes
• Tax Topic 756, Employment Taxes for Household Employees

Keyword(s): Standard Meal Allowance; Keyword(s): Standard Mileage Rate

12.7 Income & Expenses

Q. For business travel, are there limits on the amounts deductible for meals?

A. Meal expenses are deductible only if your trip is overnight or long enough that you need to stop for sleep or rest to properly perform your duties. The amount of the meal expenses must be substantiated, but instead of keeping records of the actual cost of your meal expenses you can generally use a standard meal allowance ranging from $31 to $46 in 2005 depending on where and when you travel.

Generally, the deduction for unreimbursed business meals is limited to 50% of the cost that would otherwise be deductible.

For more information on business travel expenses and restrictions, refer to Tax Topic 511, or Publication 463, *Travel, Entertainment, Gift, and Car Expenses*, and Publication 1542, *Per Diem Rates.*

References:
• Publication 463, Travel, Entertainment, Gift, and Car Expenses
• Tax Topic 511, Business travel expenses
• Publication 1542, Per Diem Rates

Q. *What are the standard mileage rates for 2005, 2004, and 2003, 2004*

A. • The standard mileage rate for business use of an automobile was 40.5 cents per mile for 2005.
• The standard mileage rate for moving or medical reasons was 15 cents per mile for 2005.
• The standard mileage rate for charitable contributions was 14 cents per mile for 2005.
The standard mileage rate for business use of an automobile was 37.5 cents per mile for 2004.
• The standard mileage rate for moving or medical reasons was 14 cents per mile for 2004.
• The standard mileage rate for charitable contributions was 14 cents per mile for 2004.
2003
• The standard mileage rate for business use of an automobile declined to 36 cents per mile for 2003.
• The standard mileage rate for moving or medical reasons declined to 12 cents per mile for 2003.
• The standard mileage rate for charitable contributions is unchanged at 14 cents per mile for 2003.

References:
• Publication 463, Travel, Entertainment, and Gift Expenses
• Tax Topic 510, Business Use of Car
• Publication 521, Moving Expenses

• Publication 502, Medical and Dental Expenses

Q. *If you lease a vehicle, can you deduct the cost of the lease payments plus the standard mileage rate?*

A. No, if you lease a car you use in business, you may use either the standard mileage rate or claim actual expenses, which would include lease payments. You cannot use both the standard mileage rate and the lease payments.

References:
• Publication 463, Travel, Entertainment, Gift, and Car Expenses
• Tax Topic 510, Business Use of Car

Q. *How do you distinguish between a business and a hobby?*

A. Since hobby expenses are deductible only to the extent of hobby income, it is important to distinguish hobby expenses from expenses incurred in an activity engaged in for profit. In making this distinction, all facts and circumstances with respect to the activity are taken into account and no one factor is determinative. Among the factors which should normally be taken into account are the following:
• Whether you carry on the activity in a businesslike manner
• Whether the time and effort you put into the activity indicate you intend to make it profitable
• Whether you depend on income from the activity for your livelihood
• Whether your losses are due to circumstances beyond your control (or are normal in the startup phase of your type of business)
• Whether you change your methods of operation in an attempt to improve profitability
• Whether you, or your advisors, have the knowledge needed to carry on the activity as a successful business
• Whether you were successful in making a profit in similar activities in the past
• Whether the activity makes a profit in some years, and how much profit it makes
• Whether you can expect to make a future profit from the appreciation of the assets used in the activity
Additional information on this topic is available in section 1.183-2 (b) of the federal tax regulations.

References:
• Treas. Req. 1.183-2 (b)
• Publication 535, Business Expenses

135

A. *If I pay personal expenses out of my business bank account, should I count the money used as part of my income, or can I write these expenses off?*

You would include the money in income and you would not write the amounts off as expenses. Only business related expenses can be deducted from your business income. It is recommended that you not mix business and personal accounts. This makes it easier to keep records.

References:
• Publication 535, Business Expenses

Q. *I use my home for business. Can I deduct the expenses?*

A. To deduct expenses related to the business use of part of your home, you must meet specific requirements. Even then, your deduction may be limited.
Your use of the business part of your home must be:
• Exclusive (Refer to *exceptions below),
• Regular,
• For your trade or business, AND
The business part of your home must be one of the following:
• Your principal place of business,
• A place where you meet or deal with patients, clients, or customers in the normal course of your trade or business, or
• A separate structure (not attached to your home) you use in connection with your trade or business.
Additional tests for employee use. If you are an employee and you use a part of your home for business, you may qualify for a deduction. You must meet the tests discussed above plus:
• Your business use must be for the convenience of your employer, and
• You do not rent any part of your home to your employer and use the rented portion to perform services as an employee.
Whether the business use of your home is for your employer's convenience depends on all the facts and circumstances. However, business use is not considered to be for your employer's convenience merely because it is appropriate and helpful.
*exceptions
You do not have to meet the exclusive use test if you satisfy the rules that apply in either of the following circumstances.
• You use part of your home for the storage of inventory or product samples.
• You use part of your home as a day-care facility.
Form 1040, Schedule C filers calculate the business use of home expenses and limits on Form 8829 . The deduction is claimed on line 30 of Schedule C.

Employees claim deduction for business use of home as an itemized deduction on Form 1040, Schedule A .
For more information refer to Tax Topic 509, Business Use of Home, or Publication 587, Business Use of Your Home (Including Use by Day-Care Providers).

References:
• Publication 587, Business Use of Your Home (Including Use by Day-Care Providers)
• Form 1040, Schedule C, Profit or Loss from Business (Sole Proprietorship)
• Form 8829, Expenses for Business Use of Your Home
• Tax Topic 509, Business Use of Home

Q. Are excise taxes for a vehicle deductible?

A. It has to be a personal property tax, not an excise tax, in order to deduct it. Deductible personal property taxes are only those based on the value of personal property such as a boat or car. The tax must be charged to you on a yearly basis, even if it is collected more than once a year or less than once a year. To be deductible, the tax must be charged to you and must have been paid during your tax year. Taxes may be claimed only as an itemized deduction on Form 1040, Schedule A, Itemized Deductions.

References:
• Publication 17, Your Federal Income Tax (For Individuals)
• Form 1040, Schedule A, Itemized Deductions

Q. If you lease office equipment and machinery with the option to buy, when do you depreciate the purchase price?

A. If you lease equipment with the option to later buy the equipment, you must first determine whether your agreement is a lease agreement or a conditional sales contract. If, under the agreement, you acquired or will acquire title to or equity in the property, you should treat the agreement as a conditional sales contract. Payments made under a conditional sales contract are not deductible as rent expense. You would start depreciating the equipment on the date you acquired the equipment.

Whether the agreement is a conditional sales contract depends on the intent of the parties. Determine intent based on the facts and circumstances that exist when you make the agreement

In general, an agreement may be considered a conditional sales contract rather than a lease if any of the following is true.

• The agreement applies part of each payment toward an equity interest that you will receive.
• You get title to the property upon the payment of a stated amount required under the contract.
• The amount you pay to use the property for a short time is a large part of the amount you would pay to get title to the property.
• You pay much more than the current fair rental value for the property.
• You have an option to buy the property at a nominal price compared to the value of the property when you may exercise the option. Determine this value when you make the agreement.
• You have an option to buy the property at a nominal price compared to the total amount you have to pay under the lease.
• The lease designates some part of the payments as interest, or part of the payments are easy to recognize as interest.

References:
• Publication 535, Business Expenses

Q. Are business gifts deductible?

A. If you give business gifts in the course of your trade or business, you can deduct the cost subject to special limits and rules. In general, you can deduct no more than $25 for business gifts you give directly or indirectly to any one person during your tax year. Exceptions may apply. For additional information, refer to Tax Topic 512 and Publication 463, *Travel, Entertainment, Gift, and Car Expense.*

For additional information on this subject Refer to Gifts.

References:
• Publication 463, Travel, Entertainment, Gift, and Car Expense
• Tax Topic 512, Business Entertainment Expenses

Q. Can I deduct my investment expenses as business expenses?

A. In order to properly determine the correct treatment income and expenses, it is first necessary to classify the type of investment activity occurring. An Investor buys and sells securities solely for their own account. They are not engaged in a trade or business. An investor's investment expenses are taken as miscellaneous itemized deductions on Form 1040, Schedule A, subject to the 2% AGI limitations (with the exception of investment interest which is not a miscellaneous deduction but subject to its own special limitations). An investor's sale of securities results in capital gains and losses.

A Dealer in securities has inventories of securities that they hold for sale to customers in the ordinary course of their trade or business. Their business expenses are deductible as ordinary business expenses. A dealer doing business as a sole proprietor would deduct their expenses on Form 1040 Schedule C. A Dealer's sale of securities is reported as ordinary income.

A third classification is Trade. A Trader is in the trade or business of buying and selling securities for their own account. You are a trader in securities if you meet all of the following conditions:
• You must Refer to profit from daily market movements in the prices of securities and not from dividends, interest, or capital appreciation.
• Your activity must be substantial.
• You must carry on the activity with continuity and regularity.

The following facts and circumstances should be considered in determining if your activity is a securities trading business:
• Typical holding periods for securities bought and sold.
• The frequency and dollar amount of your trades during the year.
• The extent to which you pursue the activity to produce income for a livelihood
• The amount of time you devote to the activity.

A trader's business expense are reported on Form 1040, Schedule C, not as itemized deductions on Form 1040 Schedule A. The deductions are not subject to the limitations that apply to Schedule A (2% AGI limitation and special limits on investment interest). A trader gain or loss on sale of securities is reported as capital gain or loss on Form 1040, Schedule D unless they have made the mark-to-market election.

If a trader has made a mark-to-market election, gains and losses are reported on Part II of Form 4797 as ordinary income. For information regarding the manner and timing of making the mark-to-market election, Refer to Publication 550, *Investment Income and Expense* or Revenue Procedure 99-17, 1999-1 CB 503.

The proper classification of your investment activities is important to determine how income and expenses are to be reported. Investors trade solely for their own account and do not carry on a trade or business. Their securities sales result in capital gain or loss and their deductible expenses are itemized deductions. Dealers sell securities to customers in the ordinary course of trade or business.

Their sales result in ordinary gain or loss and their deductible expenses are trade or business expenses. Traders buy and sell securities frequently but have no customers. Their purchases and sales result in capital gain and loss, and their deductible expenses are trade or business expenses.

Even if you engage in extensive securities activities, you are an investor, not a dealer or trader, if you do not Refer to profit primarily in swings in daily market movements, and do not personally engage in or direct the purchases or sales. An investor trades for profit-motivated reasons such as long-term appreciation, dividends and interest. Whether the activities of an individual constitute trade or business or investment is determined from the facts in each case. These distinctions have been established through court cases.

If your trading activity is a business, your trading expenses would be reported on Form 1040, Schedule C, *Profit or Loss from Business* (Sole Proprietorship) instead of Form 1040, Schedule A, *Itemized Deductions.* Your gains or losses, however, would be reported on Form 1040, Schedule D, Capital Gains and Losses, unless you file an election to change your method of accounting.

If your trading activity is a business and you elect to change to the mark-to-market method of accounting, you would report both your gains or losses on Part II of Form 4797, *Sales of Business Property.*

A change in your method of accounting requires the consent of the Commissioner and cannot be revoked without the consent of the Secretary. Though there is no publication specific to day traders, the details for traders in securities and commodities are covered in Internal Revenue Code Section 475 (f) and Revenue Procedure 99-17.

References:
• Publication 535, Business Expenses
• Form 3115, Application for Change in Accounting Method

Keyword(s): Schedule SE; Keyword(s): Schedule C-EZ

12.8 Schedule C & Schedule SE

Q. I am self-employed. How do I report my income and how do I pay Medicare and social security taxes?

A. Your self-employment income is reported on Form 1040, Schedule C, *Profit or Loss from Business*, or on Form 1040, Schedule C-EZ, *Net Profit from Business*. Your Medicare and social security taxes are reported on Form 1040, Schedule SE, Self-Employment Tax.

As a self-employed person, you pay your Medicare and social security taxes the same way you pay your income taxes. If you expect to owe less than $1,000 in total taxes, you can pay them when you file your income tax return. If you expect to owe $1,000 or more in total taxes, you will need to make estimated tax payments. These payments are made quarterly using Form 1040-ES, Estimated Tax for Individuals. You will need to figure these taxes at the beginning of the year. To learn about figuring and making estimated tax payments, Refer to Publication 505, *Tax Withholding and Estimated Tax*.

References:
• Form 1040, Schedule C, Profit or Loss from Business
• Form 1040, Schedule C-EZ, Net Profit from Business
• Form 1040, Schedule SE, Self-Employment Tax
• Tax Topic 554, Self-Employment Tax
• Publication 505, Tax Withholding and Estimated Tax
• Form 1040-ES, Estimated Tax for Individuals

Q. *If you have run a small business in the past, but this year there is no income or expenses, is it necessary to file a Schedule C?*

A. If your sole proprietorship business is inactive during the full year, it is not necessary to file a Form 1040, Schedule C, *Profit or Loss from Business*, for that year.

References:
• Publication 334, Tax Guide for Small Business
• Form 1040, Schedule C, Profit or Loss from Business

Q. *What Businesses are Now Eligible to Use Schedule C-EZ?*

A. Your business may have become eligible to use the abbreviated Schedule C-EZ instead of the longer Schedule C when reporting business profit and loss on your tax year 2005 federal income tax return, according to the IRS. That's because the deductible business expense threshold for filing Schedule C-EZ of the Form 1040 has doubled to $5,000 from $2,500. This change allows an additional 500,000 small businesses to file the C-EZ rather than Schedule C. *(**Check Pub. 334 for the current amount**)*

Schedule C-EZ, Net Profit from Business (Sole Proprietorship), is the simplified version of Schedule C, Profit or Loss from Business (Sole Proprietorship).

Schedule C-EZ consists of an instruction page and a one-page form with three short parts — General Information, Figure Your Net Profit, and Information on Your Vehicle. The instruction page includes a worksheet for figuring the amount of deductible expenses. If that amount does not exceed $5,000, you should be able to use the C-EZ instead of Schedule C.

The more complex Schedule C is two pages long and is divided into five parts — Income, Expenses, Cost of Goods Sold, Information on Your Vehicle, and Other Expenses — and a section for general information. It requests more detailed information than does the C-EZ. The instruction package is nine pages long. Schedule C must be used when deductible business expenses exceed $5,000.

This change should save time and money and reduce paperwork burden for the newly-eligible businesses.

References:
·   Publication 334, Tax Guide for Small Business

Keyword(s): Social Security Benefits

12.9 Starting or Ending a Business

Q. Which form do I use to file my business income tax return?

A. To determine which form you should file for your business entity, select one of the following links:
• Publication 541, Partnerships
• Publication 542, Corporations
• Publication 3402, Tax Issues for LLCs
• Publication 334, Tax Guide for Small Business
• Entities: Sole Proprietor, Partnership, Limited Liability Company/Partnership (LLC/LLP), Corporation, Subchapter S Corporation

References:
• Publication 541, Partnerships
• Publication 542, Corporations
• Publication 3402, Tax Issues for LLCs

• Publication 334 Tax Guide for Small Business
• Entities: Sole Proprietor, Partnership, Limited Liability Company/Partnership (LLC/LLP), Corporation, Subchapter S Corporation

Q. *What is the due date for business returns?*

A. Some forms and entities have due dates other than the well-known April 15th due date. The instructions for the each type of form used will have the appropriate due date(s) noted. In general, sole proprietor's schedule of income and expenses is attached to the 1040. Therefore, the due date is the same as the 1040.

A Corporation must generally use the calendar year, unless the entity can establish a business purpose for having a different tax year. The due date is usually March 15th.
A partnership generally must conform its tax year of the partners unless the partnership can establish a business purpose for having a different tax year. The tax year is the same as one or more partners that own (in total) more than a 50-percent interest in partnership profits and capital. If there is no majority interest tax year, the partnership must adopt the same tax year as that of its principal capital holder. Where neither condition is met, a partnership must use the calendar year. A limited Liability Company reporting as a partnership has the same tax year as a majority of its partners.

References:
• Publication 541, Partnerships
• Publication 542, Corporation
• Publication 334, Tax Guide for Small Business
• Entities: Sole Proprietor, Partnership, Limited Liability Company/Partnership (LLC/LLP), Corporation, Subchapter S Corporation

Q. *I just started a small business and want to know if I have to file my income taxes quarterly or at the end of the year?*

A. The Federal Income Tax return is filed annually. As a self-employed individual, if after deducting withholding and credits you expect to owe $1,000.00 at the end of the year, you should make estimated tax payments on a quarterly basis. Form 1040-ES, Estimated Tax for Individuals, will assist you in determining if estimated tax payments are due and how they are paid.
When you file the income tax return at the end of the year, you include the income from the business on the return. The forms to be filed are Form 1040, U.S. Individual Income Tax Return, Form 1040, Schedule C, *Profit or Loss from*

Business Form 1040, Schedule SE, *Self-Employment Tax.* If estimated tax payments where made during the year, they will be claimed on the individual income tax return as payments. Refer to Form 1040, Line 57.

References:
- Publication 583, Starting a Business and Keeping Records
- Publication 505, Tax Withholding and Estimated Tax
- Form 1040-ES, Estimated Tax for Individuals
- Form 1040, U.S. Individual Income Tax Return
- Form 1040, Schedule C, Profit or Loss from Business
- Form 1040, Schedule C-EZ, Net Profit from Business
- Form 1040, Schedule SE, Self-employment Tax
- Tax Topic 355, Estimated Tax
- Publication 334, Tax Guide for Small Business

Q. I am starting a small business. What assistance can IRS give me?

A. If you are starting or already have a small business and need information on taxes, recordkeeping, accounting practices, completing Federal business and employment tax returns, and meeting other Federal tax obligations, there is help available. Much of the assistance is free.

The service is called Small Business Tax Education Program, or STEP. Go to the IRS website (www.IRS.gov). Click on *Around the Nation* for seminars in your area or check out Tax Information for Business on the IRS website. You can find out more about this program for small business by referring to Publication 1066, Small Business Tax Workshop, or Tax Topic 103, *Small Business Tax Education Program* (STEP).

References:
- Publication 1066, Small Business Tax Workshop
- Publication 334, Tax Guide for Small Business
- Small Business and Self-Employed One-stop Resource
- Tax Topic 103, Small Business Tax Education Program (STEP)
- Tax Info For Business

Q. How do I find out about whether or not my business needs to collect sales tax?

A. Your question is a state tax question. Your state revenue department should provide information regarding sales tax to you. To access the state you need to direct your question to, please go to the IRS website (www.IRS.gov) and click on *Alphabetical State Index.*

Chapter 13

Aliens and U.S. Citizens Living Abroad

~~~~~

Keyword(s): Visa Status; Keyword(s): Non-resident Alien; Keyword(s): Permanent Resident

13.1 Canadian & U.S. Tax Issues

Q. I am a Canadian citizen living and working in the U.S. for a U.S. employer on a visa. Do I need to file both a U.S. tax return and a Canadian tax return?

A. You must comply with both U.S. and Canadian filing requirements, if any. In the United States, you generally are required to file a return if you have income from the performance of personal services within the United States. However, under certain circumstances, that income may be exempt from payment of U.S. tax pursuant to the U.S.-Canada income tax treaty. You need to determine what type of visa you have, and how that impacts your residency status in the United States. If, based on the tax code and your visa status you are treated as a U.S. resident, then your entitlement to treaty benefits will be impacted. You must contact the Canadian government to determine whether you must file a Canadian tax return and pay Canadian taxes.

References:
• Publication 519, U.S. Tax Guide for Aliens
• Publication 597, Information on the United States-Canada Income Tax Treaty
• Publication 901, U.S. Tax Treaties

Q. I am a U.S. citizen. If I move to Canada to live and work there as a Canadian permanent resident, do I pay both U.S. and Canadian Taxes?

A. United States citizens living abroad are required to file annual U.S. income tax returns and report their worldwide income if they meet the minimum income filing requirements for their filing status and age. You must contact the Canadian Government to determine whether you must file a Canadian tax return and pay Canadian taxes. For the United States income tax return, you will have several options available to you regarding claiming a foreign tax credit or excluding some or all of your foreign earned income.

References:
• Publication 54, Tax Guide for U.S. Citizens and Resident Aliens Abroad
• Publication 514, Foreign Tax Credit for Individuals
• Publication 597, Information on the United States-Canada Income Tax Treaty

Q. *Are the Canada Pension Plan and Canadian Old Age Security Benefits taxable? If they are, please tell me where they should be entered on Form 1040.*

A. Benefits paid under the Canada Pension Plan (CPP), Quebec Pension Plan (QPP), and Old Age Security (OAS) program to a U.S. resident are taxable, if at all, only in the United States. According to the U.S. - Canada income tax treaty, taxation of these benefits is based on residence. U.S. citizens or green card holders who reside in Canada are not subject to U.S. tax on this income.

These Canadian benefits are treated as U.S. social security benefits for U.S. tax purposes. Thus, under section 86 of the Internal Revenue Code, the portion of the benefits that is taxable will depend on your income and filing status. If your modified adjusted gross income is above certain limits, a maximum of 85% of your benefits will be subject to U.S. tax. Refer to Tax Topic 423 for information about determining the taxable amount of your benefits. Any benefit under the social security legislation of Canada that would not be subject to Canadian tax if paid to a resident of Canada is not subject to U.S. tax.

Canadian benefits that are treated as U.S. social security benefits are reported on line 20a and 20b of Form 1040, *U. S. Individual Income Tax* Return or line 14a and 14b of Form 1040A.

References:
• Publication 519, U.S. Tax Guide for Aliens
• Publication 597, Information on the United States-Canada Income Tax Treaty
• Publication 915, Social Security and Equivalent Railroad Retirement Benefits
• Tax Topic 423, Social Security and Equivalent Railroad Retirement Benefits

Keyword(s): Exchange Rate

13.2 Aliens and U.S. Citizens Living Abroad: Exchange Rate

Q. *Is there an Internet site with the exchange rates to convert foreign currencies to American dollars?*

A. You can obtain currency exchange rates at the Federal Reserve Board websites.

References:
• Federal Reserve Board

Keyword(s): Substantial Presence Test; Keyword(s): Green Card

13.3 Foreign Income & Foreign Income Exclusion

Q. What is foreign earned income? Is it income from a foreign source or income paid by a U.S. company while living abroad?

A. Earned income is pay for personal services performed, such as wages, salaries, or professional fees. Foreign earned income is income you receive for services you perform in a foreign country during a period when your tax home is in a foreign country and during which you meet either the bona fide residence test or the physical presence test. It does not matter whether earned income is paid by a U.S. employer or a foreign employer. Foreign earned income does not include the following amounts.
• The previously excluded value of meals and lodging furnished for the convenience of your employer.
• Pension or annuity payments including social security benefits.
• Payments by the U.S. Government, or any U.S. government agency or instrumentality, to its employees.
• Amounts included in your income because of your employer's contributions to a nonexempt employee trust or to a nonqualifying annuity contract.
• Recaptured unallowable moving expenses
• Payments received after the end of the tax year following the tax year in which you performed the services that earned the income.

References:
• Publication 54, Tax Guide for U.S. Citizens and Resident Aliens Abroad
• Publication 514, Foreign Tax Credit for Individuals
• Form 2555, Foreign Earned Income
• Form 2555EZ, Foreign Earned Income Exclusion
• Form 1116, Foreign Tax Credit
• Tax Topic 853, Foreign Earned Income Exclusion - General

Q. Do I have to meet the 330-day presence test or have a valid working resident visa to meet the requirement for foreign income exclusion?

A. To claim the foreign earned income exclusion, the foreign housing exclusion, or the foreign housing deduction, you must have foreign earned income, your tax home must be in a foreign country, and you must be one of the following:
• A U.S. citizen who is a bona fide resident of a foreign country or countries for an uninterrupted period that includes an entire tax year,
• A U.S. resident alien who is a citizen or national of a country with which the United States has an income tax treaty with a nondiscrimination article in effect and who is a bona fide resident of a foreign country or countries for an uninterrupted period that includes an entire tax year, or
• A U.S. citizen or a U.S. resident alien who is physically present in a foreign country or countries for at least 330 full days during any period of 12 consecutive months.
U.S. tax law does not specifically require a foreign resident visa or work visa for this purpose, but you (must/should) comply with the other country's laws.

References:
• Publication 54, Tax Guide for U.S. Citizens and Resident Aliens Abroad
• Publication 514, Foreign Tax Credit for Individuals
• Form 2555, Foreign Earned Income
• Form 2555EZ, Foreign Earned Income Exclusion
• Form 1116, Foreign Tax Credit
• Tax Topic 853, Foreign Earned Income Exclusion - General

Q. *I am a nonresident alien. Can I take the foreign earned income exclusion if I meet the bona fide resident test or physical presence test? If yes, what is the tax form used for nonresident taxpayer?*

A. No, nonresident aliens do not qualify for the foreign earned income exclusion. Only if you are a U.S. citizen or a resident alien of the United States and live abroad, may you qualify to exclude up to $80,000 of your foreign earned income for 2005. But, if you are the nonresident alien spouse of a U.S. citizen or resident alien, you can elect to be treated as a U.S. resident in order to file a joint return. In this case, you can take the foreign earned income exclusion if otherwise qualified. Refer to Publication 519, *U.S. Tax Guide for Aliens,* for detailed instructions on how to make this election.

However, nonresident aliens would be able to exclude their foreign earned income under the dual-status rules. Refer to Tax Topic 852 for dual-status information. A nonresident alien is generally not subject to U.S. tax on compensation for services performed outside the U.S.

References:
• Publication 519,U.S. Tax guide for Aliens

149

• Tax Topic 853, Foreign Earned Income Exclusion - General

13.4 Nonresident Alien - General

Q. *I live in a foreign country. How do I get a social security number for my dependent who qualifies for a social security card?*

A. Use Form SS-5-FS which may be obtained from the Social Security Administration.

References:
• Social Security Administration

My spouse is a nonresident alien. How can I get a nonworking social security number for her?

Each foreign person who does not have and cannot obtain a social security number must use an IRS Individual Taxpayer Identification Number (ITIN) on any U.S. tax return or refund claim filed.

References:
• Publication 1915, Understanding Your IRS Individual Taxpayer Identification Number
• Publication 519, U.S. Tax Guide for Aliens
• Form W-7, Application for IRS Individual Taxpayer Identification Number
• Tax Topic 851, Resident and Non-Resident Aliens
• Tax Topic 852, Dual Status Aliens

Q. *My spouse is a nonresident alien. How can I get a nonworking social security number for her?*

A. Each foreign person who does not have and cannot obtain a social security number must use an IRS Individual Taxpayer Identification Number (ITIN) on any U.S. tax return or refund claim filed.

References:
• Publication 1915, Understanding Your IRS Individual Taxpayer Identification Number
• Publication 519, U.S. Tax Guide for Aliens
• Form W-7, Application for IRS Individual Taxpayer Identification Number
• Tax Topic 851, Resident and Non-Resident Aliens
• Tax Topic 852, Dual Status Aliens

Keyword(s): Aliens; Keyword(s): Non-residents

Q. What is the difference between a resident alien and a nonresident alien for tax purposes?

A. For tax purposes, an alien is an individual who is not a U.S. citizen. Aliens are classified as resident aliens and nonresident aliens. Resident aliens are taxed on their worldwide income, the same as U.S. citizens. Nonresident aliens are taxed only on their U.S. source income.

Q. What is the difference between the taxation of income that is effectively connected with a trade or business in the United States and income that is not effectively connected with a trade or business in the United States?

A. The difference between these two categories is that effectively connected income, after allowable deductions, is taxed at graduated rates. These are the same rates that apply to U.S. citizens and residents. Income that is not effectively connected is taxed at a flat 30% (or lower treaty) rate.

Q. I am a student with an F-1 Visa. I was told that I was an exempt individual. Does this mean I am exempt from paying U.S. tax?

A. The term "exempt individual" does not refer to someone exempt from U.S. tax. You were referred to as an exempt individual because as a student temporarily in the United States on an F Visa, you do not have to count the days you were present in the United States as a student during the first 5 years in determining if you are a resident alien under the substantial presence test. Refer to IRS Pub. 519.

Q. I am a resident alien. Can I claim any treaty benefits?

Generally, you cannot claim tax treaty benefits as a resident alien. However, there are exceptions. Refer to Effect of Tax Treaties in IRS Pub. 519. Also Refer to also Resident Aliens under Some Typical Tax Treaty Benefits. in Pub. 519.

Q. I am a nonresident alien with no dependents. I am working temporarily for a U.S. company. What return do I file?

A. You must file Form 1040NR if you are engaged in a trade or business in the United States, or have any other U.S. source income on which tax was not fully paid by the amount withheld. You can use Form 1040NR-EZ instead of Form

1040NR if you meet all 10 conditions listed under Form 1040NR-EZ in IRS Pub. 519.

Q. *I came to the United States on June 30th of last year. I have an H-1B Visa. What is my tax status, resident alien or nonresident alien? What tax return do I file?*

A. You were a dual-status alien last year. As a general rule, since you were in the United States for 183 days or more, you have met the substantial presence test and you are taxed as a resident. However, for the part of the year that you were not present in the United States, you are a nonresident. File Form 1040. Print "Dual-Status Return" across the top. Attach a statement showing your U.S. source income for the part of the year you were a nonresident. You may use Form 1040NR as the statement. Print "Dual-Status Statement" across the top. Refer to First Year of Residency in IRS Pub. 519 for rules on determining your residency starting date. An example of a dual-status return is in IRS Pub. 519.

Q. *When is my Form 1040NR due?*

A. If you are an employee and you receive wages subject to U.S. income tax withholding, you must generally file by the 15th day of the 4th month after your tax year ends. If you file for the 2005 calendar year, your return is due April 15, 2006.

If you are not an employee who receives wages subject to U.S. income tax withholding, you must file by the 15th day of the 6th month after your tax year ends. For the 2005 calendar year, file your return by June 15, 2006. For more information on when and where to file, Refer to IRS Pub. 519.

Q. *My spouse is a nonresident alien. Does he need a social security number?*

A. A social security number (SSN) must be furnished on returns, statements, and other tax-related documents. If your spouse does not have and is not eligible to get an SSN, he must apply for an individual taxpayer identification number (ITIN).

If you are a U.S. citizen or resident and you choose to treat your nonresident spouse as a resident and file a joint tax return, your nonresident spouse needs an SSN or an ITIN. Alien spouses who are claimed as exemptions or dependents are also required to furnish an SSN or an ITIN.
Refer to Identification Number in IRS Pub. 519 for more information.

Q. *I am a nonresident alien. Can I file a joint return with my spouse?*

A. Generally, you cannot file as married filing jointly if either spouse was a nonresident alien at any time during the tax year.

However, nonresident aliens married to U.S. citizens or residents can choose to be treated as U.S. residents and file joint returns. For more information on this choice, Refer to Nonresident Spouse Treated as a Resident in IRS Pub. 519

Q. *I have an H-1B Visa and my husband has an F-1 Visa. We both lived in the United States all of last year and had income. What kind of form should we file? Do we file separate returns or a joint return?*

A. Assuming both of you had these visas for all of last year, you are a resident alien. Your husband is a nonresident alien if he has not been in the United States as a student for more than 5 years. You and your husband can file a joint tax return on Form 1040, 1040A, or 1040EZ if he makes the choice to be treated as a resident for the entire year. Refer to Nonresident Spouse Treated as a Resident in IRS Pub. 519. If your husband does not make this choice, you must file a separate return on Form 1040 or Form 1040A. Your husband must file Form 1040NR or 1040NR-EZ.

Q. *Is a "dual-resident taxpayer" the same as a "dual-status taxpayer"?*

No. A dual-resident taxpayer is one who is a resident of both the United States and another country under each country's tax laws. Refer to Effect of Tax Treaties in IRS Pub. 519. You are a dual-status taxpayer when you are both a resident alien and a nonresident alien in the same year. Refer to IRS Pub. 519.

Q. *I am a nonresident alien and invested money in the U.S. stock market through a U.S. brokerage company. Are the dividends and the capital gains taxable? If yes, how are they taxed?*

A. The following rules apply if the dividends and capital gains are not effectively connected with a U.S. trade or business.
- Capital gains are generally not taxable if you were in the United States for less than 183 days during the year. Refer to Sales or Exchanges of Capital Assets in IRS Pub. 519 for more information and exceptions.
- Dividends are taxed at a 30% (or lower treaty) rate. The brokerage company or payor of the dividends should withhold this tax at source. If tax is not withheld at the correct rate, you must file Form 1040NR to receive a refund or pay any additional tax due.

If the capital gains and dividends are effectively connected with a U.S. trade or business, they are taxed according to the same rules and at the same rates that apply to U.S. citizens and residents.

Q. *I am a nonresident alien. I receive U.S. social security benefits. Are my benefits taxable?*

A. If you are a nonresident alien, 85% of any U.S. social security benefits (and the equivalent portion of tier 1 railroad retirement benefits) you receive is subject to the flat 30% tax, unless exempt, or subject to a lower treaty rate. Refer to The 30% Tax in IRS Pub. 519

Q. *Do I have to pay taxes on my scholarship?*

A. If you are a nonresident alien and the scholarship is not from U.S. sources, it is not subject to U.S. tax. Refer to *Scholarships, Grants, Prizes, and Awards* in IRS Pub. 519 to determine whether your scholarship is from U.S. sources.

If your scholarship is from U.S. sources or you are a resident alien, your scholarship is subject to U.S. tax according to the following rules.
• If you are a candidate for a degree, you may be able to exclude from your income the part of the scholarship you use to pay for tuition, fees, books, supplies, and equipment required by the educational institution. However, the part of the scholarship you use to pay for other expenses, such as room and board, is taxable. Refer to *Scholarships and Fellowship Grants* in IRS Pub. 519 for more information.

• If you are not a candidate for a degree, your scholarship is taxable.

Q. *I am a nonresident alien. Can I claim the standard deduction?*

A. Nonresident aliens cannot claim the standard deduction. However, Refer to Students and business apprentices from India, under Itemized Deductions in IRS Pub. 519 for an exception.

Q. *I am a dual-status taxpayer. Can I claim the standard deduction?*

A. You cannot claim the standard deduction allowed on Form 1040. However, you can itemize any allowable deductions.

Q. *I am filing Form 1040NR. Can I claim itemized deductions?*

A. Nonresident aliens can claim some of the same itemized deductions that resident aliens can claim. However, nonresident aliens can claim itemized deductions only if they have income effectively connected with their U.S. trade or business. Refer to Itemized Deductions in IRS Pub. 519.

Q. *I am not a U.S. citizen. What exemptions can I claim?*

A. Resident aliens can claim personal exemptions and exemptions for dependents in the same way as U.S. However, nonresident aliens generally can claim only a personal exemption for themselves on their U.S. tax return. There are special rules for residents of Mexico, Canada, Japan, and the Republic of Korea (South Korea); for U.S. nationals; and for students and business apprentices from India. Refer to Exemptions in IRS Pub. 519.

Q. *What exemptions can I claim as a dual-status taxpayer?*

A. As a dual-status taxpayer, you usually will be able to claim your own personal exemption. Subject to the general rules for qualification, you can claim exemptions for your spouse and dependents when you figure taxable income for the part of the year you are a resident alien. The amount you can claim for these exemptions is limited to your taxable income (figured before subtracting exemptions) for the part of the year you are a resident alien. You cannot use exemptions (other than your own) to reduce taxable income to less than zero for that period.

Q. *I am single with a dependent child. I was a dual-status alien in 2005. Can I claim the earned income credit on my 2005 tax return?*

A. If you are a nonresident alien for any part of the year, you cannot claim the earned income credit. Refer to IRS Pub. 519 for additional information on dual-status aliens.

Q. *I am a nonresident alien student. Can I claim an education credit on my Form 1040NR?*

A. If you are a nonresident alien for any part of the year, you generally cannot claim the education credits. However, if you are married and choose to file a joint return with a U.S. citizen or resident spouse, you may be eligible for these credits. Refer to Nonresident Spouse Treated as a Resident in IRS Pub. 519.

Q. *I am a nonresident alien, temporarily working in the U.S. under a J visa. Am I subject to social security and Medicare taxes?*

A. Generally, services you perform as a nonresident alien temporarily in the United States as a nonimmigrant under subparagraph (F), (J), (M), or (Q) of section 101(a)(15) of the Immigration and Nationality Act are not covered under the social security program if you perform the services to carry out the purpose for which you were admitted to the United States. Refer to Social Security and Medicare Taxes in IRS Pub. 519.

Q. *I am a nonresident alien student. Social security taxes were withheld from my pay in error. How do I get a refund of these taxes?*

A. If social security or Medicare taxes were withheld in error from pay that is not subject to these taxes contact the employer who withheld the taxes for a refund. If you are unable to get a full refund of the amount from your employer, file a claim for refund with the Internal Revenue Service on Form 843, *Claim for Refund and Request for Abatement.* Refer to Refund of Taxes Withheld in Error in IRS Pub. 519.

Q. *I am an alien who will be leaving the United States. What forms do I have to file before I leave?*

A. Before leaving the United States, aliens generally must obtain a certificate of compliance. This document, also popularly known as the sailing permit or departure permit, is part of the income tax form you must file before leaving. You will receive a sailing or departure permit after filing a Form 1040-C or Form 2063. These forms are discussed in IRS Pub. 519.

Q. *I filed a Form 1040-C when I left the United States. Do I still have to file an annual U.S. tax return?*

A. Form 1040-C is not an annual U.S. income tax return. If an income tax return is required by law, you must file that return even though you already filed a Form 1040-C. IRS Pub. 519 discuss filing an annual U.S. income tax return.

References:
• Publication 519, U.S. Tax Guide for Aliens

13.5 Nonresident Alien - Tax Withholding

Q. Under my visa as a temporary nonresident alien, I'm not subject to social security and Medicare withholding. My employer withheld the taxes from my pay. What should I do to get a refund of my social security and Medicare?

A. If social security tax and Medicare were withheld in error from pay received which was not subject to the taxes, you must first contact the employer who withheld the taxes for reimbursement. If you are unable to get a refund from the employer, file a claim for refund with the Internal Revenue Service on Form 843, *Claim for Refund and Request for Abatement.*

You must attach the following to your claim:
• a copy of your Form W-2, Wage and Tax Statement, to prove the amount of tax withheld;
• Form I-797, *INS Approval Notice,* is needed if you have changed your status from F-1 or J-1 to another status prior to filing the claim;
• if your visa status changed during the tax year you should attach copies of the pay stubs that cover the period of exemption from social security taxes;
• a copy of INS Form I-94, *Arrival/Departure Record,* if you are still in the United States;
• a copy of your valid entry visa;
• Form 8316, *Information Regarding Request for Refund of Social Security Tax,,* or a signed statement stating that you have requested a refund from the employer and have not been able to obtain one; and
• a copy of Form 1040NR, *US Nonresident Alien Income Tax Return* (or Form 1040NR-EZ), for tax the year in question. Processing of your claim may be delayed if you submit it less than six weeks after you filed Form 1040NR or 1040NR-EZ.
In addition to the documentation listed above foreign student visa holders should also attach the following:
• a copy of Form I-20, *Certificate of Eligibility,* endorsed by your student advisor and stamped by the Bureau of Citizenship and Immigration Services; and
• a copy of the Employment Authorization Document of your Optional Practical Training (e.g., Form I-766, I-538 or 688B).
• if you are an exchange visitor, attach a copy of Form IAP-66 or DS-2019 to your claim.
File the claim, with attachments, with the IRS where the employer's returns were filed. If you do not know where the employer's returns were filed, send your claim to the Internal Revenue Service Center, Philadelphia, PA 19255. For more information, refer to Publication 519, *U.S. Tax Guide for Aliens.*

References:
• Form 843, Claim for Refund and Request for Abatement
• Publication 519, U.S. Tax Guide for Aliens

13.6 Nonresident Alien - Students

Q. Are nonresident alien students, with F-1 or J-1 visas and employed by a U.S. company during the summer, required to have federal income taxes withheld from their paychecks?

A. The following discussion generally applies only to nonresident aliens. Wages and other compensation paid to a nonresident alien for services performed as an employee are usually subject to graduated withholding at the same rates as resident aliens and U.S. citizens. Therefore, your compensation, unless it is specifically excluded from the term "wages" by law, or is exempt from tax by treaty, is subject to graduated withholding. Nonresident aliens must follow modified instructions when completing Form W-4. Refer to Publication 519, *U.S. Tax Guide for Aliens*, for directions on completing Form W-4, *Employee's Withholding Allowance Certificate*.

References:
*   Publication 519, U.S. Tax Guide for Aliens
*   Publication 597, Information on the United States-Canada Income Tax Treaty Publication 515, Withholding of Tax on Nonresident Aliens and Foreign Entities
*   Form W-4, Employees Withholding Allowance Certificate

Scholarship and Fellowship Grantees

Q. I am a Fulbright grantee. What documentation must I attach to my return?

A. a) There are no special tax forms for Fulbright grantees. File on a regular Form 1040.
b) If you claim exemption as a scholarship or fellowship grantee, submit brochures and correspondence describing the grant and your duties.
c) If you are located in a foreign country and wish to pay tax in foreign currency, you should submit a certified statement showing that you were a Fulbright grantee and at least 70% of the grant was paid in nonconvertible foreign currency.

Q. I taught and lectured abroad under taxable grants. What expenses can I deduct?

A. You may be able to deduct your travel, meals, and lodging expenses if you are temporarily absent from your regular place of employment. For more

158

information about deducting travel, meals, and lodging expenses, get Publication 463, *Travel, Entertainment, Gift, and Car Expenses.*

13.7 U.S. Citizens and U.S. Permanent Residents Overseas

Q. I am a U.S. citizen working abroad. Are my foreign earnings taxable?

A. A U.S. citizen or resident alien is generally subject to U.S. tax on total worldwide income. However, if you are a United States citizen or a resident alien who lives and works abroad, you may qualify to exclude all or part of your foreign earned income. For specific information, refer to Tax Topic 853, Foreign Earned Income Exclusion - General.

If you would like more information on who qualifies for the exclusion, refer to Tax Topic 854, *Foreign Earned Income Exclusion - Who Qualifies.* For more information on what type of income qualifies for the exclusion, refer to Tax Topic 855, *Foreign Earned Income Exclusion - What Qualifies.* You may also wish to refer to Publication 54, *Tax Guide for U.S. Citizens and Resident Aliens Abroad*, for a detailed discussion. If the information you need relating to this topic is not addressed in Publication 54, you may call the IRS International Tax Law hotline. The number is (215) 516-2000. This is not a toll-free number.

References:
• Publication 54, Tax Guide for U.S. Citizens and Resident Aliens Abroad
• Tax Topic 853, Foreign Earned Income Exclusion - General
• Tax Topic 854, Foreign Earned Income Exclusion - Who Qualifies
• Tax Topic 855, Foreign Earned Income Exclusion - What Qualifies

Q. I worked out of the country for one year. Do I have to pay U.S. income tax?

A. As a U.S. citizen, your worldwide income generally is subject to U.S. income tax, regardless of where you are living. However, you may qualify for the foreign earned income exclusion, foreign housing exclusion or foreign housing deduction, or the foreign tax credit. These tax benefits can reduce or eliminate the U.S. tax you would otherwise have to pay on your foreign income.

References:
• Publication 54, Tax Guide for U.S. Citizens and Resident Aliens Abroad
• Publication 514, Foreign Tax Credit for Individuals
• Form 2555, Foreign Earned Income
• Form 2555EZ, Foreign Earned Income Exclusion

• Form 1116, Foreign Tax Credit

Q. *I am a U.S. citizen working for a U.S. firm in a foreign country. Is any part of my wages or expenses tax deductible?*

A. U.S. citizens are taxed on their worldwide income, no matter where they work. Some taxpayers may qualify for the foreign earned income exclusion, foreign housing exclusion, or foreign housing deduction, if their tax home is in a foreign country and they were either a bona fide resident of a foreign country or countries for an uninterrupted period that includes an entire tax year, or were physically present in a foreign country or countries for at least 330 full days during any period of 12 consecutive months. If the taxpayer is temporarily away from his or her tax home in the United States on business (less than a year), the taxpayer may qualify to deduct away from home expenses (for travel, meals, and lodging) but would not qualify for the foreign earned income exclusion.

References:
• Publication 54, Tax Guide for U.S. Citizens and Resident Aliens Abroad
• Publication 514, Foreign Tax Credit for Individuals
• Publication 463, Travel, Entertainment, Gift and Car Expenses
• Form 2555, Foreign Earned Income
• Form 2555EZ, Foreign Earned Income Exclusion
• Form 1116, Foreign Tax Credit
• Tax Topic 514, Employee Business Expenses

Q. *I am a U.S. citizen living and working overseas. Can I have a tax credit on my U.S. taxes for the taxes I pay to the foreign country?*

A. The foreign tax credit is intended to relieve U.S. taxpayers of the double tax burden when their foreign source income is taxed by both the United States and the foreign country from which the income is derived.

Generally, only income taxes paid or accrued to a foreign country or a U.S. possession qualify for the foreign tax credit. You can choose to take the amount of any qualified foreign taxes paid or accrued during the year as a foreign tax credit or as an itemized deduction.

To choose the foreign tax credit you must generally complete Form 1116, *Foreign Tax Credit* and attach it to your Form 1040. You may claim credit without attaching Form 1116 if all of your foreign source income is passive income (such as interest and dividends) reported to you on a payee statement and the total amount of qualifying foreign taxes you paid or accrued is not more than

$300 ($600 in the case of a joint return) and is also reported to you on a payee statement. To choose the deduction, you must itemize deductions on Schedule A, Form 1040.

You may not take either a credit or a deduction for taxes paid or accrued on income you exclude under the foreign earned income exclusion or the foreign housing exclusion. There is no double taxation in this situation because the income is not subject to U.S. tax.

References:
• Publication 54, Tax Guide for U.S. Citizens and Resident Aliens Abroad
• Publication 514, Foreign Tax Credit for Individuals
• Form 1116, Foreign Tax Credit
• Tax Topic 856, Foreign Tax Credit

Keyword(s): U.S. Citizens Abroad; Keyword(s): U.S. Resident Aliens Abroad; Keyword(s): Resident Aliens Abroad.

Filing Requirements— Where, When, and How

Q. When are U.S. income tax returns due?

A. Generally, for calendar year taxpayers, U.S. income tax returns are due on April 15. If you are a U.S. citizen or resident and both your tax home and your abode are outside the United States and Puerto Rico on the regular due date, an automatic extension is granted to June 15 for filing the return. Interest will be charged on any tax due, as shown on the return, from April 15.

Q. Where do I file my U.S. income tax return?

A. If you claim the foreign earned income exclusion, the foreign housing exclusion, the foreign housing deduction, or an exclusion of income for bona fide residents of American Samoa, and you are not making a payment, you should file your return with the: Internal Revenue Service Center Philadelphia, PA 19255-0215.

If you are not claiming one of the exclusions or the deduction, but are living in a foreign country or U.S. possession and have no legal residence or principal place of business in the United States, you should send your return to the address shown above.

If you are not sure of the place of your legal residence and have no principal place of business in the United States, you also can file with the Philadelphia Service Center. However, you should not file with the Philadelphia Service Center if you are a bona fide resident of the Virgin Islands or a resident of Guam or the Commonwealth of the Northern Mariana Islands on the last day of your tax year. Refer to the discussion in IRS Pub. 54.

Q. *I am going abroad this year and expect to qualify for the foreign earned income exclusion. How can I secure an extension of time to file my return, when should I file my return, and what forms are required?*

A. a) You should file Form 2350 by the due date of your return to request an extension of time to file. Form 2350 is a special form for those U.S. citizens or residents abroad who expect to qualify under either the bona fide residence test or physical presence test and would like to have an extension of time to delay filing until after they have qualified.
b) If the extension is granted, you should file your return after you qualify, but by the approved extension date.
c) You must file your Form 1040 with Form 2555 (or Form 2555-EZ).

Q. *My entire income qualifies for the foreign earned income exclusion. Must I file a tax return?*

A. Generally. Every U.S. citizen or resident must file a U.S. income tax return unless total income without regard to the foreign earned income exclusion is below an amount based on filing status. The income levels for filing purposes are discussed under *Filing Requirements* in IRS Pub. 54.

Q. *I was sent abroad by my company in November of last year. I plan to secure an extension of time on Form 2350 to file my tax return for last year because I expect to qualify for the foreign earned income exclusion under the physical presence test. However, if my company recalls me to the United States before the end of the qualifying period and I find I will not qualify for the exclusion, how and when should I file my return?*

A. If your regular filing date has passed, you should file a return, Form 1040, as soon as possible for last year. Include a statement with this return noting that you have returned to the United States and will not qualify for the foreign earned income exclusion. You must report your worldwide income on the return. If you paid a foreign tax on the income earned abroad, you may be able to either deduct this tax as an itemized deduction or claim it as a credit against your U.S. income tax. However, if you pay the tax due after the regular due date, interest will be charged from the regular due date until the date the tax is paid.

Q. *I am a U.S. citizen and have no taxable income from the United States, but I have substantial income from a foreign source. Am I required to file a U.S. income tax return?*

A. Yes. All U.S. citizens and resident aliens are subject to U.S. tax on their worldwide income. If you paid taxes to a foreign government on income from sources outside the United States, you may be able to claim a foreign tax credit against your U.S. income tax liability for the foreign taxes paid. Form 1116 is used to figure the allowable credit.

Q. *I am a U.S. citizen who has retired, and I expect to remain in a foreign country. Do I have any further U.S. tax obligations?*

A. Your U.S. tax obligation on your income is the same as that of a retired person living in the United States. (Refer to the discussion on *filing requirements* in IRS Pub. 54.)

Q. *I have been a bona fide resident of a foreign country for over 5 years. Is it necessary for me to pay estimated tax?*

A. U.S. taxpayers overseas have the same requirements for paying estimated tax as those in the United States. Refer to the discussion under *Estimated Tax* in IRS Pub. 54. Overseas taxpayers should not include in their estimated income any income they receive that is, or will be, exempt from U.S. taxation. Overseas taxpayers can deduct their estimated housing deduction in figuring their estimated tax. The first installment of estimated tax is due on April 15 of the year for which the income is earned.

Q. *Will a check payable in foreign currency be acceptable in payment of my U.S. tax?*

A. Generally, only U.S. currency is acceptable for payment of income tax. However, if you are a Fulbright grantee, Refer to *Fulbright Grant* in IRS Pub. 54.

Q. *I have met the test for physical presence in a foreign country and am filing returns for 2 years. Must I file a separate Form 2555 (or Form 2555-EZ) with each return?*

A. Yes. A Form 2555 (or Form 2555-EZ) must be filed with each Form 1040 tax return on which the benefits of income earned abroad are claimed.

Q. *Does a Form 2555 (or 2555-EZ) with a Schedule C or Form W-2 attached constitute a return?*

A. No. The Form 2555 (or 2555-EZ), Schedule C, and Form W-2 are merely attachments and do not relieve you of the requirement to file a Form 1040 to show the sources of income reported and the exclusions or deductions claimed.

Q. *On Form 2350, Application for Extension of Time To File U.S. Income Tax Return, I stated that I would qualify under the physical presence test. If I qualify under the bona fide residence test, can I file my return on that basis?*

A. Yes. You can claim the foreign earned income exclusion and the foreign housing exclusion or deduction under either test as long as you meet the requirements. You are not bound by the test indicated in the application for extension of time. You must be sure, however, that you file the Form 1040 by the date approved on Form 2350, since a return filed after that date may be subject to a failure to file penalty. If you will not qualify under the bona fide residence test until a date later than the extension granted under the physical presence rule, apply for a new extension to a date 30 days beyond the date you expect to qualify as a bona fide resident.

Q. *I am a U.S. citizen who worked in the United States for 6 months last year. I accepted employment overseas in July of last year and expect to qualify for the foreign earned income exclusion. Should I file a return and pay tax on the income earned in the United States during the first 6 months and then, when I qualify, file another return covering the last 6 months of the year?*

A. No. You have the choice of one of the following two methods of filing your return:
a) You can file your return when due under the regular filing rules, report all your income without excluding your foreign earned income, and pay the tax due. After you have qualified for the exclusion, you can file an amended return, Form 1040X, accompanied by Form 2555 (or 2555-EZ), for a refund of any excess tax paid.

b) You can postpone the filing of your tax return by applying on Form 2350 for an extension of time to file to a date 30 days beyond the date you expect to qualify under either the bona fide residence test or the physical presence test, then file your return reflecting the exclusion of foreign earned income. This allows you to file only once and saves you from paying the tax and waiting for a refund. However, interest is charged on any tax due on the postponed tax return, but interest is not paid on refunds paid within 45 days after the return is filed. (If you have moving expenses that are for services performed in two years, you can be granted an extension to 90 days beyond the close of the year following the year of first arrival in the foreign country.)

Q. *I am a U.S. citizen. I have lived abroad for a number of years and recently realized that I should have been filing U.S. income tax returns. How do I correct this oversight in not having filed returns for these years?*

A. File the late returns as soon as possible, stating your reason for filing late. For advice on filing the returns, you should contact either the Internal Revenue Service representative serving your area or the Internal Revenue official who travels through your area (details can be obtained from your nearest U.S. consulate or Embassy). You can also write to the Internal Revenue Service, International Section, P.O. B o x 9 2 0, B e n s a l e m, P A 19020-8518.

Q. *In 1999, I qualified to exclude my foreign earned income, but I did not claim this exclusion on the return I filed in 2000. I paid all outstanding taxes with the return. Can I file a claim for refund now?*

A. It is too late to claim this refund since a claim for refund must be filed within 3 years from the date the return was filed or 2 years from the date the tax was paid, whichever is later. A return filed before the due date is considered filed on the due date.

Meeting the Requirements of Either the Bona Fide Residence Test or the Physical Presence Test

Q. *I recently came to Country X to work for the Orange Tractor Co. and I expect to be here for 5 or 6 years. I understand that upon the completion of 1 full year I will qualify under the bona fide residence test. Is this correct?*

A. Not necessarily. The law provides that to qualify under this test for the foreign earned income exclusion, the foreign housing exclusion, or the foreign housing deduction, a person must be a "bona fide resident of a foreign country or countries for an uninterrupted period which includes an entire taxable year."

If, like most U.S. citizens, you file your return on a calendar year basis, the taxable year referred to in the law would be from January 1 to December 31 of any particular year. Unless you established residence in Country X on January 1, it would be more than 1 year before you could qualify as a bona fide resident of a foreign country. Once you have completed your qualifying period, however, you are entitled to exclude the income or to claim the housing exclusion or deduction from the date you established bona fide residence.

Q. *I understand the physical presence test to be simply a matter of being physically present in a foreign country for at least 330 days within 12 consecutive months; but what are the criteria of the bona fide residence test?*

A. To be a bona fide resident of a foreign country, you must show that you entered a foreign country intending to remain there for an indefinite or prolonged period and, to that end, you are making your home in that country. Consideration is given to the type of quarters occupied, whether your family went with you, the type of visa, the employment agreement, and any other factor pertinent to show whether your stay in the foreign country is indefinite or prolonged.

To claim the foreign earned income exclusion or foreign housing exclusion or deduction under this test, the period of foreign residence must include 1 full tax year (usually January 1 – December 31), but once you meet this time requirement, you figure the exclusions and the deduction from the date the residence actually began.

Q. *To meet the qualification of "an uninterrupted period which includes an entire taxable year," do I have to be physically present in a foreign country for the entire year?*

A. No. Uninterrupted refers to the bona fide residence proper and not to the physical presence of the individual. During the period of bona fide residence in a foreign country, even during the first full year, you can leave the country for brief and temporary trips back to the United States or elsewhere for vacation, or even for business. To preserve your status as a bona fide resident of a foreign country, you must have a clear intention of returning from those trips, without unreasonable delay, to your foreign residence.

Q. *I am a U.S. citizen and during 2005 was a bona fide resident of Country X. On January 15, 2006, I was notified that I was to be assigned to Country Y. I was recalled to New York for 90 days orientation and then went to Country Y, where I have been since. Although I was not in Country Y on January 1, I was a bona fide resident of Country X and was in Country Y on December 31, 2005. My family remained in Country X until completion of the orientation period, and my household goods were shipped directly to my new post. Can I qualify as a bona* *fide resident of a foreign country for 2005, or must I wait for the entire year of 2006 to qualify?*

A. Since you did not break your period of foreign residence, you would continue to qualify as a bona fide resident for 2005.

Q. *Due to illness, I returned to the United States before I completed my qualifying period to claim the foreign earned income exclusion. Can I figure the exclusion for the period I resided abroad?*

A. No. You are not entitled to any exclusion of foreign earned income since you did not complete your qualifying period under either the bona fide residence test or physical presence test. If you paid foreign tax on the income earned abroad, you may be able to claim that tax as a deduction or as a credit against your U.S. tax.

Q. *Can a resident alien of the United States qualify for an exclusion or deduction under the bona fide residence test or the physical presence test?*

A. Resident aliens of the United States can qualify for the foreign earned income exclusion, the foreign housing exclusion, or the foreign housing deduction if they meet the   requirements of the physical presence test. Resident aliens who are citizens or nationals of a country with which the United States has an income tax treaty in effect can also qualify under the bona fide residence test.

Q. *On August 13 of last year I left the United States and arrived in Country Z to work for the Gordon Manufacturing Company. I expected to be able to exclude my foreign earned income under the physical presence test because I planned to be in Country Z for at least 1 year. However, I was reassigned back to the United States and left Country Z on July 1 of this year. Can I exclude any of my foreign earned income?*

A. No. You cannot exclude any of the income you earned in Country Z because you were not in a foreign country for at least 330 full days as required under the physical presence test.

Foreign Earned Income

Q. *I am an employee of the U.S. Government working abroad. Can all or part of my government income earned abroad qualify for the foreign earned income exclusion?*

A. No. The foreign earned income exclusion applies to your foreign earned income. Amounts paid by the United States or its agencies to their employees are not treated, for this purpose, as foreign earned income.

Q. *I qualify under the bona fide residence test. Does my foreign earned income include my U.S. dividends and the interest I receive on a foreign bank account?*

A. No. The only income that is foreign earned income is income from the performance of personal services abroad. Investment income is not earned income. However, you must include it in gross income reported on your Form 1040.

Q. *My company pays my foreign income tax on my foreign earnings. Is this taxable compensation?*

A. Yes. The amount is compensation for services performed. The tax paid by your company should be reported on Form 1040, Part IV, item 22(f) (or on Form 2555-EZ, Part IV, line 17).

Q. *I live in an apartment in a foreign city for which my employer pays the rent. Should I include in my income the cost to my employer ($1,200 a month) or the fair market value of equivalent housing in the United States ($800 a month)?*

A. You must include in income the fair market value (FMV) of the facility provided, where it is provided. This will usually be the rent your employer pays. Situations when the FMV is not included in income are discussed in IRS Pub. 54. under *Exclusion of Meals and Lodging.*

Q. *My U.S. employer pays my salary into my U.S. bank account. Is this income considered earned in the United States or is it considered foreign earned income?*

A. If you performed the services to earn this salary outside the United States, your salary is considered earned abroad. It does not matter that you are paid by a U.S. employer or that your salary is deposited in a U.S. bank account in the United States. The source of salary, wages, commissions, and other personal service income is the place where you perform the services.

Q. *What is considered a foreign country?*

A. For the purposes of the foreign earned income exclusion and the foreign housing exclusion or deduction, any territory under the sovereignty of a country other than the United States is a foreign country. Possessions of the United States are not treated as foreign countries.

Q. *What is the source of earned income?*

A. The source of earned income is the place where the work or personal services that produce the income are performed. In other words, income received for work in a foreign country has its source in that country. The foreign earned income exclusion and the foreign housing exclusion or deduction are limited to earned income from sources within foreign countries.

Foreign Earned Income Exclusion

Q. *I qualify for the foreign earned income exclusion and earned more than $80,000 during the year. Am I entitled to the maximum $80,000 exclusion?*

A. Not necessarily. Although you qualify for the foreign earned income exclusion, you may not have met either the bona fide residence test or the physical presence test for your entire tax year. If you did not meet either of these tests for your entire tax year, you must prorate the $80,000 maximum exclusion based on the number of days that you did meet either test during the year.

Q. *How do I qualify for the foreign earned income exclusion?*

A. To be eligible, you must have a tax home in a foreign country and be a U.S. citizen or resident alien. You must be either a bona fide resident of a foreign country or countries for an uninterrupted period that includes an entire tax year, or you must be physically present in a foreign country or countries for at least 330 full days during any period of 12 consecutive months. U.S. citizens may qualify under either test. The physical presence test applies to all resident aliens, while the bona fide residence test applies to resident aliens who are citizens or nationals of a country with which the United States has an income tax treaty in effect. Your tax home must be in the foreign country or countries throughout your period of residence or presence. For this purpose, your period of physical presence is the 330 full days during which you are present in a foreign country, not the 12 consecutive months during which those days occur.

Q. *Is it true that my foreign earned income exclusion cannot exceed my foreign earned income?*

A. Yes. The amount of the exclusion is limited each year to the amount of your foreign earned income after reducing that income by the foreign housing

169

exclusion. The foreign earned income must be earned during the part of the tax year that you have your tax home abroad and meet either the bona fide residence test or the physical presence test.

Q. *My wife and I are both employed, reside together, and file a joint return. We meet the qualifications for claiming the foreign earned income exclusion. Do we each figure a separate foreign earned income exclusion and foreign housing exclusion?*

A. You figure your foreign earned income exclusion separately since you both have foreign earned income. The amount of the exclusion for each of you cannot exceed your separate foreign earned incomes. If you each have a housing amount, you can figure your housing exclusion either separately or jointly. Refer to *Married Couples* in IRS Pub. 54. for further details.

Exemptions and Dependency Allowances

Q. *I am a U.S. citizen married to a nonresident alien who has no income from U.S. sources. Can I claim an exemption for my spouse on my U.S. tax return?*

A. Yes. If you file a joint return, you can claim an exemption for your nonresident alien spouse. If you do not file a joint return, you can claim an exemption for your nonresident alien spouse only if your spouse has no income from sources within the United States and is not the dependent of another U.S. taxpayer. You must use the married filing separately column in the Tax Table or section C of the Tax Computation Worksheet, unless you qualify as a head of household. A U.S. citizen or resident married to a nonresident alien also can choose to treat the nonresident alien as a U.S. resident for all federal income tax purposes. This allows you to file a joint return, but also subjects the alien's worldwide income to U.S. income tax.

Q. *I support my parents who live in Italy. I am sure that I provide the bulk of their support. Can I claim exemptions for them?*

A. It depends on whether they are U.S. citizens or residents. If your parents are not U.S. citizens or residents, you cannot claim exemptions for them even if you provide most of their support. To qualify as a dependent, a person generally must be either a citizen or national of the United States or a resident of the United States, Canada, or Mexico for some part of the tax year. The other tests of dependency also must be met.

170

Q. Should I prorate my own personal exemption and the exemptions for my spouse and dependents, since I expect to exclude part of my income?

A. No. Do not prorate exemptions for yourself, your spouse, and your dependents. Claim the full amount for each exemption permitted.

Social Security and Railroad Retirement Benefits

Q. Are U.S. social security benefits taxable?

A. Benefits received by U.S. citizens and resident aliens may be taxable, depending on the total amount of income and the filing status of the taxpayer. Under certain treaties, U.S. social security benefits are exempt from U.S. tax if taxed by the country of residence. Benefits similar to social security received from other countries by U.S. citizens or residents may be taxable. (Refer to our tax treaties with various countries for any benefit granted by the treaty.)

Q. As a U.S. citizen or resident, how do I figure the amount of my U.S. social security benefits to include in gross income?

A. Refer to Publication 915, Social Security and Equivalent Railroad Retirement Benefits, to figure if any of your benefits are includible in income.

Q. How are railroad retirement benefits taxed?

A. The part of a tier 1 railroad retirement benefit that is equivalent to the social security benefit you would have been entitled to receive if the railroad employee's work had been covered under the social security system rather than the railroad retirement system is treated the same as a social security benefit, discussed above.

The other part of a tier 1 benefit that is not considered a social security equivalent benefit is treated like a private pension or annuity, as are tier 2 railroad retirement benefits. Pensions and annuities are explained in IRS Pub. 54. under *Earned and Unearned Income.* Vested dual benefits and supplemental annuities are also treated like private pensions, but are fully taxable. The proper amounts of the social security equivalent part of tier 1 benefits and any special guaranty benefits are shown on the Form RRB-1099, *Payments by the Railroad Retirement Board,* that you receive from the Railroad Retirement Board. The taxable amounts of the non-social security equivalent part of tier 1, tier 2, vested dual benefits, and supplemental annuities are shown on the Form RRB-1099-R, *Annuities or*

Pensions by the Railroad Retirement Board, that you receive from the Railroad Retirement Board.

Social Security Tax and Self-Employment Tax

Q. *I am a minister with earned income from abroad and expect to qualify for the foreign earned income exclusion. How do I pay my self-employment tax?*

File a Form 1040 with Schedule SE and Form 2555. Figure your self-employment tax on Schedule SE and enter it on Form 1040 as the tax due with the return.

Q. *Because I expect to qualify for the foreign earned income exclusion, I have requested and received an extension of time until January 30, 2007, to file my 2005 return. However, since I will be paying self-employment tax on my spouse's income, should I file a 2005 return when due, pay the self-employment tax, and then file another return when I qualify for the exclusion?*

A. No. You do not need to file a 2005 Form 1040 (the regular income tax return) when due if you have received an extension. To stop interest from accruing on the self-employment tax due for 2005, you can pay enough estimated tax to cover the self-employment tax and any income tax that would be due after taking out the amount of excludable income.

Income Tax Withholding

Q. *How can I get my employer to stop withholding federal income taxes from wages while I am overseas and eligible for the foreign earned income exclusion?*

A. File a statement in duplicate with your employer stating that withholding should be reduced because you meet the bona fide residence test or physical presence test. Refer to also the following question.

Q. *Does the Internal Revenue Service provide forms to be used by employees requesting employers to stop withholding income tax from wages they expect to be excluded as income earned abroad?*

A. Yes. Form 673 is a sample statement that can be used by individuals who expect to qualify under the bona fide residence test or the physical presence test. A copy of this form is displayed in chapter 2. You can get this form on the Internet at www.irs.gov or by writing to the Internal Revenue Service, International Section, P.O. Box 920, Bensalem, PA 19020-8518.

Q. *I am a U.S. citizen residing overseas, and I receive dividend and interest income from U.S. sources from which tax is being withheld at a rate of 30%. How can I have this situation corrected?*

A. File Form W-9 (indicating that you are a U.S. citizen) with the withholding agents who are paying you the dividends and interest. This is their authority to stop withholding the 30% income tax at the source on payments due you.

Q. *As a U.S. citizen receiving dividend and interest income from the United States from which tax has been withheld, do I report the net dividend and interest income on my return, or do I report the gross amount and take credit for the tax withheld?*

A. You must report the gross amount of the income received and take a tax credit for the tax withheld. This is to your advantage since the tax withheld is deducted in full from the tax due. It is also advisable to attach a statement to your return explaining this tax credit so there will be no question as to the amount of credit allowable.

Deductions

Q. *Can I claim a foreign tax credit even though I do not itemize deductions?*

A. Yes. You can claim the foreign tax credit even though you do not itemize deductions.

Q. *I had to pay customs duty on a few things I brought back with me from Europe last summer. Can I include customs fees with my other deductible taxes?*

A. No. Customs duties, like federal excise taxes, are not deductible.

Q. *Some taxes paid in the United States are not deductible if I itemize my deductions. Which ones are they?*

A. Sales taxes, as well as the state and local taxes levied specifically on cigarettes, tobacco, and alcoholic beverages, are not deductible. In addition, no deduction can be taken for drivers' licenses or gasoline taxes. Auto registration fees cannot be deducted except when they qualify as personal property taxes. To qualify as personal property taxes, they must be based on the value of the auto. Some state and local taxes are deductible, such as those on personal property, real estate, and income.

Q. *What types of foreign taxes are deductible?*

A. Generally, real estate and foreign income taxes are deductible as itemized deductions. Foreign income taxes are deductible only if you do not claim the foreign tax credit. Foreign income taxes paid on excluded income are not deductible as an itemized deduction.
Note. Foreign income taxes are usually claimed under the credit provisions, if they apply, because this is more advantageous in most cases.

Q. *I rented an apartment in the United Kingdom and had to pay a local tax called a "general rates" tax, which is based on occupancy of the apartment. Can I deduct this tax as a foreign real estate tax?*

A. No. This tax does not qualify as a real estate tax since it is levied on the occupant of the premises rather than on the owner of the property.

General Tax Questions

Q. *Will the Internal Revenue Service representatives at the Embassies answer questions about tax laws of our home state and the laws of the foreign country where we reside as well as U.S. federal income tax laws?*

A. No. The IRS representatives are authorized only to answer tax questions on U.S. federal income tax. You should write your home state's tax office for state tax information and contact the tax officials of the country where you reside for information regarding their taxes.

Q. *Can Internal Revenue Service personnel recommend tax practitioners who prepare returns?*

A. No. IRS employees are not permitted to recommend tax practitioners who prepare income tax returns.

Q. *I just filed my return. How long will it take to get my refund?*

A. It may take up to 10 weeks to issue a refund on a return that is properly made out. A refund may take longer than that if the return is filed just before the filing deadline. An error on the return will also delay the refund. Among the most common causes of delay in receiving refunds are unsigned returns and incorrect social security numbers.

174

Q. *I have not received my refund from last year's return. Can I claim the credit against this year's tax?*

A. No. That would cause problems to both years' returns. If your last year's refund is overdue, contact the IRS and ask about the status of the refund. If you are outside the United States, call or write the nearest IRS office. (Refer to *Services Available Outside the United States* in IRS Pub. 54. for a list of phone numbers.) Otherwise, call or write your local U.S. IRS office. If you write to the IRS, be sure to include your social security number (or individual taxpayer identification number) in the letter.

Q. *I forgot to include interest income when I filed my return last week. What should I do?*

A. To correct a mistake of this sort you should prepare Form 1040X. Include the omitted interest income, refigure the tax, and send the form as soon as possible along with any additional tax due to the Internal Revenue Service Center where you filed your return. Form 1040X can be used to correct an individual Form 1040 income tax return filed for any year for which the period of limitation has not expired (usually 3 years after the due date of the return filed, or 2 years after the tax was paid, whichever is later).

Q. *I am a U.S. citizen and, because I expect to qualify for the foreign earned income exclusion, all my foreign income (which consists solely of salary) will be exempt from U.S. tax. Do I get any tax benefit from income tax I paid on this salary to a foreign country during the tax year?*

A. No. You cannot take either a tax credit or a tax deduction for foreign income taxes paid on income that is exempt from U.S. tax because of the foreign earned income exclusion.

Q. *I am a U.S. citizen stationed abroad. I made a personal loan to a nonresident alien who later went bankrupt. Can I claim a bad debt loss for this money?*

A. Yes. The loss should be reported as a short-term capital loss on Schedule D (Form 1040). You have the burden of proving the validity of the loan, the subsequent bankruptcy, and the recovery or nonrecovery from the loan.

Q. *With which countries does the United States have tax treaties?*

A. Refer to the Table of Appendix for a list those countries with which the United States has income tax treaties.

175

Q. *I am a retired U.S. citizen living in Europe. My only income is from U.S. sources on which I pay U.S. taxes. I am taxed on the same income in the foreign country where I reside. How do I avoid double taxation?*

A. If you reside in a country that has an income tax treaty with the United States, the treaty will generally contain provisions to eliminate double taxation. Many treaties will provide reduced rates for various types of income. Treaties often provide reciprocal credits in one country for the tax paid to the other country. Nontreaty countries, depending on their laws, may give the same type of credit. If double taxation with a treaty country exists and you cannot resolve the problem with the tax authorities of the foreign country, you can contact the U.S. competent authority for assistance. Refer to IRS Pub. 54. for information on requesting consideration.

Q. *My total income after claiming the foreign earned income and housing exclusions consists of $5,000 taxable wages. Am I entitled to claim the earned income credit?*

A. No. If you claim the foreign earned income exclusion, the foreign housing exclusion, or the foreign housing deduction, you cannot claim the earned income credit.

Q. *Last May my employer transferred me to our office in Puerto Rico. I understand that my salary earned in Puerto Rico is tax exempt. Is this correct?*

A. As long as your employer is not the U.S. Government, all income from sources within Puerto Rico is exempt from U.S. tax if you are a bona fide resident of Puerto Rico during the entire tax year. The income you received from Puerto Rican sources the year you moved to Puerto Rico is not exempt. The tax paid to Puerto Rico in the year you moved to Puerto Rico can be claimed as a foreign tax credit on Form 1116.

Q. *I am a U.S. citizen married to a nonresident alien. Can I qualify to use the head of household tax rates?*

A. Yes. Although your nonresident alien spouse cannot qualify you as a head of household, you can qualify if (a) or (b) applies:
a) You paid more than half the cost of keeping up a home that was the principal home for the entire year for your mother or father for whom you can claim an exemption (your parent does not have to have lived with you), or

176

b) You paid more than half the cost of keeping up the home in which you lived and in which one of the following also lived for more than half the year:
● Your unmarried child, grandchild, stepchild, foster child, or adopted child. A foster child will qualify you for this status only if you can claim an exemption for the child.
● Your married child, grandchild, stepchild, or adopted child for whom you can claim an exemption, or for whom you could claim an exemption except that you signed a statement allowing the noncustodial parent to claim the exemption, or the noncustodial parent provides at least $600 support and claims the exemption under a pre-1985 agreement.

● Any relative listed below for whom you can claim an exemption.

Parent   Brother-in-law
Grandparent   Sister-in-law
Brother Half-sister
Half-brother   Son-in-law
Sister   Daughter-in-law Stepbrother
Stepsister   If related by blood:
Stepmother   – Uncle
Stepfather   – Aunt
Mother-in-law – Nephew
Father-in-law – Niece

If your spouse was a nonresident alien at any time during the year and you do not choose to treat your nonresident spouse as a resident alien, then you are treated as unmarried for head of household purposes. You must have another qualifying relative and meet the other tests to be eligible to file as head of household. You can use the head of household column in the Tax Table or Section D of the Tax Computation Worksheet. It may be advantageous to choose to treat your nonresident alien spouse as a U.S. resident and file a joint income tax return. Once you make the choice, however, you must report the worldwide income of both yourself and your spouse. For more information on head of household filing status, get Publication 501, *Exemptions, Standard Deduction, and Filing Information.*

Penalties and Interest

Q. Does the June 15 extended due date for filing my return because both my tax home and my abode are outside the United States and Puerto Rico on the regular due date relieve me from having to pay interest on tax not paid by April 15?

177

A. No. An extension, whether an automatic extension or one requested in writing, does not relieve you of the payment of interest on the tax due as of April 15 following the year for which the return is filed. The interest should be included in your payment.

Q. If I wait to file my return until I qualify for the foreign earned income exclusion, I will be charged interest on the U.S. tax I will owe. To avoid being charged interest, can I file my return on time, reporting only my taxable income, excluding my salary for services abroad that will be exempt after I have met the qualifications?

A. No. If you file a return before you qualify for the exclusion, you must report all income, including all income for services performed abroad, and pay tax on all of it. After you meet the qualifications, you can file a claim for refund by excluding the income earned abroad. If you defer the filing of your return, you can avoid interest on tax due on your return to be filed by paying the tax you estimate you will owe with your request for an extension of time to file on Form 2350, or by paying enough estimated tax to cover any tax that you expect will be due on the return.

References:
• Publication 54, Tax Guide for U.S. Citizens and Resident Aliens Abroad

13.8 Other

Q. How do I know if the U.S. has an income tax treaty with another country?

A. Publication 901, U.S. Tax Treaties, has information regarding United States tax treaties.
You can also locate the complete text of current treaties at http://www.irs.gov/businesses/corporations/article/0,,id=96739,00.html or use the IRS search engine with keywords "income tax treaties. "

References:
• Publication 901, U.S. Tax Treaties

Chapter 14

Electronic Filing (e-file) and TeleFile
~~~~~

Keyword(s): Software for On-line Filing; Keyword(s): Error Code/Message; Keyword(s): Electronic Filing; Keyword(s): Tax Preparer

14.1 Age/Name/SSN Rejects, Errors, Correction Procedures

Q. What software is approved for IRS e-file?

A. The IRS does not endorse or approve software. You may want to consider IRS e-file by filing through an Authorized IRS e-file Provider. To learn more, refer to the IRS Electronic Services information. For general information about e-file, refer to Tax Topic 252, *Electronic Filing.*

References:
• Authorized IRS e-file Provider
• Tax Topic 252, Electronic filing
• Electronic Services

Q. How can I participate as an electronic filing Provider?

A. To participate in the e-file program, you must first choose the Authorized IRS e-file options that are best for you. An Authorized IRS e-file Provider can be an Electronic Return Originator, Intermediate Service Provider, Transmitter or Software Developer.

Submit Form 8633, *Application to Participate in the IRS e-file Program.* Submit your application to the appropriate Service Center as shown on Form 8633. Publication 1345, *Handbook for Authorized IRS E-File Providers Individual Income Tax Returns,* provides you with the information you need to apply to participate in the e-file Program. Technical information can be found in Publication 1346, *Electronic Return File Specifications and Record Layouts for Individual Income Tax Returns.* Updates to this publication will appear on the Electronic Filing System Bulletin Board. You can also contact the Andover Service Center at 1-800-691-1894 (toll free) for assistance.

Pass a Suitability Background check. If you apply to become an ERO, Transmitter or Intermediate Service Provider, the IRS conducts a background check on all principals of your firm and responsible officials listed on the application to determine their suitability to be an Authorized IRS e-file Provider. If you apply to be a Software Developer only, a suitability check is not required.

References:
• e-file Providers Web Page
• Form 8633, Application to Participate in the IRS e-file Program
• Publication 1345, Handbook for Electronic Filers of Individual Income Tax Returns
• Publication 1346 Electronic Return File Specifications and Record Layouts For Individual Income Tax Return
• Tax Topic 252, Electronic Filing

Q. *I filed electronically but my tax return was rejected. What do I do now?*

A. Your next action depends on the reason your return was rejected. If you made a mistake in entering the social security number or misspelled a name, you can fix these errors and have the return sent again to the IRS. There are other errors that will cause you to have to file using a paper return. If you have further questions, you can call IRS Customer Service number at 1-800-829-1040. For general information about e-file, refer to Tax Topic 252, *Electronic Filing.*

References:
• Tax Topic 252, Electronic Filing
• Electronic Services

Q. *My electronic tax return keeps getting rejected for a dependent's social security number used more than once or on another return. I have verified the social security numbers of all my dependents with the Social Security Administration and no one else is authorized to claim our children on their taxes. How do I correct this error so that an e-file return will go through?*

A. Unfortunately, you will need to file a paper return this year. Do not send any documents that are not required with your tax return. Whether the cause of this rejection is the result of a typo on another return or an attempt by another party to claim your dependent, the IRS has security measures in place to ensure the accuracy of returns submitted. In such cases, the IRS will question the dependency exemptions claimed by any other party using the wrong social security number. For general information about e-file, refer to Tax Topic 252, *Electronic Filing.*

References:
• Social Security Administration
• Tax Topic 252, Electronic Filing
• Electronic Services

Q. We will be filing a joint tax return. Can we file our return electronically?

A. Yes. Filing your return electronically is faster, safer, and more accurate than mailing your tax return because it is transmitted over telephone lines directly to an IRS computer. Refer to Tax Topic 252, *Electronic Filing,* for more information.

References:
• Tax Topic 252, Electronic Filing

14.2 Amended Returns

Q. Can I file an amended Form 1040X electronically?

A. At this time, the Form 1040X is not accepted electronically. For general information about e-file, refer to Tax Topic 252, *Electronic Filing.*

References:
•   Tax Topic 252, Electronic Filing
•   Electronic Services Instructions for Form 1040X

14.3 Due Dates & Extension Dates for e-file

Q. I don't owe taxes. Can I file electronically after April 15th?

A. Yes, you can electronically file your return after April 15th, however to do so you must file Form 4868, an *Application for an Extension of Time to File*, on or before April 15th. If the extension is timely filed, you have until August 15th to file your return. If the 15th falls on a weekend or federal holiday, you have until midnight the following business day to submit your extension or your tax return. If additional time is needed Refer to the instruction for Form 2688, *Application for Additional Time to File US Individual Income Tax Return.* Please note that the Form 2688 is not an automatic extension and must be approved by IRS; if it is approved you may have until October 15th to file your return electronically.

References:
- Tax Topic 304, Extension of Time to File Your Tax Return
- Electronic Services
- Form 4868, Application for Automatic Extension of Time to File US Individual Income Tax Return
- Form 2688, Application for Additional Time to File US Individual Income Tax Return

14.4 Forms W–2 & Other Attachments

Q. *If I file electronically, what do I do with my W-2 forms?*

A. When filing electronically you must provide Form W-2 to the authorized IRS e-file provider before the provider sends the electronic return to the IRS. In addition, you should keep them in a safe place with a copy of your tax return. For general information about e-file, refer to Tax Topic 252, *Electronic Filing.*

References:
- Tax Topic 252, Electronic Filing
- Electronic Services

Keyword(s): Telefile

14.5 TeleFile

Q. *What is TeleFile?*

A. TeleFile is an interactive computer program that calculates your taxes and begins the electronic filing process over the phone. IRS automatically sends a special TeleFile package to those who may be eligible to use it. Only those receiving the package can use TeleFile. This year, many taxpayers who filed Form 1040EZ, *Income Tax Return for Single and Joint Filers With No Dependents*, or by TeleFile last year will receive a special TeleFile tax package that allows them to file their taxes electronically by phone. TeleFile is easy, fast, and free. It's available 24 hours a day, with nothing to mail in. TeleFile is a great way for students to file their tax returns. Refer to Tax Topic 255, *TeleFile,* for more information.

References:
• Tax Topic 255, TeleFile

Q. Where can I get a TeleFile form?

A. If you file a paper tax return for the current year and qualify to TeleFile, the IRS should send you a TeleFile package in the mail by January 20th of the following year, which will include your PIN number. The booklet cannot be ordered from the IRS. If you do not qualify, you can still receive all of the benefits that IRS e-file has to offer by using a personal computer or filing through an Authorized IRS e-file Provider. To learn more, refer to the IRS Electronic Services information. For general information about TeleFile or e-file, refer to Tax Topic 255, *TeleFile,* or Tax Topic 252, *Electronic Filing.*

References:
• Tax Topic 255, TeleFile
• Tax Topic 252, Electronic Filing
• Electronic Services

Q. I have not received a TeleFile tax package. Is there a way I can order this form?

A. If you have met the criteria for using Telefile, i.e., filed TeleFile or a paper 1040EZ last year and have not changed your address or filing requirements, you should receive a package. The booklet cannot be ordered from the IRS. Also, consider IRS e-file using a personal computer or filing through an Authorized IRS e-file Provider. To learn more, refer to the IRS Electronic Services information. For general information about TeleFile or e-file, refer to Tax Topic 255, *TeleFile,* or Tax Topic 252, *Electronic Filing.*

References:
• Tax Topic 255, TeleFile
• Tax Topic 252, Electronic Filing
• Electronic Services

Chapter 15

Magnetic Media Filers

~~~~~

Keyword(s) Magnetic Media

15. Magnetic Media Filers:

Q. *How do I request approval to file information returns electronically (magnetically)?*

A. All filers must obtain approval to file prior to submitting Form 1099, Form 1098, Form 5498, Form 1042-S, Form W-4, Form W-2G or Form 8027 returns on magnetic media or electronically. A Form 4419, Application for Filing Information Returns Electronically/Magnetically, should be submitted to the IRS, Martinsburg Computing Center, Information Reporting Program, 230 Murall Drive, Kearneysville, West Virginia 25430, at least 30 days before the due date of the returns. For more information, refer to the following:
- Publication 3609, Filing Information Returns Electronically
- Tax Topic 802, Applications, Forms, and Information
- Tax Topic 803, Waivers and Extensions
- Tax Topic 804, Test Files and Combined Federal and State Filing
- Tax Topic 805, Electronic Filing of Information Returns

For further information concerning the filing of information returns with the IRS either electronically or magnetically, contact the IRS Martinsburg Computing Center toll-free at (866) 455-7438 between 8:30 a.m. and 4:30 p.m. Eastern Standard Time.

References:
- Form 1098, Mortgage Interest Statement
- Form 5498, IRA and Coveredell ESA Contribution Information
- Form 1042-S Person's U.S. Source Income Subject to Withholding
- Form 8027, Employer's Annual Information Return of Tip Income and Allocated Tips
- Form 4419, Application for Filing Information Returns Electronically/Magnetically
- Tax Topic 802, Applications, Forms, and Information
- Tax Topic 803, Waivers and Extensions
- Tax Topic 804, Test Files and Combined Federal and State Filing

184

- Tax Topic 805, Electronic Filing of Information Returns
- Publication 3609, Filing Information Returns Electronically

Q. *I have a small business. Who is required to file Forms W-2 electronically?*

A. Any person, including corporations, partnerships, employers, estates, and trusts, who files 250 or more information returns of any Form 1042-S, Form 1099, Form 1098, Form 5498, Form 8027, Form W-2, or Form W-2G for any calendar year, must file these returns electronically or magnetically. For more information, refer to Tax Topic 801, *Who Must File Magnetically*, or Tax Topic 805, *Electronic Filing of Information Returns*.

References:
- Form 1042-S, Foreign Person's U.S. Source Income Subject to Withholding
- Form 8027, Employer's Annual Information Return of Tip Income and Allocated Tips
- Form 1098, Mortgage Interest Statement
- Form 5498, IRA and Coverdell ESA Contribution Information
- Form W-2, Wage and Tax Statement
- Form W-2G, Certain Gambling Winnings
- Tax Topic 801, Who Must File Magnetically
- Tax Topic 805, Electronic Filing of Information Returns
- Publication 3609, Filing Information Returns Electronically

Chapter 16

Other (Alternative Minimum Tax, Estates, Trusts, Tax Shelters, State Tax Inquiries)

~~~~~

Keyword(s): Trust; Keyword(s): Tax Shelter

16. Other (Alternative Minimum Tax, Estates, Trusts, Tax Shelters, State Tax Inquiries):

Q. The IRS corrected my return and sent me an additional refund. Does this mean I am also entitled to an additional refund on my state tax return?

A. Whether you are entitled to an additional state tax refund depends on the nature of the change which was made to your federal return. For example, if on your federal tax return, you used the wrong line on the tax tables to figure your tax, this may not have an impact on your state tax return. However, if the change was made to the amount of your taxable income on your federal return, it may have an impact on your state tax return. Contact your state tax office for additional information. It is helpful to have a copy of your tax returns (federal and state) and a copy of the IRS notice when you call.

• To access the state you need to direct your question to, go to http://www.irs.gov/localcontacts/index.html

Head of Household Generally, you may claim head of household filing status on your tax return only if you are unmarried and pay more than 50% of the costs of keeping up a home for yourself and your dependent(s) or other qualifying individuals.

Q. I am considering a tax shelter investment. How can I recognize an abusive tax shelter?

A. Tax shelters reduce current tax liability by offsetting income from one source with losses from another source. The IRS allows some tax shelters, but will not allow a shelter which is "abusive. " An abusive shelter generally offers inflated tax savings which are disproportionately greater than your actual investment placed at risk. Generally, you invest money to generate income. However, an abusive tax shelter generates little or no income, and exists solely to reduce taxes unreasonably for tax avoidance or evasion. In comparison, a legitimate tax shelter often produces income and involves a risk of loss proportionate to the expected tax benefit. Abusive tax shelters are often marketed in terms of how much you can write off in relation to how much you invest. This "write off " ratio is often much greater than two-to-one as of the close of any of the first five year ending after the date on which the investment is offered for sale. A series of tax laws have been designed to halt abusive tax shelters. An organizer of a potentially abusing tax shelter who doesn't maintain a list of investors is subject to penalty of $50 per failure, per person, unless due to a reasonable cause and not willful neglect.

Any person participating in the sale or organization of an abusive tax shelter may be penalized up to the lesser of $1,000 or 100% of the Gross Income derived or to be derived from the activity. For additional information, refer to Tax Topic 454, *Tax Shelters*.

References:
• Publication 2193, Too Good to Be True Trusts
• Tax Topic 454, Tax Shelters

Chapter 17

Individual Retirement Arrangements (IRAs)

~~~~~

Keyword(s): Distributions; Keyword(s): Early Withdrawal; Keyword(s): 10% additional Tax

17.1 Distributions, Early Withdrawals, 10% Additional Tax

Q. How do I calculate the minimum amount that must be withdrawn from my IRA after age 70 1/2?

A. You will need to get Publication 590, *Individual Retirement Arrangements (IRAs)* to find out this amount. Generally the minimum distribution is computed using one of three tables found in Publication 590. Table I is used by beneficiaries. Table II is for use by owners who have spouses who are more than 10 years younger. Table III is generally for use by unmarried owners and owners who have spouses who are not more than 10 years younger.

References:
• Publication 590, Individual Retirement Arrangements (IRAs)

Keyword(s): Rollovers

17.2 Rollovers

Q. How long do I have to roll over a distribution from a retirement plan to an IRA account?

A. You must complete the rollover by the 60th day following the day on which you receive the distribution. (This 60-day period is extended for the period during which the distribution is in a frozen deposit in a financial institution.) The IRS may waive the 60 day requirement in certain situations, such as in the event of a casualty, disaster, or other event beyond your reasonable control. To obtain a waiver, a request for a ruling must be made and a user fee of $90.00 will apply, Refer to Revenue Procedure 2003-16 (within IRS Bulletin 2003-4). A written explanation of rollover must be given to you by the issuer making the distribution. For information on distributions which qualify for rollover treatment, refer to Tax Topic 413, *Rollovers from Retirement Plans.* For

188

information on the Direct Rollover Option, refer to Publication 590 *Individual Retirement Arrangement.*

References:
• Publication 17, Your Federal Income Tax
• Tax Topic 413, Rollovers from Retirement Plans

Q. If I can't withdraw funds penalty free from my 401(k) plan to purchase my first home, can I roll it over into an IRA and then withdraw that money to use as my down payment?

A. Yes, if you are receiving a distribution from a 401(k) that is eligible to roll over into a IRA and you meet all of the qualifications for an IRA distribution for a first-time homebuyer. Your plan administrator is required to notify you before making a distribution from your 401(k) plan whether that distribution is eligible to be rolled over into an IRA. To see if you qualify for a distribution to be used as a first-time homebuyer, refer to Publication 590, *Individual Retirement Arrangements (IRAs).*

References:
• Publication 560, Retirement Plans for Small Business (SEP, Simple, and Qualified Plans)
• Publication 575, Pension and Annuity Income
• Publication 590, Individual Retirement Arrangements (IRAs)
• Tax Topic 424, 401(k) plans
• Tax Topic 558, Tax on early distributions from retirement plans
• Tax Topic 412, Lump-sum distributions

Keyword(s): Roth IRA

17.3 Roth IRA

Q. Do I report my nondeductible Roth IRA contributions on Form 8606?

A. There are no forms to report a Roth contribution. The financial institution, which is the trustee of your Roth IRA, will send you information on the amount in your Roth IRA. They will also send the information to the Internal Revenue Service. Use Form 8606, *Nondeductible IRAs,* if you made a nondeductible contribution to a traditional IRA; converted from a traditional IRA, a SEP, or Simple IRA to a Roth IRA, received a distribution from a traditional IRA, a SEP, or a Simple IRA and made nondeductible contributions to a traditional IRA, or received a distribution from a Roth or traditional IRA.

References:
- Publication 590, Individual Retirement Arrangements (IRAs)
- Form 8606, Nondeductible IRAs and Coverdell ESAs
- Tax Topic 428, Roth IRA distributions

Q. *Can a person make a contribution to a SEP-IRA and a Roth IRA, too?*

A. Yes, you can make a contribution to a SEP-IRA and a Roth IRA. Refer to Publication 590, *Individual Retirement Arrangements*, for the requirements to contribute to a SEP and a Roth IRA. However, your SEP IRA contribution and Roth IRA contribution can not be made to the same IRA.

References:
- Publication 590, Individual Retirement Arrangements (IRAs)
- Publication 560, Retirement Plans for Small Business
- Tax Topic 451, Individual retirement arrangements (IRAs)

Keyword(s): Traditional IRA

17.4 Traditional IRA

Q. *I want to establish a traditional individual retirement arrangement (IRA) for my spouse, and I need additional information. What is the most I can contribute to a spousal IRA during the tax year?*

A. If both you and your spouse work and both have taxable compensation, each of you can contribute up to $4,000 (or the amount of each IRA owner's compensation, if less) to a separate traditional IRA. Even if one spouse has little or no compensation, up to $4,000 can be contributed to each IRA if combined compensation is at least equal to the amount contributed to both IRAs and you file a joint return. You can contribute $4,000 to a separate IRA for your nonworking spouse if you file a joint return. Your total contribution to both your IRA and the spousal IRA for this year is limited to the smaller of $8,000, or your taxable compensation reduced by any contributions you make to a traditional IRA or Roth IRA. You cannot contribute more than $4,000 to either IRA for the year. If you are 50 or older in 2006, the most that can be contributed to your traditional IRA for 2005 is the lesser of:
- $4,500, or
- Your compensation that you must include in income.

For additional information, refer to Tax Topic 451, *Individual Retirement Arrangements (IRAs)*, or Publication 590, Individual Retirement Arrangements (IRAs).

References:
• Publication 590, Individual Retirement Arrangements (IRAs)
• Tax Topic 451, Individual retirement arrangements (IRAs)

Q. *Can I take an IRA deduction for the amount I contributed to a 401(k) plan last year?*

A. No. A 401(k) plan is not an IRA. However, the amount you contributed is not included as income in box 1 of your W-2 form so you don't pay tax on it for 2005. For more information, refer to Tax Topic 424, *401(k) Plans*, Publication 575, *Pension and Annuity Income,* or Publication 560, *Retirement Plans for Small Business.*

References:
• Publication 575, Pension and Annuity Income
• Publication 560, Retirement Plans for Small Business (SEP, Simple, and Qualified Plans)
• Tax Topic 424, 401(k) Plans

Q. *What is the deadline for making an IRA Contribution?*

A. If you haven't contributed funds to an Individual Retirement Arrangement (IRA) for tax year 2005, or if you've put in less than the maximum allowed, you still have time to do so. You can contribute to either a traditional or Roth IRA until the April 15, 2006, due date for filing your tax return for 2005, not including extensions. Be sure to tell the IRA trustee that the contribution is for 2005. Otherwise, the trustee may report the contribution as being for 2006, when they get your funds. Generally, you can contribute up to $4,000 of your earnings for 2005 or up to $4,500 if you are age 50 or older in 2005.

You can fund a traditional IRA, a Roth IRA (if you qualify), or both, but your total contributions cannot be more than these amounts. You may be able to take a tax deduction for the contributions to a traditional IRA, depending on whether you — or your spouse, if filing jointly — are covered by an employer's pension plan and how much total income you have. You cannot deduct Roth IRA contributions, but the earnings on a Roth IRA may be tax-free if you meet the conditions for a qualified distribution. You can file your tax return claiming a traditional IRA deduction before the contribution is actually made. However, the contribution must be made by the due date of your return, not including extensions. If you report a contribution to a traditional IRA on your return, but fail to contribute by the deadline, you must file an amended tax return by using Form 1040X, *Amended U.S. Individual Income Tax Return.* You must add the amount you deducted to your income on the amended return and pay the additional tax accordingly. Publication 590, *Individual Retirement Arrangements* (IRAs), has more information. Download Publication 590 or order it by calling toll free 1-800-TAX-FORM (1-800-829-3676). Taxpayers needing this or any other IRS publication should act soon to be sure they have the item in time to meet the April deadline.

References:
- Publication 590, Individual Retirement Arrangements
- Form 1040X, Amended U.S. Individual Income Tax Return
- Form 1040X Instructions

Chapter 18

FAQs regarding Social Security and Medicare Taxes
~~~~~

Keyword(s): Social Security taxes, Medical taxes

18. FAQs regarding Social Security and Medicare Taxes

These frequently asked questions and answers are provided for general information only and should not be cited as any type of legal authority. They are designed to provide the user with information required to respond to general inquiries. Due to the uniqueness and complexities of Indian law and Federal tax law, it is imperative to ensure a full understanding of the specific question presented, and to perform the requisite research to ensure a correct response is provided.

Q. Are all employees subject to social security and Medicare taxes?

A. Generally, you must withhold social security and Medicare taxes from your employees' wages and you must also pay a matching amount of these taxes. Tribal council representatives are not subject to social security and Medicare taxes. Other types of wages and compensation not subject to social security taxes can be found in Publication 15, Circular E, *Employer's Tax Guide.*

Deceased employees are subject to social security and Medicare taxes for wages paid to the beneficiary or estate in the same calendar year as the worker's death. Wages paid to the beneficiary or estate after the calendar year of the worker's death are not subject to social security and Medicare taxes.

Q. If an employee is collecting social security benefits, is the employer required to withhold social security and Medicare taxes?

A. Yes. The employer is required to follow the withholding requirements for social security and Medicare taxes even if an employee is collecting social security benefits. Per Chapter 9 of security and Medicare taxes regardless of the employee's age or whether he or she is receiving social security benefits.

Q. *If the employee has reached the wage base limit for social security tax, is the employer still required to contribute their portion of the social security tax for this employee? Is there a wage base limit for Medicare taxes, too?*

A. The employer is subject to the same social security tax rate and wage base limits as the employee. The wage base limit for 2005 is $90,000. When the employee reaches their limitation, the employer also reaches the limitation and no longer has to pay social security taxes for that employee. Refer to Publication 15, Circular E, *Employer's Tax Guide,* for the current wage limit for social security wages. There is no wage base limit for Medicare tax; all covered wages are subject to Medicare tax.

For questions regarding tax return account matters, tax deposits or filing requirements, please contact the IRS Customer Account Services staff toll-free at 1-877-829-5500.

This call center is open 8:30am to 5:30pm Eastern Time.

Chapter 19

FAQs - STUDENTS
~~~~~

Keyword(s): student; Keyword(s): student; Keyword(s): grants; Keyword(s): babysitting; Keyword(s): savings bonds; Keyword(s): state Tuition Program; Keyword(s): Pell Grant; Keyword(s): tips; Keyword(s): ROTC; Keyword(s): scholarship; Keyword(s): fellowship;

Q. As a full-time student, am I exempt from federal taxes?

A. Every U.S. citizen or resident must file a U.S. income tax return if certain income levels are reached. There is no exemption from tax for full-time students. Factors that determine whether you have an income tax filing requirement include:
- the amount of your income (earned and unearned),
- whether you are able to be claimed as a dependent,
- your filing status, and
- your age. If your income is below the filing requirement for your age, filing status, and dependency status, you will not owe income tax on the income and will not have to file a tax return. You may choose to file if you have income tax withholding that you would like refunded to you.

You may have given your employer a Form W-4, Employee's Withholding Allowance Certificate, claiming exemption from withholding. To claim exemption from withholding, you generally would have to have had no tax liability the previous year and expect none in the current year. An exemption certificate is good for the calendar year. For related topics Refer to Tax Information for Students.

References:
- Publication 17, Your Federal Income Tax
- Publication 505, Tax Withholding and Estimated Tax
- Form W-4, Employee's Withholding Allowance Certificate
- Tax Information for Students.

Q. *What types of incomes are taxable to students?*

A. **Taxable Income for Students:** The following kinds of income often received by students are generally taxable.
- Pay for services performed
- Self-employment income
- Investment income
- Certain scholarships and fellowships

Pay for Services Performed: When figuring how much income to report, include everything you received as payment for your services. This usually means wages, salaries, and tips.

Wages and Salaries: The amount of wages (including tips) or salaries you received during the year is shown in box 1 of Form W-2, Wage and Tax Statement. Your employer will give you Form W-2 soon after the end of the year.

Q. *Are the tips I received at my job taxable?*

A. All tips you receive are income, and subject to income tax. This includes tips customers give you directly, tips customers charge on credit cards that your employer gives you, and your share of tips split with other employees.

Keep a daily record or other proof of your tips. You can use Form 4070A, *Employee's Daily Record of Tips.* Your daily record must show your name and address, your employer's name, and the establishment's name. For each day worked, you must show the amount of cash and charge tips you received from customers or other employees, a list of the names and amounts you paid to other employees through tip splitting, and the value of any noncash tips you get, such as tickets, passes, or other items of value. Record this information on or near the date you receive the tip income.

Q. *How and when do I report tips I received to my employer?*

A. If you receive cash, check, or credit card tips of $20 or more in any one calendar month while working for one employer, you must report the total amount of your tips to your employer by the 10th day of the next month. If the 10th falls on a Saturday, Sunday, or legal holiday, give your employer the report on the next day that is not a Saturday, Sunday, or a legal holiday.
To report your tips, you can use Form 4070, *Employee's Report of Tips to Employer.* To get a year's supply of this form, ask your employer or call the IRS for Publication 1244, *Employee's Daily Record of Tips and Report to Employer.*

Fill in the information asked for on the form, sign and date the form, and give it to your employer. If you do not use Form 4070, give your employer a statement with the following information:

- Your name, address, and social security number
- Your employer's name, address, and business name (if it is different from the employer's name)
- The month (or the dates of any shorter period) in which you received tips
- The total tips required to be reported for the period

Withholding on Tips: Your employer must withhold social security tax and Medicare taxes or railroad retirement tax, and any income tax due on the tips you report. Your employer usually deducts the withholding due on tips from your wages. If your wages are too small for your employer to withhold taxes, you may give him or her extra money to pay the taxes up to the close of the calendar year. Your employer should tell you how much is needed.

Any taxes that remain unpaid may be collected by your employer from your next paycheck. If withholding taxes remain uncollected at the end of the year, you may be subject to a penalty for underpayment of estimated taxes. Refer to Publication 505, *Tax Withholding and Estimated Tax*, for more information.

Form W-2

The tips you reported to your employer will be included with your wages in box 1 of Form W-2. Federal income tax, social security tax, and Medicare tax withheld on your wages and tips will be shown in boxes 2, 4, and 6, respectively.

Your Form W-2 may show an amount in box 8, "Allocated tips." This is an additional amount allocated to you if tips you reported to your employer were less than the minimum amount expected to be earned by employees where you work.

If you do not have adequate records of your actual tips, you must report at least the amount of allocated tips shown in box 8 on your Form W-2.

If you have adequate records, report your actual tips on your return. For more information on allocated tips, Refer to Publication 531, *Reporting Tip Income*.

Q. *What will happen if I do not report the tips I received?*

A. If you did not report tips to your employer as required, you may be charged a penalty in addition to the tax you owe. If you have reasonable cause for not reporting tips to your employer, you should attach a statement to your return explaining why you did not.

Q. *I am in the Reserve Officers' Training Corps (ROTC) participating in advance training. I do receive allowances from the Corps. Is the allowance taxable?*

A. Subsistence allowances paid to ROTC students participating in advanced training are not taxable. However, active duty pay, such as that received during summer advanced camp, is taxable.

Example
Jim Hunter is a member of the ROTC who is participating in the advanced course. He received a subsistence allowance of $100 each month for 10 months and $600 of active duty pay during summer advanced camp. He must include only the $600 active duty pay in his gross income.

Q. *I am a student and I do occasional paid babysitting job. I also do some part time time jobs here and there during the school year and also in the summer. Is the monies I make on this jobs taxable?*

A. Self-Employment Income: Earnings you received from self-employment are subject to income tax. These earnings include income from baby-sitting and lawn mowing. These earnings are not self-employment income if you provided these services as an employee.

You are taxed on your net earnings (income you received minus any business expenses you are allowed to deduct). For information on what expenses can be deducted, Refer to Publication 535, *Business Expenses.* As a self-employed person, you are responsible for keeping records to show how much income you received and how many expenses you had. Your income and expenses are reported on Schedule C or C-EZ (Form 1040). An example of a filled-in Schedule C-EZ appears at the end of this publication.

Q. *I only made $1000 working for myself, do I have to pay any other type of tax on the amount other than the income tax?*

A. Self-employment tax: If you had net earnings of $400 or more from self-employment, you also will have to pay self-employment tax. This tax pays for your benefits under the social security system. Social security and Medicare benefits are available to individuals who are self-employed the same as they are to wage earners who have social security tax and Medicare tax withheld from their wages. The self-employment tax is figured on Schedule SE (Form 1040).

For more information on self-employment tax, Refer to Publication 533, *Self-Employment Tax.*

Newspaper Carriers and Distributors
Special rules apply to services you perform as a newspaper carrier or distributor. You are a direct seller and treated as self-employed for federal tax purposes if you meet the following conditions.
1.   You are in the business of delivering/distributing newspapers or shopping news, including directly related services such as soliciting customers and collecting receipts.
2.   Substantially all your pay for these services directly relates to sales or other output rather than to the number of hours worked.
3.   You perform the delivery services under a written contract between you and the service recipient that states that you will not be treated as an employee for federal tax purposes.

Carriers and Vendors Under Age 18
Carriers or distributors (not including those who deliver or distribute to any point for subsequent delivery or distribution) and vendors (working under a buy-sell arrangement) under age 18 are not subject to self-employment tax.

If you were self-employed, you can deduct half of your self-employment tax and part of your health insurance premiums. Refer to the Form 1040 instructions for lines 27 and 28 for more information.

Q. *I have a few small investments here and there. What is taxable and what is not taxable?*

A. Investment Income
This section explains whether you have to report income from bank accounts and certain other investments. Various types of investment income are treated differently. Some of the more common ones are discussed here.

Interest
Interest you get from checking and savings accounts and most other sources is taxable.

Bank accounts
Some credit unions, building and loan associations, savings and loan associations, mutual savings banks, and cooperative banks call what they pay you on your deposits "dividends." However, for tax purposes, these payments are considered interest, and you should report them as interest.

Interest Statements: Your bank, savings and loan, or other payer of interest will send you a statement if you earned at least $10 in interest for the year. You should receive these statements sometime in January for the previous tax year. Banks may use Form 1099-INT, *Interest Income*. However, they may include your total interest on the statement they send you at the end of the year. Do not throw these statements away.

Dividends: Dividends are distributions of money, stock, or other property paid to you by a corporation. You may also get dividends through a partnership, an estate, a trust, or an association that is taxed as a corporation. Ordinary dividends, the most common type, are paid out of the corporation's earnings. You must report these as income on your tax return.

Dividend Statements: Regardless of whether you receive your dividends in cash or additional shares of stock, the payer of the dividends will send you a Form 1099-DIV, *Dividends and Distributions*, if you earned at least $10 in dividends for the year.

Other Investment Income: If you received income from investments not discussed here, Refer to Publication 550. Also, the payer of the income may be able to tell you whether the income is taxable or nontaxable.

Q. *I was giving some savings bond several years ago by relatives and family friends. I was planning to cash the bonds. Will I owe taxes on them?*

A. **U.S. Savings Bonds:** Interest on U.S. savings bonds is taxable for federal income tax purposes, but exempt from all state and local income taxes. The most common bonds are series EE and series I bonds. Series EE bonds are issued in several different denominations and cost one-half the amount shown on the face of the bond. For example, a $100 bond costs $50. The face value of the bond is paid only when the bond matures. The difference between what you paid for the bond and the amount you get when you cash it is taxable interest.

Series I bonds are inflation-indexed bonds issued at their face value. The face value plus accrued interest is payable to you at maturity.

You can report all interest on these bonds when you cash them, or you can choose to report their increase in value as interest each year. Publication 550, *Investment Income and Expenses*, explains how to make this choice.

Under certain circumstances, the interest on U.S. savings bonds (series EE and series I) issued after December 31, 1989, is exempt from tax if the bonds are used for educational purposes. Refer to Publication 550 for further information.

Other Interest from the U.S. Government: Interest on U.S. Treasury bills, notes, and bonds is taxable for federal income tax purposes. This interest is exempt from all state and local income taxes.

Tax-Exempt Bonds: Generally, interest from bonds issued by state and local governments is not taxable for federal income tax purposes.

Q. I am a student on scholarship. I also received some grants. Do I have to pay taxes on the monies I received?

A. **Taxable Scholarships and Fellowships:** If you received a scholarship or fellowship, all or part of it may be taxable, even if you did not receive a Form W-2. Generally, the entire amount is taxable if you are not a candidate for a degree.

If you are a candidate for a degree, you generally can exclude from income that part of the grant used for:
- **Tuition and fees** required for enrollment or attendance, or
- **Fees, books, supplies, and equipment** required for your courses.

You cannot exclude from income any part of the grant used for other purposes, such as room and board.

A **scholarship** generally is an amount paid for the benefit of a student at an educational institution to aid in the pursuit of studies. The student may be in either a graduate or an undergraduate program.

A **fellowship** grant generally is an amount paid for the benefit of an individual to aid in the pursuit of study or research.

Example 1
Tammy Graves receives a $6,000 fellowship grant that is not designated for any specific use. Tammy is a degree candidate. She spends $5,500 for tuition and $500 for her personal expenses. Tammy is required to include $500 in income.

Example 2
Ursula Harris, a degree candidate, receives a $2,000 scholarship, with $1,000 specifically designated for tuition and $1,000 specifically designated for living expenses. Her tuition is $1,600. She may exclude $1,000 from income, but the

other $1,000 designated for living expenses is taxable and must be included in income.

Payment for Services

All payments you receive for past, present, or future services must be included in income. This is true even if the services are a condition of receiving the grant or are required of all candidates for the degree.

Example

Gary Thomas receives a scholarship of $2,500 for the spring semester. As a condition of receiving the scholarship, he must serve as a part-time teaching assistant. Of the $2,500 scholarship, $1,000 represents payment for his services. Gary is a degree candidate, and his tuition is $1,600. He can exclude $1,500 from income as a qualified scholarship. The remaining $1,000, representing payment for his services, is taxable.

Fulbright Students and Researchers: A Fulbright grant is generally treated as any other scholarship or fellowship in figuring how much of the grant can be excluded. If you receive a Fulbright grant for lecturing or teaching, it is payment for services and subject to tax.

Pell Grants, Supplemental Educational Opportunity Grants, and Grants to States for State Student Incentives. These grants are nontaxable scholarships to the extent used for tuition and course-related expenses during the grant period.

Reduced Tuition

You may be entitled to reduced tuition because you or one of your parents is or was an employee of the school. If so, the amount of the reduction is not taxable so long as the tuition is for education below the graduate level. (But Refer to Graduate student exception, next.) The reduced tuition program must not favor any highly paid employee. The reduced tuition is taxable if it represents payment for your services.

Graduate Student Exception

Tax-free treatment of reduced tuition can also apply to a graduate student who performs teaching or research activities at an educational institution. The qualified tuition reduction must be for education furnished by that institution and not represent payment for services.

Contest prizes

Scholarship prizes won in a contest are not scholarships or fellowships if you do not have to use the prizes for your education. If you can use the prize for any purpose, the entire amount is taxable.

Q. *I received distributions from a Qualified State tuition Program. Do I have to pay tax on the amount?*

A. **Qualified State Tuition Program:** If you receive distributions from a qualified state tuition program, only the amount that is more than the amount contributed to the program is taxable. Part of the benefits may qualify as a nontaxable scholarship or fellowship (for example, matching-grant amounts paid under the program to a degree candidate). Other benefits are partly a nontaxable return of the contributions made to the program on your behalf (for example, by your parents). You must include in your income the part of the benefits that is neither a nontaxable scholarship or fellowship nor a return of contributions. For more information about qualified state tuition programs, Refer to Publication 525, *Taxable and Nontaxable Income*, but for more information on a specific program, contact the state or agency that established and maintains it.

Other Grants or Assistance
If you are not sure whether your grant qualifies as a scholarship or fellowship, ask the person who made the grant.

Additional information
Refer to Publication 970, Tax Benefits for Education, for more information on how much of your scholarship or fellowship is taxable.

Q. *How do I report the taxable amounts or portions of my scholarship or fellowship on the tax form?*

A. **How to Report:** If you file Form 1040EZ, include the taxable amount of your scholarship or fellowship on line 1. Print "SCH" and any taxable amount not reported on a W-2 form in the space to the right of the words "W-2 form(s)" on line 1.

If you file Form 1040A or Form 1040, include the taxable amount on line 7. Print "SCH" and any taxable amount not reported on a W-2 form in the space to the left of line 7 on Form 1040A or on the dotted line next to line 7 on Form 1040.

Other Income
If you are not sure whether to include any item of income on your return, Refer to Publication 525

Q. *I am a student doing occasional part time jobs. Looking through my pay check I found out that no taxes are being taken out. Does that mean that I would not have to pay income taxes on the amount received?*

A. No. Every U.S. citizen or resident must file a U.S. income tax return if certain income levels are reached. There is no exemption from tax for full-time students. Factors that determine whether you have an income tax filing requirement include:
- the amount of your income (earned and unearned),
- whether you are able to be claimed as a dependent,
- your filing status, and
- your age.

Chances are that your earnings from that employment is small or that you claimed a lot more withholdings such that your taxable income will result to no tax liability on you at the end of the tax year.

If your income is below the filing requirement for your age, filing status, and dependency status, you will not owe income tax on the income and will not have to file a tax return. You may choose to file if you have income tax withholding that you would like refunded to you.

You may have given your employer a Form W-4, *Employee's Withholding Allowance Certificate,* claiming exemption from withholding. To claim exemption from withholding, you generally would have to have had no tax liability the previous year and expect none in the current year. An exemption certificate is good for the calendar year.

For related topics Refer to Tax Information for Students.

References:
- Publication 17, Your Federal Income Tax
- Publication 505, Tax Withholding and Estimated Tax
- Form W-4, Employee's Withholding Allowance Certificate
- Tax Information for Students.

Chapter 20

Other Frequently Asked Questions
~~~~~

Keyword(s): Common Mistakes; Keyword(s): Preparing Tax return; Keyword(s): Taxpayers Right; Keyword(s): Taxpayer Dies; Keyword(s): Deceased Taxpayer; Keyword(s):Child is Kidnapped; Keyword(s): Free Help; Keyword(s): Large-print Forms and Instructions; Keyword(s): Extension; Keyword(s): Taxable income; Keyword(s): Nontaxable income; Keyword(s): Common Errors; Keyword(s): Last minute tips; Keyword(s): Last-minute; Keyword(s): Recordkeeping; Keyword(s): Sold my home; Keyword(s): Refinanced my home; Keyword(s): Deductible home office; Keyword(s): Deductible taxes; Keyword(s): Avoid problems

20. Other Frequently Asked Questions

Q. What are some of the Common Mistakes I should avoid in preparing my tax return?

A. Mistakes may delay your refund or result in notices being sent to you.

• Make sure you entered the correct name and social security number (SSN) for each dependent you claim on line 6c. Check that each dependent's name and SSN agrees with his or her social security card. Also, make sure you check the box in line 6c, column (4), for each dependent under age 17 who is also a qualifying child for the child tax credit.

• Check your math, especially for the child tax credit, earned income credit (EIC), taxable social security benefits, total income, itemized deductions or standard deduction, deduction for exemptions, taxable income, total tax, federal income tax withheld, and refund or amount you owe.

• Be sure you use the correct method to figure your tax.

• Be sure to enter your SSN in the space provided on page 1 of Form 1040. If you are married filing a joint or separate return, also enter your spouse's SSN. Be sure to enter your SSN in the space next to your name. Check that your name and SSN agree with your social security card.

• Make sure your name and address are correct on the peel-off label. If not, enter the correct information. If you did not get a peel-off label, enter your (and your spouse's) name in the same order as shown on your last return. Check that your name agrees with your social security card.

• If you are taking the standard deduction and you checked any box on line 38a or 38b or you (or your spouse if filing jointly) can be claimed as a dependent on someone else's 2005 return.

• If you received capital gain distributions but were not required to file Schedule D, make sure you checked the box on line 13.

• If you are taking the EIC, be sure you used the correct column of the EIC Table for your filing status and the number of children you have.

• Remember to sign and date Form 1040 and enter your occupation(s).

• Attach your Form(s) W-2 and other required forms and schedules. Put all forms and schedules in the proper order.

• If you owe tax and are paying by check or money order, be sure to include all the required information on your payment.

Q*. What Are My Rights as a Taxpayer?*

A. You have the right to be treated fairly, professionally, promptly, and courteously by IRS employees. The goal at the IRS is to protect your rights so that you will have the highest confidence in the integrity, efficiency, and fairness of the U.S. tax system. To ensure that you always receive such treatment, you should know about the many rights you have at each step of the tax process. For details, Refer to Pub. 1.

Q*. How Long Should I keep my Tax Returns?*

A. Keep a copy of your tax return, worksheets you used, and records of all items appearing on it (such as Forms W-2 and 1099) until the statute of limitations runs out for that return. Usually, this is 3 years from the date the return was due or filed, or 2 years from the date the tax was paid, whichever is later. You should keep some records longer. For example, keep property records (including those on your home) as long as they are needed to figure the basis of the original or replacement property. For more details, Refer to Pub. 552.

Q. *What happens if a Taxpayer dies?*

A. If a taxpayer died before filing a return for the tax year, the taxpayer's spouse or personal representative may have to file and sign a return for that taxpayer. A personal representative can be an executor, administrator, or anyone who is in charge of the deceased taxpayer's property. If the deceased taxpayer did not have to file a return but had tax withheld, a return must be filed to get a refund. The person "Deceased," who files the deceased return must enter taxpayer's name, and the date of death across the top of the return. If this information is not provided, it may delay the processing of the return.

Q. *Can one file a tax return if one spouse dies during the tax year?*

A. If your spouse died, for example, in 2005 and you did not remarry in 2005, or if your spouse died, for example in 2006 before filing a return for 2005, you can file a joint return. A joint return should show your spouse's 2005 income before death and your income for all of 2005. Enter " Filing as surviving spouse" in the area where you sign the return. If someone else is the personal representative, he or she must also sign.

The surviving spouse or personal representative should promptly notify all payers of income, including financial institutions, of the taxpayer's death. This will ensure the proper reporting of income earned by the taxpayer's estate or heirs. Note: A deceased taxpayer's social security number should not be used for tax years after the year of death, except for estate tax return purposes.

Q. *Can someone else Claim a Refund for a Deceased Taxpayer*

A. If you are filing a joint return as a surviving spouse, you only need to file the tax return to claim the refund. If you are a court-appointed representative, file the return and attach a copy of the certificate that shows your appointment. All other filers requesting the deceased taxpayer's refund must file the return and attach Form 1310. For more details, use TeleTax topic 356 or Refer to Pub. 559.

Q. *If my child is Kidnapped can I still take that child into account when filing my tax?*

A. The parent of a child who is presumed by law enforcement authorities to have been kidnapped by someone who is not a family member may be able to take the child into account in determining his or her eligibility for the head of household or qualifying widow(er) filing status, deduction for dependents, child tax credit, and the earned income credit (EIC). For details, use TeleTax topic 357 or Refer to Pub. 501 (Pub. 596 for the EIC).

Q. *Can I send a written tax question to the IRS?*

A. Yes you can send Your Written Tax Questions to the IRS. You should get an answer in about 30 days. If you do not have the mailing address, call the IRS.

Q. *Where can I get some free help with my tax return?*

A. Free help in preparing your return is available nationwide from IRS-sponsored volunteers. The Volunteer Income Tax Assistance (VITA) program is designed to help low-income taxpayers and the Tax Counseling for the Elderly (TCE) program is designed to assist taxpayers age 60 or older with their tax returns. Many VITA sites offer free electronic filing and all volunteers will let you know about the credits and deductions you may be entitled to claim. If you are a member of the military, you can also get assistance on military tax benefits, such as combat zone tax benefits, at an office within your installation. For more information on these programs, go to www.irs.gov and enter keyword "VITA" in the upper right corner. Or, call the IRS. To find the nearest AARP Tax-Aide site, visit AARP's web-site at www.aarp.org/taxaide or call 1-888-227-7669.

When you go for help, take your photo ID and social security numbers (or individual taxpayer identification numbers) for your spouse, your dependents, and yourself. Also take a copy of your 2004 tax return (if available), all your Forms W-2 and 1099 for 2005, and any other information about your 2005 income and expenses.

Q. *Where can I get a face-to-face help in solving my tax problems?*

A. You can get face-to-face help solving tax problems every business day in IRS Taxpayer Assistance Centers. An employee can explain IRS letters, request adjustments to your account, or help you set up a payment plan. Call your local Taxpayer Assistance Center for an appointment. To find the number, go to www.irs.gov/localcontacts or look in the phone book under "United States Government, Internal Revenue Service."

Q. *How or Where can I find Large-Print Forms and Instructions?*

A. Pub. 1614 has large-print copies of Form 1040, Schedules A, B, D, E, and R, and Form 1040-V, and their instructions. You can use the large-print forms and schedules as worksheets to figure your tax, but you cannot file them. You can get Pub. 1614 by phone or mail.

Q. *Are there any Help for People With Disabilities?*

A. Telephone help is available using TTY/ TDD equipment by calling 1-800-829-4059. Braille materials are available at libraries that have special services for people with disabilities.

Q. *What Can I do if I Can't Pay My Taxes?*

A. If this year's tax filing deadline will be a "pay" day for you and you cannot pay the full amount you owe, you should still file your return by the due date and pay as much as you can. You can charge your taxes on your American Express, MasterCard, Visa or Discover cards. To pay by credit card, contact one of the service providers at its telephone number or Web site listed below and follow the instructions. The service providers charge a convenience fee based on the amount you are paying. Do not add the convenience fee to your tax payment.

- **Official Payments Corporation**
  1-800-2PAY-TAX (1-800-272-9829)
  www.officialpayments.com·

- **Link2Gov Corporation**
  1-888-PAY-1040 (1-888-729-1040)
  www.pay1040.com

If this option is not a good one, you may be able to pay any remaining balance over time in monthly installments through an installment agreement. If you can not fully pay your taxes, you can apply to pay less than the full amount owed through the Offer in Compromise program. To apply for an installment payment plan, attach Form 9465, *Installment Agreement Request,* to the front of your tax return. The IRS has streamlined the approval process if your total taxes (not counting interest, penalties or other additions) do not exceed $25,000 and can be paid off in five years or less. Be sure to show the amount of your proposed monthly payment and the date you wish to make your payment each month. The IRS charges a $43 fee for setting up an installment agreement. You will also be charged interest plus a late payment penalty on the unpaid taxes. The late payment penalty is usually one-half of one percent per month or part of a month of your unpaid tax. The penalty rate is reduced to one-quarter of one percent for any month an Installment Agreement is in effect if you filed your return by the due date (including extensions). The maximum failure to pay penalty is 25 percent of the tax paid late. If you do not file your return by the due date (including extensions), you may have to pay a penalty for filing late. The penalty for failing to file and pay timely is usually five percent of the unpaid tax for each month or part of a month that your return is late. The maximum penalty for failure to file and pay on time is 25 percent of your unpaid tax. For more information about filing and paying your taxes, refer to the Form 1040 Instructions or IRS Publication 17, *Your Federal Income Tax*. You can download forms and publications from this Web site or request a free copy by calling toll free 1-800-TAX-FORM (1-800-829-3676). Taxpayers who need Form 9465 or any other federal tax form or publication should act soon to be sure they have the item in time to meet the April deadline.

References:
- www.officialpayments.com· www.pay1040.com
- Form 9465, Installment Agreement Request   Installment   payment process
- Publication 17, Your Federal Income Tax

Q. I Haven't Filed Last Year's Tax Return? What Should I Do?

A. The IRS hears many reasons from taxpayers for not filing a tax return. You may not have known whether you were required to file. Whatever the reason, it's best to file your return as soon as you can. If you need help, even with a late return, the IRS is ready to assist you.

The failure to file a return can be costly — whether you end up owing more or missing out on a refund. If you owe taxes, a delay in filing may result in a "failure to file" penalty and interest charges. The longer you delay, the larger these charges grow.

There is no penalty for failure to file if you are due a refund. However, you cannot get a refund without filing a tax return. But if you wait too long to file, you may risk losing the refund altogether. The deadline for claiming refunds is three years after the return due date.

Individuals who are entitled to the Earned Income Tax Credit must file their return to claim the credit even if they are not otherwise required to file.

Whether or not you must file a tax return will depend upon a number of factors, including your filing status, age and gross income. Some taxpayers are required to file whether or not they owe money. Even if you do not meet any of the requirements, you should file a return if you are due a refund.

For more information on how to file a tax return for a prior year, call the IRS toll-free Tax Help Line for Individuals at 1-800-829-1040 or visit your local IRS office.

Q. *What are some of the Common Errors I should avoid when preparing my Tax Return?*

A. The IRS recommends reviewing your entire tax return to be sure it is accurate and complete. Even a simple mistake can cause problems which might lead to delays in processing your return and receiving your refund. Want to avoid frequent trouble spots?

Check these areas which can reduce problems:
- Use the peel-off label. You may line through and make necessary corrections right on the label. Be sure to fill in your Social Security number in the box provided on the return. It is not on the label.
- If you do not have a peel-off label, fill in all requested information clearly, including the Social Security numbers.
- Check only one filing status on the tax return and check the appropriate exemption boxes. Make sure the writing is legible. Enter the correct Social Security number for each exemption. Incorrect or missing numbers will delay tax return processing.
- Use the correct Tax Table column for your filing status.
- Double check all figures on the return. Math errors are common mistakes.
- Make sure that the financial institution routing and account numbers you have entered for a direct deposit of your refund are accurate. Incorrect numbers can cause a delayed or misdirected refund.
- Sign and date the return. If filing a joint return, both spouses must sign and date the return.
- Attach all Forms W-2, *Wage and Tax Statement*, and other forms that reflect tax withheld to the front of the return. If you are also filing a Form 9465, *Installment Agreement Request*, attach that to the front of the tax return. Attach all other necessary forms and schedules in the attachment sequence order listed in the upper right corner of each form or schedule.
- Do you owe tax? If so, enclose a check or money order made payable to the "United States Treasury" and Form 1040-V, *Payment Voucher*, with the return. Or, you may choose to pay by credit card by contacting one of the credit card service providers. If you file electronically, you may authorize the U.S. Treasury to withdraw the payment directly from your bank account.

For a complete checklist and a listing of some of the most common errors, see Tax Topic 303, *Checklist of Common Errors When Preparing Your Tax Return,* or call the toll-free TeleTax number, 1-800-829-4477.

References:
* Form 9465, Installment Agreement Request
* Form 1040-V, Payment Voucher
* Tax Topic 303 — Checklist of Common Errors When Preparing Your Tax Return Subscribe

Q. The tax filing deadline is close at hand and I am almost set to file my tax return. Are there any last minute tips for me?

A. With the tax filing deadline close at hand, the IRS offers some tips for those still working on their paper tax forms:
* Put all required Social Security numbers on the return (they're not on the label)
* Double-check your figures
* Sign your form
* Attach all required schedules
* Send your return or request a filing extension by April 15.

The numbers to check most carefully on the tax return are the identification numbers — usually Social Security numbers — for each person listed. This includes the taxpayer, spouse, dependents and persons listed in relation to claims for the Child Care or Earned Income Tax Credits.

Missing, incorrect or illegible SSNs can delay or reduce a tax refund. Taxpayers should also check that they have correctly figured the refund or balance due and have used the right figure from the tax table. Taxpayers must sign and date their returns. Both spouses must sign a joint return, even if only one had income. Anyone who is paid to prepare a return must also sign it. The only attachments that should be at the front of the tax return are:
* Form W-2, Wage and Tax Statement,
* Form W-2G, Certain Gambling Winnings,
* Form 1099-R, Distributions from Pensions, Annuities, Retirement or Profit-Sharing Plans, IRAs, Insurance Contracts, Etc.,
* Form 2439, Notice to Shareholder of Undistributed Long-Term Capital Gains, or

- Form 9465, Installment Agreement Request. All other required forms and schedules should be behind the Form 1040 or 1040A, in the attachment sequence order listed in the upper right of each page.

Individuals expecting a refund should consider direct deposit of the refund to their bank account. Choosing direct deposit is the best way to guard against a misplaced or stolen refund. A few words of caution — some financial institutions do not allow a joint refund to be deposited into an individual account. Check with your bank or other financial institution to make sure your direct deposit will be accepted. Also make sure you enter the correct nine-digit routing number for your financial institution and your correct account number when selecting direct deposit. Wrong numbers can cause your refund to be misdirected or delayed. Persons sending a payment should make the check out to "*United States Treasury*" and enclose it with the tax return. The check should not be attached to the tax return or the Form 1040-V *payment voucher*, if used. The check should include the taxpayer's Social Security number, daytime phone number, the tax year and the type of form filed.

Those who don't e-file may use the U.S. Postal Service or one of the designated private delivery services to send their forms to the IRS by the deadline. The tax form instructions list these private delivery services, which are offered by three companies: DHL Express (DHL), Federal Express (FedEx) and United Parcel Service (UPS). By April 15, taxpayers should either file a return or request a four-month extension of time to file, which will give them until August 15. The extension of time to file is not an extension of time to pay. The extension may be requested by calling toll free 1-888-796-1074, by e-filing a Form 4868, *Application for Automatic Extension of Time to File U.S. Individual Income Tax Return,* that is included in most tax preparation software, or by sending a paper Form 4868 to the IRS.

Taxpayers are not required to make a payment to get the extension. Taxpayers who request an extension by phone or computer and who wish to make a tax payment will need the adjusted gross income from their 2005 return. Taxpayers who choose to charge an extension-related payment to a credit card through one of the two processors do not have to file Form 4868 to get an extension. Official Payments Corporation may be reached at 1-800-2PAY-TAX (1-800-272-9829), or at www.officialpayments.com. Link2Gov Corporation may be reached at 1-888-PAY-1040 (1-888-729-1040) or at www.pay1040.com. There is no IRS fee for credit card payments, but the processors charge a convenience fee. Download forms and publications, link to private sector e-file partners, and get helpful information on a variety of tax subjects on this Web site. The toll-free IRS customer assistance help number for individuals, 1-800-829-1040, is available from 7 a.m. to 10 p.m. weekdays and from 10 a.m. to 3 p.m. on Saturdays through April 9. All times are local, except for Alaska and Hawaii, which are on Pacific Time.

References:
- Form 9465, Installment Agreement Request
- Form 1040-V, Payment Voucher
- Form 4868, Application for Automatic Extension of Time to File U.S. Individual Income Tax Return

Q. Do You Have a Deductible Home Office?

A. Whether you are self-employed or an employee, if you use a portion of your home exclusively and regularly for business purposes, you may be able to take a home office deduction. You can deduct certain expenses if your home office is the principal place where your trade or business is conducted or where you meet and deal with clients or patients in the course of your business.

If you use a separate structure not attached to your home for an exclusive and regular part of your business, you can deduct expenses related to it. Your home office will qualify as your principal place of business if you use it exclusively and regularly for the administrative or management activities associated with your trade or business. There must be no other fixed place where you conduct substantial administrative or management activities.

If you use both your home and other locations regularly in your business, you must determine which location is your principle place of business, based on the relative importance of the activities performed at each location. If the relative importance factor doesn't determine your principle place of business, you can also consider the time spent at each location.

If you are an employee, you have additional requirements to meet. You cannot take the home office deduction unless the business use of your home is for the convenience of your employer. Also, you cannot take deductions for space you are renting to your employer.

Generally, the amount you can deduct depends on the percentage of your home used for business. Your deduction will be limited if your gross income from your business is less than your total business expenses.

Expenses that you can deduct for business use of the home may include the business portion of real estate taxes, mortgage interest, rent, utilities, insurance, depreciation, painting and repairs. However, you may not deduct expenses for lawn care or those related to rooms not used for business.

There are special rules for qualified daycare providers and for persons storing business inventory or product samples.

For more information, see IRS Publication 587, *Business Use of Your Home.*

If you are self-employed, use Form 8829, *Expenses for Business Use of Your Home,* to figure your home office deduction and report those deductions on line 30 of Schedule C, Form 1040. Employees can use the worksheet in Pub. 587 to figure their allowable expenses and claim them as a miscellaneous itemized deduction on Schedule A, Form 1040.

To be on the safe side, you may also want to review IRS Publication 4035, *Home-Based Business Tax Avoidance Schemes,* which describes schemes that claim to offer tax relief but which actually result in illegal tax avoidance. IRS publications and forms are available on this Web site or by calling the IRS at 1-800-TAX-FORM (1-800-829-3676).

References:
- Publication 587, Business Use of Your Home
- Form 8829, Expenses for Business Use of Your Home
- Form 8829 Instructions
- Schedule C, Profit or Loss from Business
- Schedules A&B, Itemized Deductions and Interest & Dividend Income
- Publication 4035, Home-Based Business Tax Avoidance Schemes

Q. Are there some ways I can avoid problems during tax return filing time?

A. Looking for ways to avoid the last-minute rush for doing your taxes? The IRS offers these tips:
1. **Don't Procrastinate.** Resist the temptation to put off your taxes until the last minute. Your haste to meet the filing deadline may cause you to overlook potential sources of tax savings and will likely increase your risk of making an error.

2. **Organize Your Tax Records.** Tax preparation time can be significantly reduced if you develop a system for organizing your records and receipts. Start with the income, deduction or tax credit items that were on last year's return.

3. **Visit the IRS Online.** Millions of taxpayers visited the IRS Web site in calendar year 2004, downloading nearly 600 million forms, publications and a variety of topic-oriented tax information. Anyone with Internet

215

access can find tax law information and answers to frequently asked tax questions.

4. **Take Advantage of Free Assistance.** The IRS offers recorded messages on about 150 tax topics through its toll-free TeleTax service at 1-800-829-4477. It also offers federal tax forms and publications at 1-800-TAX-FORM (1-800-829-3676). Some libraries, post offices, banks, grocery stores, copy centers and office supply stores carry the most widely requested forms and instructions. Libraries may also have reference sets of IRS publications. The IRS also staffs a tax Help Line for Individuals at 1-800-829-1040. Help for small businesses, corporations, partnerships and trusts which need information or assistance preparing business returns is available at the Business and Specialty Tax Line at 1-800-829-4933. Both lines are staffed from 7 a.m. to 10 p.m. weekdays. In addition, the Help Line for Individuals is available from 10 a.m. to 3 p.m. on Saturdays though April 9. All times are local, except in Alaska and Hawaii, which should use Pacific Time. Hearing-impaired individuals with access to TTY/TDD equipment may call 1-800-829-4059 to ask questions or to order forms and publications.

5. **Use IRS Taxpayer Assistance Centers and Volunteer Programs.** Free tax help is available at IRS offices nationwide. Also, check your newspaper or local IRS office to find locations for Volunteer Income Tax Assistance or Tax Counseling for the Elderly sites. To obtain the location, dates, and hours of the VITA or TCE volunteer site closest to you, call the IRS toll-free Tax Help Line for Individuals at 1-800-829-1040. Check this Web site to find the local IRS office nearest you.

6. **File Your Return Electronically.** About 61 million taxpayers filed their returns electronically in 2004. Aside from ease of filing, IRS e-file is the fastest and most accurate way to file a tax return. If you're due a refund, the waiting time for e-filers is half that of paper filers. The IRS and the Free File Alliance, LLC, a private-sector consortium of tax software companies, have formed a partnership to help qualified taxpayers electronically prepare and file their federal tax returns for free.

7. **Double-Check Your Math and Data Entries.** Review your return for possible math errors and make sure you have provided the names and correct (and legibly written) Social Security or other identification numbers for yourself, your spouse and your dependents.

8. **Have Your Refund Deposited Directly to Your Bank Account.** Another way to speed up your refund and reduce the chance of theft is to

have the amount deposited directly to your bank account. Check the tax instructions for details on entering the routing and account numbers on your tax return. Make sure the numbers you enter are correct. Wrong numbers can cause your refund to be misdirected or delayed.

9. **Don't Panic if You Can't Pay.** If you can't immediately pay the taxes you owe, consider some stress-reducing alternatives. You can apply for an IRS installment agreement, suggesting your own monthly payment amount and due date, and getting a reduced late payment penalty rate. You also have various options for charging your balance on a credit card, either as part of an electronic return or directly through a processing agent, either by phone or online. Official Payments Corporation may be reached at 1-800-2PAY-TAX (1-800-272-9829), or online. The Link2Gov Corporation may be reached at 1-888-PAY-1040 (1-888-729-1040) and is also available online. There is no IRS fee for credit card payments, but the processing companies charge a convenience fee. Electronic filers with a balance due can file early and authorize the government's financial agent to take the money directly from their checking or savings account on the April 15 due date, with no fee. Note that if you file your tax return or a request for a filing extension on time, even if you can't pay, you avoid potential late filing penalties.

10. **Request an Extension of Time to File — But Pay on Time.** If the clock runs out, you can get an automatic four-month extension of time to file, to Aug. 15. An extension of time to file does not give you an extension of time to pay, however. You can call 1-888-796-1074, e-file a Form 4868, Application for Automatic Extension of Time to File, that is included in most tax preparation software, or send a paper Form 4868 to the IRS to request the extension. You will need the adjusted gross income and total tax amounts from your 2003 return if you request the extension by computer or phone. You may also get an extension by charging your expected balance on a credit card, and then you won't have to file the form. Contact Official Payments Corporation or Link2Gov Corporation. There is no IRS fee for credit card payments, but the processors charge a convenience fee. Note that the extension itself does not give you more time to pay any taxes due. You will owe interest on any amount not paid by the April deadline, plus a late payment penalty if you have not paid at least 90 percent of your total tax by that date.

Taxpayers needing Form 4868 or any other federal tax form should act soon to be sure they have the item in time to meet the April deadline. Forms are available on this Web site or by calling toll-free 1-800-TAX-FORM (1-800-829-3676).

References:
* Form 4868, Application for Automatic Extension of Time to File U.S. Individual Income Tax Return

Q. What is the difference between taxable and nontaxable income?

A. Generally, most income you receive is taxable, according to the IRS. But there are some areas where certain types of income are partially taxed or not taxed at all. A complete list is available in IRS Publication 525, *Taxable and Nontaxable Income.* Some common examples of items not included in your income are:
* Reimbursement for qualifying adoption expenses
* Child support payments
* Gifts, bequests and inheritances
* Workers' compensation benefits
* Meals and lodging for the convenience of your employer
* Compensatory damages awarded for physical injury or physical sickness· Welfare benefits
* Cash rebates from a dealer or manufacturer.

If you surrender a life insurance policy for cash, you must include in income any proceeds that are more than the cost of the life insurance policy. Life insurance proceeds paid to you because of the death of the insured person are not taxable unless the policy was turned over to you for a price.

Another example of income that you may or may not exclude is a scholarship or fellowship grant. If you are a candidate for a degree, you can exclude amounts you receive as a qualified scholarship or fellowship. Amounts used for room and board do not qualify. These examples are not all-inclusive.

For more information, view or download Publication 525, *Taxable and Nontaxable Income* or call toll free 1-800-TAX-FORM (1-800-829-3676).

References:
* Publication 525, Taxable and Nontaxable Income

Q. I recently sold my home. Are there any tax benefits or obligations I should know about?

A. If you sold your main home, you may be able to exclude up to $250,000 of gain ($500,000 for married taxpayers filing jointly) from your federal tax return. This exclusion is allowed each time that you sell your main home, but generally no more frequently than once every two years.

To be eligible for this exclusion, your home must have been owned by you and used as your main home for a period of at least two out of the five years prior to its sale. You also must not have excluded gain on another home sold during the two years before the current sale.

If you and your spouse file a joint return for the year of the sale, you can exclude the gain if either of you qualify for the exclusion. But both of you would have to meet the use test to claim the $500,000 maximum amount. To exclude gain, a taxpayer must both own and use the home as a principal residence for two of the five years before the sale. The two years may consist of 24 full months or 730 days. Short absences, such as for a summer vacation, count as periods of use. Longer breaks, such as a one-year sabbatical, do not.

If you do not meet the ownership and use tests, you may be allowed to exclude a reduced maximum amount of the gain realized on the sale of your home if you sold your home due to health, a change in place of employment, or certain unforeseen circumstances. Unforeseen circumstances include, for example, divorce or legal separation, natural or man-made disaster resulting in a casualty to your home, or an involuntary conversion of your home.

If you can exclude all the gain from the sale of your home, you do not report any of that gain on your federal tax return. If you cannot exclude all the gain from the sale of your home, use Schedule D, *Capital Gains or Losses,* of the Form 1040 to report it.

For more details and information, download a copy of Publication 523, *Selling Your Home,* or order it by calling toll free 1-800-TAX-FORM (1-800-829-3676).

References:
- Publication 523, Selling Your Home
- Schedule D, Capital Gains and Losses
- Tax Topic 701 — Sale of Your Home
- Publication 3, Armed Forces Tax Guide

Q. *I recently refinanced my home. Are there any tax benefits or obligations I should know about?*

A. Taxpayers who refinanced their homes may be eligible to deduct some costs associated with their loans.

Generally, for taxpayers who itemize, the "points" paid to obtain a home mortgage may be deductible as mortgage interest. Points paid to obtain an original home mortgage can be, depending on circumstances, fully deductible in the year paid. However, points paid solely to refinance a home mortgage usually must be deducted over the life of the loan.

For a refinanced mortgage, the interest deduction for points is determined by dividing the points paid by the number of payments to be made over the life of the loan. This information is usually available from lenders.

Taxpayers may deduct points only for those payments made in the tax year. For example, a homeowner who paid $2,000 in points and who would make 360 payments on a 30-year mortgage could deduct $5.56 per monthly payment, or a total of $66.72 if he or she made 12 payments in one year.

However, if part of the refinanced mortgage money was used to finance improvements to the home and if the taxpayer meets certain other requirements, the points associated with the home improvements may be fully deductible in the year the points were paid. Also, if a homeowner is refinancing a mortgage for a second time, the balance of points paid for the first refinanced mortgage may be fully deductible at pay off.

Other closing costs — such as appraisal fees and other non-interest fees — generally are not deductible. Additionally, the amount of Adjusted Gross Income can affect the amount of deductions that can be taken.

For more information on deductions related to refinancing, look up Frequently Asked Questions (keyword: refinancing fees) or Tax Topics 504, *Home Mortgage Points, and 505, Interest Expenses.* Other tax information on residential real estate can be found in IRS Publications 936, *Home Mortgage Interest Deduction*; 523, *Selling Your Home;* 527, *Residential Rental Property*; and 530, *Tax Information for First-Time Homeowners.* All publications are available on this Web site or by calling toll free 1-800-TAX FORM (1-800-829-3676).

References:
*   Publication 936, Home Mortgage Interest Deduction

- Publication 523, Selling Your Home
- Publication 527, Residential Rental Property
- Publication 530, Tax Information for First-Time Homeowners
- Tax Topic 504 — Home Mortgage Points
- Tax Topic 505 — Interest Expenses

Q. *How importance is Recordkeeping? Must I keep them?*

A. You can avoid headaches at tax time by keeping track of your receipts and other records throughout the year, the IRS advises. Good recordkeeping will help you remember the various transactions you made during the year, which may help you out on your taxes.

Records help you document the deductions you've claimed on your return. You'll need this documentation should the IRS select your return for examination. Normally, tax records should be kept for three years, but some documents — records relating to a home purchase or sale, stock transactions, IRA and business or rental property — should be kept longer.

In most cases, the IRS does not require you to keep records in any special manner. Generally speaking, however, you should keep any and all documents that may have an impact on your federal tax return. Such items would include bills, credit card and other receipts, invoices, mileage logs, canceled, imaged or substitute checks or any other proof of payment, and any other records to support any deductions or credits you claim on your return.

Good recordkeeping throughout the year saves you time and effort at tax time when organizing and completing your return. If you hire a paid professional to complete your return, the records you have kept will assist the preparer in quickly and accurately completing your return.

For more information on what kinds of records to keep, see IRS Publication 552, *Recordkeeping for Individuals,* and Publication 17, *Your Federal Income Tax for Individuals.* You can download these publications or order them by calling toll-free 1-800-TAX-FORM (1-800-829-3676).

References:
- Publication 552, Recordkeeping for Individuals

Chapter 21

About the IRS (History, Mission, Structure)
~~~~~

Keyword(s): IRS Mission; Keyword(s): Statutory Authority; Keyword(s): History & Culture

21.1 IRS Mission

Q. What is the Mission of the Internal Revenue Service (IRS)?

A. The IRS Mission is to provide America's taxpayers top quality service by helping them understand and meet their tax responsibilities and by applying the tax law with integrity and fairness to all.

This mission statement describes our role and the public's expectation about how we should perform that role.
*   In the United States, the Congress passes tax laws and requires taxpayers to comply.
*   The taxpayer's role is to understand and meet his or her tax obligations.
*   The IRS role is to help the large majority of compliant taxpayers with the tax law, while ensuring that the minority who are unwilling to comply pay their fair share.

21.2 IRS – The Agency

Q. What really is the Internal Revenue Service (IRS)?

A. **The Agency:** The IRS is a bureau of the Department of the Treasury and one of the world's most efficient tax administrators. In 2004, the IRS collected more than $2 trillion in revenue and processed more than 224 million tax returns.
*   The IRS spent just 48 cents for each $100 it collected in 2004.

(Source: Table 31, IRS Data Book: 2004.)

21.3 Statutory Authority of the IRS

Q. What is the statutory authority of the IRS to do what it does?

A. **Statutory Authority:** The IRS is organized to carry out the responsibilities of the secretary of the Treasury under section 7801 of the Internal Revenue Code. The secretary has full authority to administer and enforce the internal revenue laws and has the power to create an agency to enforce these laws. The IRS was created based on this legislative grant.

Section 7803 of the Internal Revenue Code provides for the appointment of a commissioner of Internal Revenue to administer and supervise the execution and application of the internal revenue laws.

21.4 IRS History and Structure

Q. *When was the IRS created and how is it structured?*

A. The agency has a long history. Its roots go back to the Civil War when President Lincoln and Congress, in 1862, created the Commissioner of Internal Revenue and enacted an income tax to pay war expenses. The income tax was repealed 10 years later. Congress revived the income tax in 1894, but the Supreme Court ruled it unconstitutional the following year.

In 1913, the states ratified the 16th Amendment, which gave Congress the authority to enact an income tax. That same year, the first Form 1040 appeared after Congress levied a 1% tax on net personal incomes above $3,000 with a 6% surtax on incomes of more than $500,000. As the nation sought greater revenue to finance the World War I effort, the top rate of the income tax rose to 77% in 1918. It dropped sharply in the post-war years, down to 24% in 1929, and rose again during the Depression. During World War II, Congress introduced payroll withholding and quarterly tax payments.

In the 1950s, the agency was reorganized to replace the patronage system with career, professional employees. Now, only the IRS Commissioner and Chief Counsel are selected by the President and confirmed by the Senate. The Bureau of Internal Revenue name also was changed to the Internal Revenue Service to emphasize service to taxpayers.

The IRS Restructuring and Reform Act of 1998 prompted the most comprehensive reorganization and modernization of IRS in nearly half a century. The law resulted in the IRS reorganizing itself into four major operating divisions, aligned by types of taxpayers:

- The Wage and Investment Division, serving approximately 116 million taxpayers who file individual and joint tax returns.

223

- The Small Business/Self-Employed Division, serving approximately 45 million small businesses and self-employed taxpayers.

- The Large and Mid-Size Business Division, serving corporations with assets of more than $10 million.

- The Tax-Exempt and Government Entities Division, serving employee benefit plans, tax-exempt organizations, such as charities and social welfare groups, and governmental entities.
  Other divisions include Appeals, Communications and Liaison and Criminal Investigation. The Office of Chief Counsel provides legal services to the agency.

The 1998 law also greatly expanded taxpayers' rights and established a Taxpayer Advocate Service as an independent voice inside the agency on behalf of the taxpayer. The Taxpayer Advocate Service seeks to assist with problems that have not been resolved through normal channels. Each state also has a local taxpayer advocate who reports directly to the National Taxpayer Advocate.

APPENDIX A
Useful Addresses and Telephone Numbers

HELP Telephone Numbers and Web Addresses to Use When You Have Questions:

<u>Internal revenue Service</u>

Business and Specialty Tax Line
800-829-4933

Electronic Federal Tax Payment System
(EFTPS) Hotline
800-555-4477

Employee Plans Taxpayer Assistance Telephone Service
877-829-5500 (toll free)

Employer Identification Number (EIN) Requests
800-829-4933
Monday - Friday, 7:00 a.m.
to 10:00 p.m., local time or
http://www.irs.gov, key word
(upper right) "EIN."

Form 941 and Form 940 Filing On-Line Filling Program /Austin Submission Center
New Toll Free Number for e-Help
866-255-0654
Supports IRS e-file,TeleFile and future e-Services customers. Go to
http://www.irs.gov/efile/
article/0,,id=118520,00.html for specifics.

Forms (IRS)
Order at 800-829-3676.

General IRS Tax Law Questions and Account Information
800-829-1040

Information Reporting Program Customer Service Section
866-455-7438 (toll free)
304-263-8700 (non-toll free)
Monday - Friday, 8:30 a.m. to 4:30 p.m., ET.

Telecommunications Devices for the Deaf (TDD) may be reached non-toll free at 304-267-3367.
Taxpayers can contact this unit via e-mail at mccirp@irs.gov.

Information Reporting Program Web Page
http://www.irs.gov/smallbiz

IRS Tax Fax
703-368-9694 (non-toll free) This service offers faxed topical tax information.

Keywords on IRS.gov

IRS.gov is now using keywords as another way to help makes your visit less taxing!
Look for the IRS keywords in its public service, outreach, and other materials for
taxpayers and tax professionals. For a current list and more information about IRS
keywords, check
out http://www. irs.gov/help/   article/0,,id=108258,00.html.

National Taxpayer Advocate's Help Line
877-777-4778 (toll free)

Retirement Plans Web Page
http://www.irs.gov/ep?

Social Security Tax Questions
Social Security Tax questions should be referred to the IRS at 800-829-1040.

Taxpayer Advocacy Panel
888-912-1227 (toll-free)

Telephone Device for the Deaf (TDD)
800-829-4059

Tele-Tax System
800-829-4477

Child Support Web Site for Employers
http://www.acf.hhs.gov/programs/cse/newhire/employer/home.htm

Social Security Administration

Copy A / Form W-2 Reporting
Questions about wage reporting (submitting Copy A of Form W-2 to SSA) should be
referred to the SSA's Employer Reporting Service at 800-772-6270 or e-mailed to

employerinfo@ssa.gov.

General SSA Benefit Questions
General Social Security benefit questions should be referred to SSA's Tele Service Center at 800-772-1213.

APPENDIX B
Tax Publications and Descriptions

IRS Publication, Your Rights as a Taxpayer, and 1SP, Derechos del Contribuyente, highlight some of the most important rights. You can download these publications from the IRS website at *www.irs.gov* or order the paper document from the IRS by calling (800)-829-3676.

Publication 553, Highlights of … Tax Changes, is a collection of the latest tax law changes that can affect your tax situation. You can download Publication 553 and nearly 100 other tax publications listed in this booklet from the IRS website at *www.irs.gov*. You can request a free copy of any IRS tax publication by calling the IRS at (800)-829-3676.

Pub 1, Your Rights as a Taxpayer — explains some of your most important rights as a taxpayer. It also explains the examination, appeal, collection, and refund processes. To ensure that you always receive fair treatment in tax matters, you should know what your rights are.

Pub 1SP, Derechos del Contribuyente (Your Rights as a Taxpayer) — Publication 1 in Spanish.

Pub 3, Armed Forces' Tax Guide — gives information about the special tax situations of active members of the Armed Forces. This publication contains information on items that are included in and excluded from gross income, combat zone exclusion, alien status, dependency exemptions, sale of residence, itemized deductions, tax liability, extension of deadline, and filing returns. Forms 1040, 1040A, 1040EZ, 1040NR, 1040X, 1310, 2106, 2688, 2848, 3903, 4868, 8822, 9465, W-2.

Pub 15, Circular E, Employer's Tax Guide —Forms 940, 941.

Pub 15-A, Employer's Supplemental Tax Guide

Pub 15-B, Employer's Tax Guide to Fringe Benefits

Pub 17, Your Federal Income Tax (For Individuals) — can help you prepare your individual tax return. This publication takes you step-by-step through each part of the return. It explains the tax law in a way that will help you better understand your taxes so that you pay only as much as you owe and no more. This publication also includes information on various kinds of credits you may be able to take to reduce your tax. (Note to Tax Professionals only: There is a fee to order this publication.) Forms 1040 (Schedules A, B, D, E, EIC, R), 1040A, 1040EZ, 2106, 2119, 2441, 3903, W-2.

Pub 51, Circular A, Agricultural Employer's Tax Guide — Form 943.

Pub 54, Tax Guide for U.S. Citizens and Resident Aliens Abroad — explains the special tax rules for U.S. citizens and resident aliens who live and work abroad or who have income earned in foreign countries. In particular, this publication explains the rules for excluding income and excluding or deducting certain housing costs.
Forms 1040, 1116, 2555, 2555-EZ.

Pub 80, Circular SS, Federal Tax Guide for Employers in the Virgin Islands, Guam, American Samoa, and the Commonwealth of the Northern Mariana Islands — Forms 940, 941SS, 943.

Pub 179, Guía Contributiva Federal Para Patronos Puertorriqueños (Circular PR) (Federal Tax Guide for Employers in Puerto Rico) — in Spanish.
Forms 940PR, 941PR, 943PR, W-3PR.

Pub 225, Farmer's Tax Guide — explains how the federal tax laws apply to farming, incuding the kind of farm income you must report and the different deductions you can take.
Forms 1040 (Schedules D, F, J, SE), 4562, 4684, 4797.

Pub 334, Tax Guide for Small Business (For Individuals Who Use Schedule C or C-EZ) — explains federal tax laws that applies to sole proprietors and statutory employees. (Note to Tax Professionals only: There is a fee for this publication.) Forms 1040 (Schedule C, C-EZ, SE), 4562.

Pub 378, Fuel Tax Credits and Refunds— explains the credit or refund of the federal excise taxes on certain fuels that you may claim. Also discusses the alcohol fuel credit. Forms 720, 4136, 6478, 8849.

Pub 463, Travel, Entertainment, Gift, and Car Expenses — identifies business related travel, entertainment, gift, and transportation expenses that may be deductible. Forms 2106, 2106EZ.

Pub 501, Exemptions, Standard Deduction, and Filing Information — explains the rules for determining who must file a federal income tax return, what filing status to use, how many exemptions to claim and who cannot take the standard deduction. Forms 2120, 8332.

Pub 502, Medical and Dental Expenses — explains which medical and dental expenses are deductible, how to deduct them, and how to treat insurance reimbursements you may receive for medical care. Form 1040 (Schedule A).

Pub 503, Child and Dependent Care Expenses — explains how you may be able to claim a credit if you pay someone to care for your dependent who is under age 13, or your spouse or dependent who is unable to care for himself or herself. Tax rules covering dependent care benefits from your employer are also explained. See Publication 926 for information on the employment taxes you may have to pay if you are a household employer. Forms 1040A (Schedule 2), 2441.

Pub 504, Divorced or Separated Individuals — Form 8332.

Pub 505, Tax Withholding and Estimated Tax — Forms 1040-ES, 2210, 2210F, W-4, W-4P, W-4S, W-4V.

Pub 509, Tax Calendars for 2005

Pub 510, Excise Taxes for 2005 — covers in detail the various federal excise taxes reported on Form 720. These include environmental taxes; communications and air transportation taxes; fuel taxes; manufacturers taxes; tax on heavy trucks, trailers, and tractors; and the ship passenger tax. This publication also provides information on wagering activities reported on Form 11-C and 730. Forms 11-C, 637, 720, 730, 6197, 6627.

Pub 513, Tax Information for Visitors to the United States — briefly reviews the general requirements of U.S. income tax rules for foreign visitors who may have to file a U.S. income tax return during their visit. Most visitors who come to the United States are not allowed to work in this country. Check with the Bureau of Citizenship and Immigration Services (BCIS) before taking a job. Forms 1040C, 1040-ES (NR), 1040NR, 2063.

Pub 514, Foreign Tax Credit for Individuals — explains the foreign tax credit that is allowed for income taxes paid to a foreign government on income taxed by both the United States and a foreign country. Form 1116.

Pub 515, Withholding of Tax on Nonresident Aliens and Foreign Entities — provides information for withholding agents who are required to withhold and report tax on payments to nonresident aliens, foreign partnerships and foreign corporations. This publication includes information on required withholding upon the disposition of a U.S. real property interest by a foreign person. Also, it includes three tables listing U.S. tax treaties and some of the treaty provisions that provide for reduction of or exemption from withholding for certain types of income. Forms 1042, 1042S, 8233, 8288, 8288A, 8288-B, 8804, 8805, 8813, W-8 series (BEN, ECI, EXP, IMY).

Pub 516, U.S. Government Civilian Employees Stationed Abroad — discusses many of the allowances, reimbursements, expenses and property sales that U.S. Government civilian employees may have while working overseas.

Pub 517, Social Security and Other Information for Members of the Clergy and Religious Workers — discusses social security and Medicare taxes and exemptions from them for ministers and religious workers. This publication also explains the income tax treatment of certain income and expense items of interest to the clergy. Forms 1040 (Schedules C-EZ, SE), 2031, 2106EZ, 4029, 4361.

Pub 519, U.S. Tax Guide for Aliens — gives guidelines on how nonresident aliens determine their U.S. tax status and figure their U.S. income tax. Forms 1040, 1040C, 1040NR, 1040NREZ, 2063.

Pub 521, Moving Expenses — explains whether certain expenses of moving are deductible. For example, if you changed job locations last year or started a new job, you may be able to deduct your moving expenses. You may also be able to deduct expenses of moving to the United States if you retire while living and working overseas or if you are a survivor or dependent of a person who died while living and working overseas. Form 1040 (Schedule D)

Pub 523, Selling Your Home — explains how to treat any gain or loss from selling your main home. Form 1040 (Schedule D).

Pub 524, Credit for the Elderly or the Disabled — explains who qualifies for the credit and how to figure it. Forms 1040 (Schedule R), 1040A (Schedule 3).

Pub 525, Taxable and Nontaxable Income

Pub 526, Charitable Contributions — explains how to claim a deduction for charitable contributions and describes organizations that are qualified to receive charitable contributions. It also describes contributions you can (and cannot) deduct and explains deduction limits. Forms 1040 (Schedule A), 8283.

Pub 527, Residential Rental Property — explains rental income and expenses and how to report them on your return. This publication also defines other special rules that apply to rental activity. Forms 1040 (Schedule E), 4562.

Pub 529, Miscellaneous Deductions — identifies expenses you may be able to take as miscellaneous deductions on Form 1040 (Schedule A), such as employee business expenses and expenses of producing income. This publication does not discuss other itemized deductions, such as the ones for charitable contributions, moving expenses, interest, taxes, or medical and dental expenses. Forms 1040 (Schedule A), 2106, 2106EZ.

Pub 530, Tax Information for First-Time Homeowners — Forms 1040 (Schedule A), 8396.
Pub 531, Reporting Tip Income — explains how tip income is taxed and the rules for keeping records and reporting tips to your employers. This publication focuses on employees of food and beverage establishments, but recordkeeping rules and other information may also apply to other workers who receive tips, such as hairdressers, cab drivers, and casino dealers. (See Publication 1244.) Forms 4070, 4070A.

Pub 533, Self-Employment Tax — explains how people who work for themselves figure and pay selfemployment tax on their earned income. Self-employment tax consists of social security and Medicare taxes. Form 1040 (Schedule SE).

Pub 534, Depreciating Property Placed in Service Before 1987 — Form 4562.

Pub 535, Business Expenses — discusses in detail common business expenses and explains what is and is not deductible.

Pub 536, Net Operating Losses (NOLs) for Individuals, Estates and Trusts — discusses net operating losses (NOLs) for individuals, estates, and trusts. Such topics include: how to figure an NOL; when to use an NOL; how to claim an NOL deduction; and how to figure an NOL carry-over. Form 1045.

Pub 537, Installment Sales — explains the tax treatment of installment sales. (Installment sales are sales where part or all of the selling price is paid after the year of the sale.) If you finance the buyer's purchase of your property, instead of having the buyer get a loan or mortgage from a bank (or other lender), you probably have an installment sale. Form 6252.

Pub 538, Accounting Periods and Methods — explains some of the rules for accounting periods and methods. This publication is not intended as a guide to general business and tax accounting rules. Forms 1128, 2553, 3115.

Pub 541, Partnerships — Form 1065 (Schedules K, K-1).

Pub 542, Corporations — Forms 1120, 1120-A.

Pub 544, Sales and Other Dispositions of Assets — explains how to figure gain and loss on various transactions, such as trading, selling, or exchanging an asset used in a trade or business. This publication defines capital and noncapital assets and the tax results of different types of gains and losses. Forms 1040 (Schedule D), 4797, 8824.

Pub 547, Casualties, Disasters, and Thefts — helps you identify a deductible disaster, casualty, or theft loss. This publication also explains how to figure and prove your loss and how to treat the reimbursement you receive from insurance or other sources. Form 4684.

Pub 550, Investment Income and Expenses — covers investment income such as interest and dividends, expenses related to investments, and sales and trades of investment property including capital gains and losses. Forms 1040 (Schedules B, D), 1099DIV, 1099-INT, 4952, 6781, 8815.

Pub 551, Basis of Assets — explains how to determine the basis of property, which is usually its cost.

Pub 552, Recordkeeping for Individuals — highlights and serves as a ready reference on general recordkeeping for individual income tax filing.

Pub 553, Highlights of 2003 Tax Changes — provides detailed information about tax law changes that may affect you this filing season.

Pub 554, Older Americans' Tax Guide — provides helpful information on tax topics that may be of interest to older Americans. This guide also covers certain provisions that give special tax treatment to them.

Pub 555, Community Property — provides helpful information to married taxpayers who reside in a community property state — Arizona, California, Idaho, Louisiana, Nevada, New Mexico, Texas, Washington, or Wisconsin. If you and your spouse file separate tax returns, you should understand how community property laws affect the way you figure your income on your federal income tax return.

Pub 556, Examination of Returns, Appeal Rights, and Claims for Refund — Forms 1040X.

Pub 557, Tax-Exempt Status for Your Organization — explains the rules and procedures that apply to organizations applying for exemption from federal income tax under section 501 of the Internal Revenue Code. Forms 990, 990 EZ, 990 PF, 1023, 1024, 8871, 8872.

Pub 559, Survivors, Executors, and Administrators — provides helpful information for reporting and paying the proper federal income taxes if you are responsible for settling a decedent's estate. This publication answers many questions that a spouse or other survivor faces when a person dies.
Forms 1040, 1041.

Pub 560, Retirement Plans for Small Business (SEP, SIMPLE, and Qualified Plans) — provides guidance relevant to retirement plans available to small businesses (including the self-employed). It covers simplified employee pensions (SEPs), qualified plans, and savings incentive match plan for employees (SIMPLE) retirement plans.

Pub 561, Determining the Value of Donated Property — defines fair market value and provides other guidance that may help you determine the value of property you donated to a qualified organization. Form 8283.

Pub 564, Mutual Fund Distributions — explains the tax treatment of distributions paid or allocated to an individual shareholder of a mutual fund, and explains how to figure gain or loss on the sale of mutual fund shares. Forms 1040 (Schedules B, D), 1099DIV.

Pub 570, Tax Guide for Individuals with Income from U.S. Possessions — provides tax guidance for individuals with income from American Samoa, Guam, the Commonwealth of the Northern Mariana Islands, Puerto Rico, and the U.S. Virgin Islands. This publication also gives information and addresses for filing U.S. possession tax returns, if required. Forms 1040, 1040-SS, 4563, 5074, 8689.

Pub 571, Tax-Sheltered Annuity Plans (403(b) Plans) for Employees of Public Schools and Certain Tax-Exempt

Organizations — explains the contribution rules that apply to tax-sheltered annuity plans offered by qualified employers to eligible employees. Rules discussed include the limit on elective deferrals and the limit on annual additions. Form 5330.

Pub 575, Pension and Annuity Income — explains how to determine the tax treatment of distributions received from a qualified pension and annuity plans. It also discusses the optional tax treatment you can choose to use for lumpsum distributions received from a pension, from stock bonus and profit-sharing plans. Additionally, this publication discusses how to roll over distributions from a qualified plan. Forms 1040, 1040A, 1099-R, 4972.

Pub 579SP, Cómo Preparar la Declaración de Impuesto Federal (How to Prepare the Federal Income Tax Return) — in Spanish. Forms 1040, 1040A (Schedules 1 and 2), 1040EZ, and Schedule EIC.

Pub 583, Starting a Business and Keeping Records — provides basic federal tax information for people who are starting a business. It also provides information on keeping records and illustrates a recordkeeping system.

Pub 584, Casualty, Disaster, and Theft Loss Workbook (Personal-Use Property) — contains schedules for listing contents of your residence and is designed to help you figure your losses on personal-use property in the event of a casualty, disaster or theft.

Pub 584-B, Business Casualty, Disaster, and Theft Loss Workbook — contains schedules for listing your income producing property and is designed to help you figure your losses on the property in the event of a casualty, disaster or theft.

Pub 584SP, Registro de Pérdidas Personales Causadas por Hechos Fortuitos (Imprevistos) o Robos — Publication 584 in Spanish.

Pub 587, Business Use of Your Home (Including Use by Daycare Providers) — explains rules for *claiming deductions for business use of your home and what expenses may be deducted.*

Pub 590, Individual Retirement Arrangements (IRAs) — explains the tax rules that apply to IRAs and the penalties for not following them. Rules discussed include those affecting contributions, deductions, transfers (including rollovers) and withdrawals. This publication includes tax rules for traditional IRAs, Roth IRAs, SEPs, and SIMPLEs. Forms 1040, 1040A, 5329, 8606.

Pub 593, Tax Highlights for U.S. Citizens and Residents Going Abroad — provides a brief overview of various U.S. tax provisions that apply to U.S. citizens and resident aliens who live or work abroad and expect to receive income from foreign sources.

Pub 594, Understanding the Collection Process — defines your rights and duties as a taxpayer who owes federal taxes. This publication also explains how the IRS fulfills its legal obligation to collect these taxes.

Pub 594SP, Comprendiendo el Proceso de Cobro (Understanding the Collection Process) — Publication 594 in Spanish.

Pub 595, Tax Highlights for Commercial Fishermen — is primarily intended for sole proprietors who use Form 1040 (Schedules C or C-EZ) to report profit or loss from fishing. This publication does not cover corporations or partnerships in detail. Forms 1040 (Schedules C, C-EZ), 1099-MISC.

Pub 596, Earned Income Credit — explains who may receive the credit, how to figure and claim the credit, and how to receive advance payments of the credit. Forms 1040, 1040A, Schedule EIC, EIC Worksheets, W-5.

Pub 596SP, Crédito por Ingreso del Trabajo (Earned Income Credit) — Publication 596 in Spanish.

Pub 597, Information on the U.S.-Canada Income Tax Treaty — this publication explains certain tax provisions that may apply to U.S. residents who temporarily work in Canada.

Pub 598, Tax on Unrelated Business Income of Exempt Organizations — explains how the tax applies to most taxexempt organizations. It explains the rules that apply if an organization regularly operates a trade or business that is not substantially related to its exempt purpose.
Form 990-T.

Pub 686, Certification for Reduced Tax Rates in Tax Treaty Countries — explains how U.S. citizens, residents, and domestic corporations may certify to a foreign country that they are entitled to tax treaty benefits.

Pub 721, Tax Guide to U.S. Civil Service Retirement Benefits — explains how the federal income tax rules apply to civil service retirement benefits received by retired federal employees (including those disabled) or their survivors. Forms 1040, 1040A.Pub 850, English-Spanish Glossary of Words and Phrases Used in Publications Issued by the Internal Revenue Service

Pub 901, U.S. Tax Treaties — explains the reduced tax rates and exemptions from U.S. taxes provided under U.S. tax treaties with foreign countries. This publication provides helpful information for residents of those countries who receive income from U.S. sources. It may be useful to U.S. citizens and residents with income from abroad.

Pub 907, Tax Highlights for Persons with Disabilities — briefly explains tax laws that apply to persons with disabilities and directs readers to sources of detailed information on topics such as deductible expenses, tax credits and taxable and nontaxable income.

Pub 908, Bankruptcy Tax Guide — explains the federal tax obligations of persons filing bankruptcy petitions and bankruptcy estates. Forms 982, 1040, 1041.

Pub 911, Direct Sellers — provides information on figuring income and deductible expenses for your direct-sales business. A direct seller is a person who sells consumer products to others on a person-to-person basis, such as door-to-door, at sales parties, or by appointment in someone's home. Form 1040 (Schedules C, SE).

Pub 915, Social Security and Equivalent Railroad Retirement Benefits — explains taxability of social security and equivalent railroad retirement benefits.Forms SSA-1042S and RRB-1042S, SSA-1099 and RRB-1099, Social Security Benefits Worksheets.

Pub 918, Drafts of Worksheets in IRS Publications — available on IRS Web site and IRS CD only.

Pub 919, How Do I Adjust My Tax Withholding ? — discusses Form W-4 and offers guidance for getting the right amount of tax withheld from your pay.
Form W-4.

Pub 925, Passive Activity and At-Risk Rules — discusses two sets of rules that may limit the losses you can deduct on your tax return from any trade, business, rental or other income-producing activity. Form 8582.

Pub 926, Household Employer's Tax Guide For Wages Paid in 2005 — identifies "household employees." Included are tax rules you should know when you employ a household worker such as a babysitter, maid, yard worker, or similar domestic worker. This publication explains what federal employment taxes to withhold and pay and what records to keep. Forms 1040 (Schedule H), W-2, W-3, W-4, W-5.

Pub 929, Tax Rules for Children and Dependents — explains filing requirements and the standard deduction amount for dependents. This publication also explains when and how a child's parents may elect to include their child's interest and dividend income on their return, and when and how a child's interest, dividends, and other investment income reported on the child's return are taxed at the parents' tax rate. Forms 8615, 8814.

Pub 936, Home Mortgage Interest Deduction — discusses the rules for deducting home mortgage interest limits on the deduction and how to report it on your tax return.

Pub 938, Real Estate Mortgage Investment Conduits (REMICs) Reporting Information (And Other Collateralized Debt Obligations (CDOs) — contains directories of REMICs and CDOs to assist brokers and middlemen with their reporting requirements. Available on the IRS Web site.

Pub 939, General Rule for Pensions and Annuities — covers the method used to figure the tax-free part of pension and annuity payments from nonqualified plans, using life expectancy actuarial tables. The General Rule is used primarily for nonqualified plans, such as purchased commercial annuities, private annuities, and nonqualified employee plans. Pub 946, How to Depreciate Property — This publication explains how to figure and claim deductions for depreciation under MACRS and the special depreciation allowance. It also explains how you can elect to take a section 179 deduction for certain property and additional rules for listed property. Form 4562.

Pub 947, Practice Before the IRS and Power of Attorney — explains who can represent a taxpayer before the IRS and what forms are used to authorize a person to represent a taxpayer or to receive information from IRS regarding a taxpayer. Forms 2848, 8821.

Pub 950, Introduction to Estate and Gift Taxes — provides general information on the federal gift and estate taxes. It explains when these taxes apply and how they can be eliminated or reduced by the unified credit. — Forms 706, 709.

Pub 954, Tax Incentives for Distressed Communities

Pub 957, Reporting Back Pay and Special Wage Payments to the Social Security Administration

Pub 967, The IRS Will Figure Your Tax — explains the procedures for choosing to have the IRS figure the tax on Forms 1040, 1040A, and 1040EZ.

Pub 968, Tax Benefits for Adoption — explains the adoption tax credit and the exclusion from income on certain employer-provided amounts you pay to adopt a child. Form 8839.

Pub 969, Medical Savings Accounts (MSAs) — explains the program for certain employees of small businesses and selfemployed individuals. This publication also explains what a medical savings account is, who can have one, and how to report it on a tax return. This publication also explains Medicare plus choice MSAs.

Forms 8853, 1098-MSA, 1099-MSA. Pub 970, Tax Benefits for Education — explains the tax benefits that may be available to you if you are saving for or paying higher education costs for yourself or another student. Includes information previously contained in Publications 508 and 520, such as deducting work-related education expenses and the taxability of scholarships and other types of educational assistance. Form 8839.

Pub 971, Innocent Spouse Relief (And Separation of Liability and Equitable Relief) — explains who may quality for relief and how to apply for relief. Form 8857.

Pub 972, Child Tax Credit — provides Child Tax Credit Worksheets for those who cannot use the worksheet in their Form 1040 or Form 1040A instructions. It also provides the additional child tax credit worksheet for those who cannot use the worksheet in the Form 8812 instructions.

Pub 1004, Identification Numbers Under ERISA

Pub 1045, Information for Tax Practitioners

Pub 1212, List of Original Issue Discount Instruments — helps brokers and other middlemen identify publicly offered original issue discount debt instruments so that they can file Forms 1099-OID or Forms 1099-INT as required. This publication also assists owners of publicly offered OID instruments to determine the OID to report on their income tax returns.

Pub 1244, Employee's Daily Record of Tips and Report to Employers — Forms 4070, 4070-A.

Pub 1542, Per Diem Rates — provides the maximum per diem allowances for business travel within the continental U.S.A.

Pub 1544, Reporting Cash Payments of Over $10,000 (Received in a Trade or Business) — explains when and how persons in a trade or business must file a Form 8300 when they receive cash payments of more than $10,000 from one buyer. It also discusses the substantial penalties for not filing the Form. Form 8300.

Pub 1544SP, Informe de Pagos en Efectivo en Exceso de $10,000 (Recibidos en una Ocupacion o Negocio) — explains in Spanish when and how persons in a trade or business must file a Form 8300 or 8300SP when they receive cash payments of more than $10,000 from one buyer. It also discusses the substantial penalties for not filing the form.

Pub 1546, Taxpayer Advocate Service of the IRS — Index of Topics and Related Publications. Look over the following index to find the topic you have questions about. The number listed after each topic is the related publication. Where more than one number is listed after a topic, bold type has been used to identify the publication that provides the most detailed information about that topic. Refer to previous section titled Tax Publications for a brief description of many of the publications listed below.

APPENDIX C
Tax Topics, and Publications by numbers (#s)
that discuss them

Look over the following index to find the topic you have questions about. The number listed after each topic is the related publication. Where more than one number is listed after a topic, bold type has been used to identify the publication that provides the most detailed information about that topic. Refer to Appendix B for a brief description of many of the publications listed below.

A

E

F

Fair market value:
  Charitable contributions | 526, **561**
  Defined | 526, 527, 537, **544, 551, 561**, 946
  Mutual funds | 564
  Valuation | 561
Family:
  Employees | 15, 225, 926
  Partnerships | 541
  Related persons | 544, 550, 946
Farmers and farming | 225
  Employment taxes | 51
Federal employees compensation act (FECA) payments | 525, 557, 721
Federal employees overseas | 516
Federal insurance contributions act (FICA) | 517
  Clergy and religious workers | 517
Federal retirees | 721
Federal retirees, disabled | 721
Federal unemployment tax (FUTA) | 15, 926
Fees:
  Appraisal | **526,** 529, **547, 561**
  Check-writing | 529
  Club dues and membership | 463, 529, 535
  Commitment | 535
  Custodial | **529,** 550, 564
  Directors' | 525
  Legal | 529, 535
  License and regulation | 535
  Personal services | 525
  Service, broker | 529, 550, 564
Fellowships | 970
Fiduciaries | 559
Filing requirements:
  Age 65 or over | 501, 554, 915
  Corporations | 542
  Dependents | 501, 929
  Employee benefit plans | 1004
  Estates | (Forms 706 & 709 instructions)
  Excise taxes | 510
  Exempt organizations | 557, 598
  Farmers | 225
  Gift taxes | (Forms 706 & 709 instructions)
  Information returns | 911
  IRA | 590
  Partnerships | 541
  S corporations | (Form 1120-S instructions)
Filing status | **501,** 554
Final return, individual | 559
Fines | **529, 535**

H

I

J

M

N

O

P

Q

S

T

U

Y

Numbers

APPENDIX D
Commonly Used Tax Forms

Form Number and Title

1040	U.S. Individual Income Tax Return Sch A&B Itemized Deductions & Interest and Ordinary Dividends
1040A	U.S. Individual Income Tax Return
1040-ES	Estimated Tax for Individuals
1040EZ	Income Tax Return for Single and Joint Filers With No Dependents
1040X	Amended U.S. Individual Income Tax Return
1099–R	Distributions From Pensions, Annuities, Retirement or Profit-Sharing Plans, IRAs, Insurance Contracts, etc.
1116	Foreign Tax Credit (Individual, Estate, or Trust)
1310	Statement of Person Claiming Refund Due a Deceased Taxpayer
2106	Employee Business Expenses
2106-EZ	Unreimbursed Employee Business Expenses
2159	Payroll Deduction Agreement
2210	Underpayment of Estimated Tax by Individuals, Estates, and Trusts
2439	Notice to Shareholder of Undistributed Long-Term Capital Gains
2441	Child and Dependent Care Expenses
2848	Power of Attorney and Declaration of Representative
3115	Application for Change in Accounting Method
3903	Moving Expenses
433-F	Collection Information Statement
4562	Depreciation and Amortization
4684	Casualties and Thefts
4797	Sales of Business Property
4810	Request for Prompt Assessment Under Internal Revenue Code Section 6501(d)
4868	Application for Automatic Extension of Time To File U.S. Individual Income Tax Return
4952	Investment Interest Expense Deduction
4972	Tax on Lump-Sum Distributions
530	Tax Information for First-Time Homeowners
5329	Additional Taxes on Qualified Plans (including IRAs) and Other Tax-Favored Accounts
5329	Additional Taxes on Qualified Plans (Including IRAs) and Other Tax-Favored Accounts

56	Notice Concerning Fiduciary Relationship
6251	Alternative Minimum Tax—Individuals
6252	Installment Sale Income
656	Offer in Compromise
8109	Federal Tax Deposit Coupon ~ Form 8821, Tax Information Authorization
8283	Noncash Charitable Contributions
8396	Mortgage Interest Credit
8546	Claim for Reimbursement of Bank Charges Incurred Due to Erroneous Service Levy or Misplaced Payment Check
8582	Passive Activity Loss Limitations
8606	Nondeductible IRAs
8801	Credit For Prior Year Minimum Tax — Individuals, Estates, and Trusts
8812	Additional Child Tax Credit
8815	Exclusion of Interest From Series EE and I U.S. Savings Bonds Issued After 1989
8818	Optional Form To Record Redemption of Series EE and I U.S. Savings Bonds Issued After 1989
8822	Change of Address
8824	like-Kind Exchanges
8828	Recapture of Federal Mortgage Subsidy
8829	Expenses for Business Use of Your Home
8834	Qualified Electric Vehicle Credit
8839	Qualified Adoption Expenses
8863	Education Credits
8880	Credit for Qualified Retirement Savings Contributions
8885	Health Coverage Tax Credit
911	Application for Taxpayer Assistance Order
9465	Installment Agreement Request
12203	Request For Appeals
Schedule 1 (Form 1040A)	Interest and Ordinary Dividends for Form 1040A Filers
Schedule 2	Child and Dependent Care Expenses for Form 1040A Filers
Schedule 3 (Form 1040A)	Credit for the Elderly or the Disabled for Form 1040A Filers
Schedule A (Form 1040)	Itemized Deductions
Schedule B (Form 1040)	Interest and Ordinary Dividends
Schedule C	Profit or Loss From Business
Schedule C-EZ	Net Profit From Business
Schedule D (Form 1040)	Capital Gains and Losses
Schedule D-1	Continuation Sheet for Schedule D
Schedule E (Form 1040)	Supplemental Income and Loss
Schedule EIC	Earned Income Credit
Schedule F	Profit or Loss From Farming

Schedule H	Household Employment Taxes
Schedule J	Farm Income Averaging
Schedule R (Form 1040)	Credit for the Elderly or the Disabled
Schedule SE	Self-Employment Tax
W–10	Dependent Care Provider's Identification and Certification
W–4	Employee's Withholding Allowance Certificate
W–4P	Withholding Certificate for Pension or Annuity Payments
W–4S	Request for Federal Income Tax Withholding From Sick Pay
W–4V	Voluntary Withholding Request

BUSINESS-RELATED FORMS & SCHEDULES

W-2	Wage and Tax Statement
W-4	Employee's Withholding Allowance Certificate
940	Employer's Annual Federal Unemployment(FUTA) Tax Return
940-EZ	Employer's Annual Federal Unemployment (FUTA) Tax Return
941	Employer's Quarterly Federal Tax Return
1040	U.S. Individual Income Tax Return
1040X	Amended U.S. Individual Income Tax Return
1065	U.S. Return of Partnership Income
Sch D	Capital Gains and Losses
Sch K-1	Partner's Share of Income, Credits, Deductions, etc.
1120	U.S. Corporation Income Tax Return
1120-A	U.S. Corporation Short-Form Income Tax Return
1120S	U.S. Income Tax Return for an S Corporation
Sch D	Capital Gains and Losses and Built-In Gains
Sch K-1	Shareholder's Share of Income, Credits, Deductions, etc.
3800	General Business Credit
4797	Sales of Business Property
6252	Installment Sale Income
8300	Report of Cash Payments Over $10,000 Received in a Trade or Business

279

APPENDIX E

TELETAX Topics

Teletax Topic menu Numbers

Call **1–800–829–4477** to listen to pre-recorded messages covering various teletax topics.

Menu #s	Subject (Tax Topic)
01	IRS services - Volunteer tax assistance, toll-free telephone, walk-in assistance, and outreach programs
102	Tax assistance for individuals with disabilities and the hearing impaired
103	Intro to Federal taxes for small business/self-employed
104	Taxpayer Advocate Program – Help for problem situations
105	Public libraries - Tax information tapes and reproducible tax forms

IRS Procedures
151	Your appeal rights
152	Refunds - How long they should take
153	What to do if you haven't filed your tax return (Non-filers)
154	Form W-2 - What to do if not received
155	Forms and publications - How to get
156	Copy of your tax return - How to get one
157	Change of address - How to notify the IRS
158	Ensuring proper credit of payments

Collection
201	The collection process
202	What to do if you can't pay your tax
203	Failure to pay child support, federal non-tax obligations and state income tax
204	Offers in compromise
205	Innocent spouse relief

Alternative Filing Methods
251	Signing your return with a self selected PIN
252	Electronic filing
253	Substitute tax forms
254	How to choose a paid tax preparer

602	Child and dependent care credit
603	Credit for the elderly or the disabled
604	Advance earned income credit
605	Education credits
606	Child tax credits
607	Adoption credit
608	Excess social security and RRTA tax withheld
609	Rate reduction credit

IRS Notices
651	Notices - what to do
652	Notice of under reported income - CP 2000
653	IRS notices and bills, and penalties and interest charges

Basis of Assets, Depreciation, and Sale of Assets
701	Sale of your home
703	Basis of assets
704	Depreciation
705	Installment sales

Employer Tax Information
751	Social security and Medicare withholding rates
752	Form W-2 - Where, when, and how to file
753	Form W-4 - Employee's withholding allowance certificate
754	Form W-5 - Advance earned income credit
755	Employer Identification Number (EIN) - How to apply
756	Employment taxes for household employees
757	Form 941 - Deposit requirements
758	Form 941 - Employer's quarterly federal tax return
759	Form 940 and 940-EZ – Deposit requirements
760	Form 940 and 940-EZ -Employer's Annual Federal Unemployment Tax Returns
761	Tips - Withholding and reporting 762 Independent contractor vs employee

Magnetic Media Filers - 1099 Series and Related Information Returns
801	Who must file magnetically
802	Applications, forms, and information
803	Waivers and extensions
804	Test files and combined federal and state filing
805	Electronic filing of information returns Tax Information for Aliens and U.S. Citizens Living Abroad
851	Resident and nonresident aliens
852	Dual-status alien
853	Foreign earned income exclusion - General
854	Foreign earned income exclusion - Who qualifies?
855	Foreign earned income exclusion - What qualifies?
856	Foreign tax credit

857   IRS Individual Taxpayer Identification Number (ITIN) - Form W-7
858   Alien tax clearance

Tax Information for Puerto Rico Residents (in Spanish only)
901   Who must file a U.S. income tax return in Puerto Rico
902   Deductions and credits for Puerto Rico filers
903   Federal employment taxes in Puerto Rico
904   Tax assistance for Puerto Rico residents

Note: *Topic numbers are effective January 1, 2005.*

APPENDIX F

TAXFAX

Tax Products Available by Fax: The following tax products are available through the IRS TAXFAX service by calling 703-368-9694 from the telephone connected to the fax machine. When you call, you will hear instructions on how to use the service. Select the option for getting tax products. Then, enter the Catalog No. shown below for each item you want. When you hang up the phone, the fax will begin.

Name of Tax Product	Title	Catalog No.	No. of Pages
Form SS-4	Application for Employer Identification Number	16055	2
Instr. SS-4	Instructions for Form SS-4	62736	6
Form SS-8	Determination of Employee Work Status for Purposes of Federal Employment Taxes and Income Tax Withholding	16106	5
Form W-4	Employee's Withholding Allowance Certificate	10220	2
Form W-4P	Withholding Certificate for Pension or Annuity Payments	10225	4
Form W-5	Earned Income Credit Advance Payment Certificate	10227	3
Form W-7	Application for IRS Individual Taxpayer Identification Number	10229	3
Form W-7A	Application for Taxpayer Identification Number for Pending U.S. Adoptions	24309	2
Form W-7P	Application for Preparer Tax Identification Number	26781	1
Form W-9	Request for Taxpayer Identification Number and Certification	10231	3
Instr. W-9	Instructions for the Requestor of Form W-9	20479	4
Form W-9S	Request for Student's or Borrower's Taxpayer Identification Number and Certification	25240	2
Form W-10	Dependent Care Provider's Identification and Certification	10437	1
Form 433-A	Collection Information Statement for Wage Earners and Self-Employed Individuals	20312	6

285

Form 433-B	Collection Information Statement for Business	16649	6
Form 656	Offer in Compromise	16728	6
Form 709	U.S. Gift (and Generation-Skipping Transfer) Tax Return	16783	4
Instr. 709	Instructions for Form 709	16784	12
Form 709A	U.S. Short Form Gift tax Return	10171	3
Form 720	Quarterly Federal Excise Tax Return	10175	5
Instr. 720	Instructions for Form 720	64240	12
Form 720X	Amended Quarterly Federal Excise Tax Return	32661	2
Form 843	Claim for Refund and Request for Abatement	10180	1
Instr. 843	Instructions For Form 843	11200	2
Form 940	Employer's Annual Federal Unemployment (FUTA) Tax Return	11234	2
Instr. 940	Instructions for Form 940	13660	6
Form 940-EZ	Employer's Annual Federal Unemployment (FUTA) Tax Return	10983	2
Instr. 940-EZ	Instructions for Form 940-EZ	25947	5
Form 941	Employer's Quarterly Federal Tax Return	17001	4
Instr. 941	Instructions for Form 941	14625	4
Form 941c	Supporting Statement To Correct Information	11242	4
Form 943	Employer's Annual Federal Tax Return for Agricultural Employees	11252	2
Instr. 943	Instructions for Form 943	25976	3
Form 943-A	Agricultural Employer's Record of Federal Tax Liability	170302	2
Form 945	Annual Return of Withheld Federal Income Tax	14584	2
Instr. 945	Instructions for Form 945	20534	4
Form 945-A	Annual Record of Federal Tax Liability	14733	3
Form 990	Return of Organization Exempt From Income Tax	11282	6
Instr. 990 & 990-EZ	Instructions for Form 990 or 990-EZ	22386	15
Instr. 990	Specific Instructions for Form 990	5002	19
Schedule A (Form 990 or 990-EZ)	Organization Exempt Under Section 501(c)(3)	11285	6
Instr.	Instructions for Schedule A (form 990 or 990EZ)	11294	14

Sch. A

Form 990-EZ	Short Form Return of Organization Exempt From Income Tax	10642	2
Instr. 990-EZ	Specific Instructions for Form 990-EZ	50003	9
Form 1040	U.S. Individual Income Tax Return	11320	2
Instr. 1040	Line Instructions for Form 1040	11325	35
Instr. 1040 (Base)	General Information for Form 1040	24811	26
Tax Table & Tax Computation Wksht.	Tax Table and Tax Computation Worksheet (Form 1040)	24327	13
Schedules A&B (Form 1040)	Itemized Deductions & Interest and Ordinary Dividends	11330	2
Instr. Sch. A&B	Instructions for Form 1040 (Schedules A & B)	24328	8
Schedule C (Form 1040)	Profit or Loss From Business (Sole Proprietorship)	11334	2
Instr. Sch. C	Instructions fpr Form 1040 (Schedule C)	24329	8
Schedule C-EZ (Form 1040)	Net Profit From Business (Sole Proprietorship)	14374	2
Schedule D (Form 1040)	Capital Gains and Losses	11338	2
Instr. Sch.D	Instructions for Form 1040 (Schedule D)	24331	9
Schedule D-1 (Form 1040)	Continuation Sheet for Sch. D	10424	2
Instr. Sch. E (Form 1040)	Supplemental Income and Loss	11344	2
Instr. Sch. E	Instructions for Form 1040 (Schedule E)	24332	6
Schedule EIC (Form 1040)	Earned Income Credit	13339	2

Schedule F (Form 1040)	Profit or Loss From Farming	11346	2
Instr. Sch. F	Instructions For Form 1040 (Schedule F)	24333	6
Schedule H (Form 1040)	Household Employment Taxes	12187	2
Instr. Sch. H	Instructions for Form 1040 (Schedule H)	21451	8
Schedule J (Form 1040)	Farming Income Averaging	25513	1
Instr. Sch. J	Instructions for Form 1040 (Schedule J)	25514	7
Schedule R (Form 1040)	Credit for the Elderly or the Disabled	11359	2
Instr. Sch. R	Instructions for Form 1040 (Schedule R	11357	4
Schdule SE (Form 1040)	Self-Employment Tax	11358	2
Inst. Sch. SE	Instructions for Form 1040 (Schedule SE)	24334	4
Form 1040A	U.S. Individual Income Tax Return	11327	2
Schedule 1 (Form 1040)	Interest and Ordinary Dividends for Form 1040A Filers	12075	1
Schedule 2 (Form 1040A)	Child and Dependent Care Expenses for Form 1040A Filers	10749	2
Instr. Sch. 2	Instructions for Form 1040a (Schedule 2)	30139	3
Schedule 3 (Form 1040A)	Credit for the Elderly or the Disabled for Form 1040A Filers	12064	2
Instr. Sch. 3	Instructions for Form 1040a (Schedule 3)	12059	4
Form 1040-ES	Estimated Tax for Individuals	11340	7
Form 1040EZ	Income Tax Return for Single and Joint Filers With No Dependents	11329	2
Instr. 1040EZ	Instructions for Form 1040EZ	12063	32
Form 1040NR	U.S. Nonresident Alien Income Tax Return	11364	5
Instr. 1040NR	Instructions for Form 1040NR	11368	40
Form 1040NR-EZ	U.S. Income Tax Return for Certain Nonresident Aliens With No Dependents	21534	2
Instr.	Instructions for Form 1040NR-EZ	21718	15

Form	Description		
1040NR-EZ			
Form 1040-V	Payment Voucher	20975	2
Form 1040X	Amended U.S. Individual Income Tax Return	11360	2
Instr. 1040X	Instructions for Form 1040X	11362	6
Form 1041	U.S. Income Tax Return for Estates & Trusts	11370	4
Form 1065	U.S. Return of Partnership Income	11390	4
Inst. 1065	Instructions for Form 1065	11392	36
Schedule D (Form 1065)	Capital Gains and Losses	11393	4
Schedule K-1 (Form 1065)	Partner's Share of Income, Credits, Deductions, and Etc.	11394	2
Instr. Sch. K-1	Instructions for Form 1065 (Schedule K-1)	11396	11
Form 1116	Foreign Tax Credit	11440	2
Instr. 1116	Instructions for Form 1116	11441	16
Form 1120	U.S. Corporation Income Tax Return	11450	4
Form 1120A	U.S. Corporation Short-Form Income Tax Return	11456	2
Inst. 1120 & 1120A	Instructions for Forms 1120 & 1120A	11455	28
Form 1310	Statement of Person Claiming Refund Due a Deceased Taxpayer	11566	2
Form 2106	Employee Business Expenses	11700	2
Instr. 2106	Instructions for Form 2106	64188	8
Form 2106-EZ	Unreimbursed Employee Business Expenses	20604	3
Form 2120	Multiple Support Declaration	11712	1
Form 2210	Underpayment of Estimated Tax by Individuals, Estates, Trusts	11744	4
Instr. 2210	Instructions for Form 2210	63610	5
Form 2290	Heavy Highway Vehicle Use Tax Return	11250	3
Instr. 2290	Instructions for Form 2290	27231	10
Form 2350	Application for Extension of Time To File U.S. Income Tax Return	11780	3

Form 2438	Undistributed Capital Gains Tax Return	11856	3
Form 2439	Notice to Shareholder of Undistributed Long-Term Capital Gains	11858	8
Form 2441	Child and Dependent Care Expenses	11862	2
Instr. 2441	Instructions for Form 2441	10842	4
Form 2553	Election by a Small Business Corporation	18629	2
Instr. 2553	Instructions for Form 2553	49978	4
Form 2555	Foreign Earned Income	11900	3
Instr. 2555	Instructions for Form 2555	11901	4
Form 2555-EZ	Foreign Earned Income Exclusion	13272	2
Instr. 2555-EZ	Instructions for Form 2555-EZ	14623	3
Form 2688	Application for Additional Extension of Time To File U.S. Individual Income Tax Return	11958	2
Form 2758	Application for Extension of Time To File Certain Exercise, Information, and Other Returns	11976	2
Form 2848	Power of Attorney and Declaration of Representative	11980	2
Inst. 2848	Instructions for Form 2848	11981	4
Pub. 3376	E-File Fact Sheet for Magnetic Tape Reporting	27457	3
Pub. 3377	E-File Fact Sheet for Simplified Tax and Wages Reporting System (STAWRS)	27458	2
Pub. 3378	E-File Fact Sheet for Filing Form 941 using a Personal Computer	27459	3
Pub. 3379	E-File Fact Sheet for Form 941 E-file	27460	2
Pub. 3380	E-File Fact Sheet for Form 941 Telefile	27461	2
Pub. 3381	E-File Fact Sheet for Electronic Federal Tax Payment System	27462	3
Pub. 3382	E-File Fact Sheet for Employee Benefit Plan 5500 Series	27463	1
Pub. 3383	E-File Fact Sheet for Form 1065	27464	3
Form 3468	Investment Credit	12276	4
Form 3800	General Business Credit	12392	4
Inst. 3800	Instructions for Form 3800	10622	2
Form 3903	Moving Expenses	12490	2
Form 3911	Taxpayer Statement Regarding Refund	41167	2

Form 4136	Credit for Federal Tax Paid on Fuels	12625	4
Form 4137	Social Security and Medicare Tax on Unreported Tip Income	12626	2
Form 4419	Application for Filing Information Returns Electronically/Magnetically	41639	2
Form 4506	Request for Copy of Tax Return	41721	2
Form 4506T	Request for Transcript of Tax Return	37667	2
Form 4562	Depreciation and Amortization (Including Information on Listed Property)	12906	2
Instr. 4562	Instructions for Form 4562	12907	15
Form 4684	Casualties and Thefts	12997	2
Instr. 4684	Instructions for Form 4684	12998	4
Form 4797	Sales of Business Property	13086	2
Instr. 4797	Instructions for Form 4797	13087	8
Form 4802	Transmittal of Information Returns Reported Magnetically/Electronically (Continuation of Form 4804)	27205	1
Form 4804	Transmittal of Information Returns Reported Magnetically	27210	2
Form 4835	Farm Rental Income and Expenses	13117	2
Form 4852	Substitute for Form W-2 and Form 1099-R	42058	2
Form 4868	Application for Automatic Extension of Time To File U.S. Individual Income Tax Return	13141	4
Form 4952	Investment Interest Expense Deduction	13177	2
Form 4972	Tax on Lump-Sum Distributions	13187	4
Form 5329	Additional taxes on Qualified Plans (including IRAs) and Other tax-Favored Acounts	13329	2
Instr. 5329	Instructions for Form 5329	13330	6
Form 6198	At-Risk Limitations	50012	1
Instr. 6198	Instructions for Form 6198	50013	8
Form 6251	Alternative Minimum Tax— Individuals	13600	2
Instr. 6251	Instructions for Form 6251	64277	8
Form 6252	Installment Sale Income	13601	4
Form 6781	Gains and Losses From Section 1256 Contracts and Straddles	13715	3
Form 7004	Application for Automatic Extension of Time to File Corporation Income Tax Return	13804	3

Form 8271	Investor Reporting of Tax Shelter Registration Number	61924	2
Form 8283	Noncash Charitable Contributions	62299	2
Instr. 8283	Instructions for Form 8283	62730	4
Form 8300	Report of Cash Payments Over $10,000 Received in a Trade or Business	62133	4
Form 8332	Release of Claim to Exemption for Child of Divorced or Separated Parents	13910	1
Form 8379	Injured Spouse Claim and Allocation	62474	2
Form 8453-OL	U.S. Individual Income Tax Declaration for an IRS e-file Online Return	15907	2
Form 8508	Request for Waiver from Filing Information Returns Magnetically	63499	2
Form 8582	Passive Activity Loss Limitations	63704	3
Instr. 8582	Instructions for Form 8582	64294	12
Form 8586	Low-Income Housing Credit	63987	2
Form 8606	Nondeductible IRAs	63966	2
Instr. 8606	Instructions for Form 8606	25399	8
Form 8615	Tax for Children Under Age 14 With Investment Income of More Than $1,500	64113	1
Instr. 8615	Instructions for Form 8615	28914	2
Form 8718	User Fee for Exempt Organization Determination Letter Request	64728	1
Form 8801	Credit for Prior Year Minimum Tax—Individuals, Estates, and Trusts	10002	4
Form 8809	Applications (or Request) for Extension of Time To File Information Returns	10322	2
Form 8812	Additional Child Tax Credit	10644	2
Form 8814	Parents' Election To Report Child's Interest and Dividends	10750	2
Form 8815	Exclusion of Interest From Series EE and I U.S. Savings Bonds Issued after 1989	10822	2
Form 8821	Tax Information Authorization	11596	4
Form 8822	Change of Address	12081	2
Form 8824	Like-Kind Exchanges	12311	4
Form 8829	Expenses for Business Use of Your Home	13232	1
Instr. 8829	Instructions for Form 8829	15683	4
Form 8834	Qualified Electric Vehicle Credit	14953	2

Form 8839	Qualified Adoption Expenses	22843	2
Instr. 8839	Instructions for Form 8839	23077	4
Form 8850	Pre-Screening Notice and Certification Request for the Work Opportunity and Welfare-to-Work Credits	22851	2
Instr. 8850	Instructions for Form 8850	24833	2
Form 8853	Archer MSAs and Long-Term Care Insurance Contracts	24091	2
Instr. 8853	Instructions for Form 8853	24188	8
Form 8857	Request for Innocent Spouse Relief	24647	4
Form 8859	District of Columbia First-Time Homebuyer Credit	24779	2
Form 8862	Information To Claim Earned Income Credit After Disallowance	25145	2
Instr. 8862	Instructions for Form 8862	25343	2
Form 8863	Education Credits (Hope and Lifetime Learning Credits)	25379	3
Form 8868	Application for Extension of Time to File an Exempt Organization Return	27916	4
Form 8869	Qualified Subchapter S Subsidiary Election	28755	2
Form 8870	Information Return for Transfers Associated With Certain Personal Benefit Contracts	28906	6
	Political Organization Notice of Section 527 Status	30405	4
Form 8872	Political Organization Report of Contributions and Expenditures	30406	3
Instr. 8872	Instructions for Form 8872	30584	3
Form 8873	Extraterritorial Income Exclusion	30732	2
Form 8880	Credit for Qualified Retirement Savings Contributions	33394	4
Form 8885	Health Coverage Tax Credit	34641	4
Form 8889	Health Savings Accounts (HSAs)	37621	1
Instr. 8889	instructions for Form 8889	37971	6
Form 9465	Installment Agreement Request	14842	3

Formas Federales Disponibles en IRS TaxFax
Entre el número de Catálogo o Código para cada producto.
Desde su máquina de Fax llame al (703) 368-9694

Nombre del Producto	Título	Num. De Código	Num. De Páginas
Form SS-4PR	Solicitud de Número de Identificación Patronal (EIN)	16064	2
Inst. SS-4PR		32588	7
Form SS-8PR	Determinación del Estado de Empleo de un trabajador para Propósitos las Contribuciones Federales Sobre el Empleo	23365	5
Form W-3PR	Informe de Comprobantesde Retencion - 2004	10116	3
Inst. W-3PR		26400	4
Form W-3CPR	Transmisión de Comprobantes de Retención Corregidos	62776	2
Form W-7(SP)	Solicitud de Número de Identificación Personal del Contribuyente del Servicio de Impuestos Internos	23117	5
Form 433-A(SP)	Información de Cobro-Informe Personal para Individuos	20503	4
Form 433-B(SP)	Información de Cobro-Informe Personal para Negocios	20596	4
Form 886-H(SP)	Explicación de los Artículos	28258	2
Form 940PR	Planilla para la Declaración Anual del PatronoContribución Federal para el Desempleo (FUTA)	16996	2
Inst. 940PR		21105	6
Form 941CPR	Planilla para la Corrección de Información Facilitada Anteriomente en Cumplimiento con la Ley del Seguro Social y del Seguro Medicare (S.S. y Medicare)	17012	4
Form 941PR	Planilla para la Declaración Trimestral del Patrono (S.S. y Medicare)	17009	2
Inst. 941PR		35286	4
Form 941PR	(Anexo B) - Registro Suplementario de la Obligación Contributiva Federal del Patrono	12465	2
Form 943PR	Planilla para la Declaración Anual de la Contribución del Patrono de Empleados Agrícolas	17029	2
nst. 943PR		34648	4
Form 943A-PR	Registro de la Obligación Contributiva Federal del Patrono Agricola	17031	2
Form 1040ES(ESP)	Contribuciones Federales Estimadas del Trabajo por Cuenta Propia y Sobre el Empleo de Empleados Domésticos - Puerto Rico	17173	4
Form 1040PR	Planilla Para La Declaración de la Contribución Federal Sobre el Trabajo por Cuenta Propia -Puerto Rico	17182	4
Instr. 1040PR		31798	9
Form	Contribuciónes Sobre el Empleo De Empleados Domésticos	21446	2

1040PR (Anejo H-PR) Instr.		22119	8
1040PR (Anejo H-PR) Form 2290 - SP	Declaración del Impuestos sobre el Uso de Vehículos Pesados en las Carreteras	30488	3
Form 3911 (SP)	Declaración del Contribuyente Sobre el Reembolso	31331	2
Form 8300 -SP	Informe de Pagos en Efectivo en Exceso de $10,000.00 Recibidos en una Ocupación o Negocio	24396	4
Pub 1SP	Derechos del Contribuyente	10919	2
Pub 179	Circular PR - Guía Contributiva Federal Para Patronos Puertorriqueños	46252	20
Pub 579SP	Cómo Preparar la Declaración de Impuesto Federal	15146	104
Pub 584SP	Registo de Pérdidas por Hechos Fortuitos (Imprevistos), Desastres y Robos (Propiedad de Uso Personal)	14883	25
Pub 594SP	El Proceso de Cobro del IRS	10975	12
Pub 596SP	Crédito por Ingreso del Trabajo	13737	64
Pub 724SP	Ayude A Otras Personas Con Los Impuestos	46719	2
Pub 850	Diccionario Inglés-Español De Palabras y Frases	46805	35
Pub 1244-PR	Registro Diario de Propinas Recibidas por el Empleado e Informe al Patrono	63181	10
Pub 1321	Special Instructions for Bona Fide Residents of Puerto Rico Who Must File a U.S. Individual Income Tax Return (Form 1040 or 1040A)	63770	4
Pub 1544SP	Informe de Pagos en Efectivo en Exceso de $10,000	24236	7
Pub 2053-B(SP)	Participe en los Programas-Acceso a Materiales sobre Impuestos	31563	2
Pub 3148SP	Lo Que Usted Necesita Saber Sobre Las Propinas	27444	10
Pub 3518(SP)	Guía de Impuesto Federal para la Industria De Belleza y Barbería	30575	2

295

APPENDIX G

State Unemployment Tax Agencies

The following list of state unemployment tax agencies was provided to the IRS by the U.S. Department of Labor. If the telephone number listed for your state would be a long distance call from your area, you can use the name of the agency to look for a local number in your telephone book. The addresses and telephone numbers of the agencies, which were current at the time this publication was prepared for print, are subject to change.

For the most up-to-date addresses and telephone numbers for these agencies, you can download this publication from the IRS website. You can access the IRS website at www.irs.gov.

Alabama
Department of Industrial Relations
649 Monroe Street
Montgomery, AL 36131
(334) 242-8467
www.dir.state.al.us

Alaska
Department of Labor Employment
Security Division
P. O. Box 25506
Juneau, AK 99802-5509
(888) 448-3527
www.labor.state.ak.us/

Arizona
Department of Economic Security
3225 N. Central Avenue Suite 1411
Phoenix, AZ 85012 (
602) 248-9396
www.arizona.gov

Arkansas
Employment Security Department
P. O. Box 2981
Little Rock, AR 72203
(501) 682-3253
www.arkansas.gov

California

Employment Development Department
3321 Power Inn Road, Suite 220
Sacramento, CA 95826-6110
(877) 547-4503
www.edd.cahwnet.gov

Colorado
Department of Labor and Employment
1515 Arapahoe Street Tower 2, Suite 400
Denver, CO 80202-2117
(800) 480-8299
www.coworkforce.com

Connecticut
Employment Security Division Labor Department
200 Folly Brook Blvd.
Wethersfield, CT 06109-1114
(860) 263-6550
www.ct.gov

Delaware
Department of Labor
4425 North Market Street
Wilmington, DE 19802
(302) 761-8484
www.delawareworks.com

District of Columbia

296

Department of Employment Services
609 H Street, NE, Room 362
Washington, DC 20001
(202) 698-7550
www.does.dc.gov

Florida
Agency for Workforce Innovation UC
Services
107 E. Madison Street, MSC 229
Tallahassee, FL 32399-0100
 (800) 352-3671
www.floridajobs.org

Georgia
Department of Labor 148 International
Blvd. Suite 800
Atlanta, GA 30303 (404) 232-3301
www.dol.state.ga.us

Hawaii
Department of Labor and Industrial
Relations
 830 Punchbowl Street Room 437
Honolulu, HI 96813
(808) 586-8913
www.dlir.state.hi.us/

Idaho
Department of Labor
317 Main Street
Boise, ID 83735
(208) 332-3576 or (800) 448-2977
www.labor.state.id.us

Illinois
Department of Employment Security
33 South State Street
Chicago, IL 60603 (312) 793-1900
www.ides.state.il.us

Indiana
Department of Workforce Development
10 North Senate Avenue
Indianapolis, IN 46204
(317) 232-7436
www.in.gov/dwd/unemploy

Iowa
Workforce Development
1000 East Grand Avenue
Des Moines, IA 50319
(515) 281-5339
www.iowaworkforce.org/ui

Kansas
Department of Human
Resources
401 SW Topeka Blvd.
Topeka, KS 66603
(785) 296-5025
www.dol.ks.gov

Kentucky
Division of Employment
Services
P. O. Box 948
Frankfort, KY 40602
(502) 564-6838
www.oet.ky.gov

Louisiana
Department of Labor
P. O. Box 98146
Baton Rouge, LA 70804
(225) 342-2944
www.ldol.state.la.us

Maine
Department of Labor
P. O. Box 259
Augusta, ME 04332-0259
(207) 287-3176
www.maine.gov

Maryland
Department of Labor,
Licensing & Regulation
1100 North Eutaw Street,
Room 414
Baltimore, MD 21201
(800) 492-5524
www.maryland.gov

297

Massachusetts
Division of Employment and Training
19 Staniford Street
Boston, MA 02114
(617) 626-5050
www.detma.org/

Michigan
Department of Labor & Economic
Growth
Unemployment Insurance Agency
3024 West Grand Blvd.
Detroit, MI 48202
(313) 456-2180
www.michigan.gov/uia

Minnesota
Department of Employment
& Economic Security
390 North Robert Street
St. Paul, MN 55101
(651) 296-6141
www.uimn.org

Mississippi
Employment SecurityCommission
P. O. Box 22781
Jackson, MS 39225-2781
(601) 961-7755
www.mesc.state.ms.us/tax

Missouri
Division of Employment Security
P. O. Box 59
Jefferson City, MO 65104
(573) 751-3340 www.missouri.gov

Montana
Department of Labor and Industry
P. O. Box 1728
Helena, MT 59624
(406) 444-6900
www.dli.state.mt.us

Nebraska
Department of Labor

Box 94600
State House Station
Lincoln, NE 68509
(402) 471-9899
www.dol.state.ne.us

Nevada
Department of Employment Training
and Rehabilitation
500 East Third Street
Carson City, NV 89713
(775) 687-4545
www.detr.state.nv.us

New Hampshire
Department of Employment Security
32 South Main Street
Concord, NH 03301
(603) 228-4033
www.nhes.state.nh.us

New Jersey
Department of Labor
P. O. Box 947
Trenton, NJ 08625-0947
(609) 633-6400
www.nj.gov

New Mexico
Department of Labor
P. O. Box 2281
Albuquerque, NM 87103
505) 841-8582 www.dol.state.nm.us

New York
Department of Labor
State Campus, Building 12,
Room 542
Albany, NY 12240
888) 899–8810
www.labor.state.ny.us

North Carolina
Employment Security Commission
P. O. Box 26504
Raleigh, NC 27611
(919) 733-7396

www.ncesc.com

North Dakota
Job Service of North Dakota
P. O. Box 5507
Bismarck, ND 58506-5507
(800) 472-2952
www.state.nd.us

Ohio
Department of Job and Family Services
4300 Kimberly Parkway
Columbus, OH 43232
(614) 466-2319
www.state.oh.us

Oklahoma
Employment Security Commission
Will Rogers Memorial
Office Building
2401 North Lincoln
Oklahoma City, OK 73105
(405) 557-7170
www.oesc.state.ok.us/ui

Oregon
Employment Department
875 Union Street NE
Salem, OR 97311
(503) 947-1488 www.emp.state.or.us

Pennsylvania
Department of Labor and Industry
7th and Forster Streets
Harrisburg, PA 17121
(888) 313-7284
www.dli.state.pa.us

Puerto Rico
Department of Labor
Prudencio Rivera Martinez Building
505 Ave. Munoz Rivera
San Juan, PR 00910
(787) 754-5262
www.interempleo.org

Rhode Island

Division of Taxation
One Capitol Hill
Providence, RI 02908-5829
(401) 222-3696
www.det.state.ri.us

South Carolina
Employment Security Commission
P. O. Box 995
Columbia, SC 29202
(803) 737-3075
www.sces.org/ui

South Dakota
Department of Labor
P. O. Box 4730
Aberdeen, SD 57402
(605) 626-2312
www.state.sd.us

Tennessee
Department of Labor & Workforce
500 James Robertson Parkway
Davy Crocket Tower, 9th Floor
Nashville, TN 37245-3500
615) 741-2486 www.state.tn.us

Texas
Workforce Commission
101 East 15th Street
Austin, TX 78778
(512) 463-2700
www.twc.state.tx.us

Utah
Department of Workforce Services
P. O. Box 143001
Salt Lake City, UT 84144
(801) 526–9400
www.jobs.utah.gov/ui

Vermont
Department of Employment and
Training
P. O. Box 488
Montpelier, VT 05601-0488
(802) 828-4000

www.det.state.vt.us

Virginia
Employment Commission
P. O. Box 1358
Richmond, VA 23218-1358
(804) 371-6325
www.vec.state.va.us

Virgin Islands
Department of Labor
P. O. Box 789
St. Croix, U.S. Virgin Islands 00821
(340) 776-3700 St. Thomas
(340) 773-1994 St. Croix
www.vidol.gov

Washington
Employment Security Department
P. O. Box 9046
Olympia, WA 98507-9046

(360) 902-9360 www.wa.gov/esd

West Virginia
Bureau of Employment Programs
112 California Avenue
Charleston, WV 25305-0112
(304) 558-2675 www.wv.gov

Wisconsin
Department of Workforce
Development
P. O. Box 7942, GEF 1
Madison, WI 53702
608) 261-6700 www.dwd.state.wi.us

Wyoming
Department of Employment
P. O. Box 2760
Casper, WY 82602
(307) 235-3217
wydoe.state.wy.us

APPENDIX H

Table of Tax Treaties

Table of tax Treaties (Updated through September 30, 2004)

Country	General Effective Date	Country	Date
		Jamaica	Jan. 1, 1982
		Japan	Jan. 1, 1973
		Kazakstan	Jan. 1, 1996
		Korea, Rep. of	Jan. 1, 1980
Australia	Dec. 1, 1983	Latvia	Jan. 1, 2000
Protocol	Jan. 1, 2004	Lithuania	Jan. 1, 2000
Austria	Jan. 1, 1999	Luxembourg	Jan. 1, 2001
Barbados	Jan. 1, 1984	Mexico	Jan. 1, 1994
Protocol	Jan. 1, 1994	Protocol	Jan. 1, 2004
Belgium	Jan. 1, 1971	Morocco	Jan. 1, 1981
Protocol	Jan. 1, 1988	Netherlands	Jan. 1, 1994
Canada[1]	Jan. 1, 1985	New Zealand	Nov. 2, 1983
Protocol	Jan. 1, 1996	Norway	Jan. 1, 1971
China, P.R. of	Jan. 1, 1987	Protocol	Jan. 1, 1982
Commonwealth		Pakistan	Jan. 1, 1959
of Independent		Philippines	Jan. 1, 1983
States[2]	Jan. 1, 1976	Poland	Jan. 1, 1974
Cyprus	Jan. 1, 1986	Portugal	Jan. 1, 1996
Czech Republic	Jan. 1, 1993	Romania	Jan. 1, 1974
Denmark	Jan. 1, 2001	Russia	Jan. 1, 1994
Egypt	Jan. 1, 1982	Slovak Republic	Jan. 1, 1993
Estonia	Jan. 1, 2000	Slovenia	Jan. 1, 2002
Finland	Jan. 1, 1991	South Africa	Jan. 1, 1998
France	Jan. 1, 1996	Spain	Jan. 1, 1991
Germany[3]	Jan. 1, 19903	Sweden	Jan. 1, 1996
Greece	Jan. 1, 1953	Switzerland	Jan. 1, 1998
Hungary	Jan. 1, 1980	Thailand	Jan. 1, 1998
Iceland	Jan. 1, 1976	Trinidad and Tobago	Jan. 1, 1970
India	Jan. 1, 1991	Tunisia	Jan. 1, 1990
Indonesia	Jan. 1, 1990	Turkey	Jan. 1, 1998
Ireland	Jan. 1, 1998	Ukraine	Jan. 1, 2001
Israel	Jan. 1, 1995	United Kingdom	Jan. 1, 2004
Italy	Jan. 1, 1985	Venezuela	Jan. 1, 2000

1. Information on the treaty can be found in Publication 597, Information on the United States-Canada Income Tax Treaty.

2. The U.S.-U.S.S.R. income tax treaty applies to the countries of Armenia, Azerbaijan, Belarus, Georgia, Kyrgyzstan, Moldova, Tajikistan, Turkmenistan, and Uzbekistan.

3. The general effective date for the area that was the German Democratic Republic is January 1, 1991.

Source: IRS Pub. 54

OTHER TAX-RELATED BOOKS/RESOURCES BY THE SAME AUTHOR

1) A Citizen's Guide to Frequently Asked Tax Questions and the Answers the IRS Wants You to Know, paperback, ISBN: 1-890605-38-7 (or ISBN: 978-1-890605-38-4)

(2) Encyclopedia of Individual Tax Deductions, paperback ISBN: 1890605-39-5 (or ISBN: 978-1-890605-39-1)

(3) A Simplified Guide to Small Business Tax Deductions, paperback, ISBN: 1-890605-40-9 (or ISBN: 978-1-890605-40-7)

(4) A Citizen's Guide to Negotiating and Working Through Tax Problems with the IRS, paperback, ISBN: 1-890605-28-X (or ISBN: 978-1-890605-28-5)

(5) The History of Federal Income Tax and Facts the IRS Wants You to Know – An Annotated Guide for Students and Adults, paperback, ISBN: 1-890605-41-7 (or ISBN: 978-1-890605-41-4)

(6) The US Tax Dictionary – A Guide to terms, words & Phrases used by the IRS, paperback, ISBN: 1-890605-30-1 (or ISBN: 978-1-890605-30-8)

(7) Individual Tax Deductions by Profession as well as other personal circumstances (Online) at www. myustaxdeductions.com; www.taxdeductionsbyprofession.com or www.frontlinepublishers.com

(8) A Simplified Guide to hundreds of Small Business Tax Deductions, (Online) at www. myustaxdeductions.com; or www.frontlinepublishers.com

303

LIBRARY RECOMMENDATION FORM
(This form should be hand delivered to your local Head Librarian or Reference Librarian)

Sir/Madam:
I regularly use the following book(s) published by Frontline Publishers:

(1)_____ISBN #:_____Price $_____
(2)_____ISBN #:_____Price $_____
(3)_____ISBN #:_____Price $_____
(4)_____ISBN #:_____Price $_____
(5)_____ISBN #:_____Price $_____
(6)_____ISBN #:_____Price $_____

Your records indicate that the library does not carry these valuable and comprehensive travel reference books. Could you please order them for our library?

Name of Recommender:_____
Address:_____
_____
Phone:_____

ORDERING INFORMATION

Mail or Fax your orders to:

Frontline Publishers, Inc.
P.O. Box 32674-1A,
Baltimore, MD 21282-2674 U.S.A.
Fax: (410) 922-8009.
Make check or money order payable to **Frontline Publishers, Inc.**
We also accept, International Money Orders. You may also pay by credit
or debit card online at **www. myustaxdeductions.com;**
www.frontlinepublishers.com

Shipping/Postage Cost for books:
U.S. Residents add $4 U.S. dollars per book for postage.
Canadian Residents add $5 U.S. dollars per book for postage.
Mexican Residents add $7 U.S. dollars per book for postage.
Other Countries: add $15 U.S. dollars for airmail delivery; $7 for surface
mail delivery.

Books may also be ordered on-line at amazon.com,
www.myustaxdeductions.com; or www.frontlinepublishers.com, and
other major online bookstores, or from major bookstores throughout the
country.

NOTES

ORDER FORM

Telephone Orders: (Directly from the publisher- Frontline Publishers at 1-410-922-4903
Fax Orders: 1-410-922-8009 (Send this form)
Postal Orders: Frontline Publishers Inc, P.O. Box 32674-1A, Baltimore, Maryland 21282-2674-8674 U.S.A. {Tel: (410) 922-4903}. Make Check or Money Order payable to Frontline Publishers.

Online Orders: Visit www. *amazon.com*; ***www. myustaxdeductions.com;*** *www.frontlinepublishers.com* Also available through several online bookstores

☐ Please enter my order for the following books:

1) A Citizen's Guide to Frequently Asked Tax Questions and the Answers the IRS Wants You to Know, paperback, ISBN: 1-890605-38-7 (or ISBN: 978-1-890605-38-4)
                    $29.99 + $_____postage   Total $____
(2) Encyclopedia of Individual Tax Deductions , paperback ISBN: 1890605-39-5 (or ISBN: 978-1-890605-39-1) $24.99 + $_____postage   Total $____
(3) A Simplified Guide to Small Business Tax Deductions, paperback, ISBN: 1-890605-40-9 (or ISBN: 978-1-890605-40-7)
                    $39.99 + $_____postage   Total $____
(4) A Citizen's Guide to Negotiating and Working Through Tax Problems with the IRS, paperback, ISBN: 1-890605-28-X (or ISBN: 978-1-890605-28-5)
                    $39.99 + $_____postage   Total $____
(5) The History of Federal Income Tax and Facts the IRS Wants You to Know – An Annotated Guide for Students and Adults, paperback, ISBN: 1-890605-41-7 (or ISBN: 978-1-890605-41-4) $19.99 + $_____postage   Total $____
(6) The US Tax Dictionary – A Guide to terms, words & Phrases used by the IRS, paperback, ISBN: 1-890605-30-1 (or ISBN: 978-1-890605-30-8)
                    $19.99 + $_____postage   Total $____

(Please refer to the section containing shipping/postage information for applicable postage rates.)

Sales Tax: (Maryland Residents Only) Add 5% $_____

Enclosed is my Total Payment of $_____by ☐ Check ☐ Money Order ☐ This is a gift from:_____

Ship To:_____**Firm Name:**_____
Your Name:_____ _____**Address:**_____
City:_____**State:**_____**Zip:**_____**Country:**_____

COMMENT FORM FOR
FRONTLINE PUBLISHERS BOOKS

YOUR OPINION MEANS A LOT TO US
Please use this post card to tell us how you feel about any of our books.
Remember, we may quote you and/or use your comments, testimonials or
suggestions in our promotions and future editions.

Title of Book:_____

Name:_____

Organization:_____Position:_____

Address:_____

City, State, Zip & Country:_____

_____

_____

(   ) Check here if we may quote you.

Signature:_____Date:_____

[Mail your comments to Frontline Publishers, P.O. Box 32674 Baltimore,
MD 21282-2674, USA.]

NOTES

INDEX/KEYWORDS

ABOUT THE AUTHOR

Gladson I. Nwanna (Ph.D.) is a professor of Accounting & Finance and a former consultant to the World Bank. Dr. Nwanna is the author of several tax-related books.

OTHER TAX-RELATED BOOKS/RESOURCES BY
THE SAME AUTHOR

1) A Citizen's Guide to Frequently Asked Tax Questions and the Answers the IRS Wants You to Know, paperback, ISBN: 1-890605-38-7 (or ISBN: 978-1-890605-38-4)

(2) Encyclopedia of Individual Tax Deductions, paperback ISBN: 1890605-39-5 (or ISBN: 978-1-890605-39-1)

(3) A Simplified Guide to Small Business Tax Deductions. paperback, ISBN: 1-890605-40-9 (or ISBN: 978-1-890605-40-7)

(4) A Citizen's Guide to Negotiating and Working Through Tax Problems with the IRS, paperback. ISBN: 1-890605-28-X (or ISBN: 978-1-890605-28-5)

(5) The History of Federal Income Tax and Facts the IRS Wants You to Know – An Annotated Guide for Students and Adults, paperback. ISBN: 1-890605-41-7 (or ISBN: 978-1-890605-41-4)

(6) The US Tax Dictionary – A Guide to terms, words & Phrases used by the IRS, paperback. ISBN: 1-890605-30-1 (or ISBN: 978-1-890605-30-8)

(7) Individual Tax Deductions by Profession as well as other personal circumstances (Online) at www. myustaxdeductions.com; www.taxdeductionsbyprofession.com or www.frontlinepublishers.com

(8) A Simplified Guide to hundreds of Small Business Tax Deductions, (Online) at www. myustaxdeductions.com; or www.frontlinepublishers.com

See inside pages for ordering information

To Check Tax Deductions
By Profession or Occupation

Go To

www.myustaxdeductions.com
OR
www.taxdeductionsbyprofession.com

Printed in the United States
53447LVS00006B/100-111

9 781890 605384